Money Cometh!
To the Body of Christ

Money Cometh!
To the Body of Christ

by

Dr. Leroy Thompson, Sr.

Harrison House
Tulsa, Oklahoma

Third Printing

Money Cometh!
To the Body of Christ
ISBN 1-55794-186-1
Copyright © 1999 by Dr. Leroy Thompson, Sr.
Ever Increasing Word Ministries
P.O. Box 7
Darrow, Louisiana 70725

Published by Harrison House, Inc.
P.O. Box 35035
Tulsa, Oklahoma 74153

Contents

The Body of Christ at large has suffered tremendously by being ignorant of God's laws of prosperity and of God's *will* concerning their
prosperity. For the most part, Christians have not had a full supply.

Many have simply been ignorant of what the Word has to say;
others have tried to hold on to every dime they have, saving for a rainy
day. They talk about how hard it is to have any money and how it's
even harder to hold on to it once they have it! Money just seems to fly
away from them because they haven't operated on God's system of
giving and receiving in their finances. But money *cometh* to the Body
of Christ!

More than a year ago, the Lord gave me this revelation of "Money
cometh." At first, I thought He gave it to me just to bless me and my
family, because "Money cometh" began working mightily in our lives,
bringing about a tremendous change for the better in our finances.

But soon after I received the revelation and saw what it was doing
in our own lives, God began dealing with me about sharing it with the
Body of Christ. This truth can change the life of every believer who
wants to be free from financial bondage! It has already had a
profound impact on many who have heard and heeded the message.

The Lord wants to establish a money-covenant with believers such
as only a few have experienced until now. As more and more
Christians receive the revelation of divine prosperity in their spirits   *Divine Prosperity*
and act on what they've received, they will march out of poverty on a
straight path toward divine prosperity!

But it takes Bible information to change a person's situation. You
need to be confident in the Word of God and convinced of the *will* of
God so that, as boldly as you can say, "I'm saved by the blood of the
Lamb!" or "By Jesus' stripes I'm healed!" you could *also* say, "God
meets my every need, and I have an *abundant* supply!"

God wants Christians to get past always looking to *get* something,
and to instead be looking to give "big" to the Gospel, having plenty

left over to live an abundant life! He wants others to ask them, "How did you get out of debt and into prosperity?" so they can say, "The Lord has brought me out! *Money cometh to the Body of Christ!*"

Whatever your vocation in life, if you are God's child, God wants to show Himself strong on your behalf and to raise you up financially. And He wants the world to see Him do it! Money cometh to the Body of Christ! That means money cometh to *you!*

The Lord is going to finance the propagation of His Gospel throughout the earth, and He wants to use some of your money to do it! It is my prayer that you, as a willing vessel, will let Him take you higher and higher into a new realm of financial prosperity as you walk in the fullness of the good things He has prepared for you.

All the commandments which I command thee this day shall
ye observe to do, that ye may live, and multiply, and GO IN and
POSSESS THE LAND which the Lord sware unto your fathers.
—DEUTERONOMY 8:1

Let them shout for joy, and be glad, that favour my righteous
cause: yea, let them say continually, Let the Lord be magnified,
which hath PLEASURE in the PROSPERITY of his servant.
—PSALM 35:27

God has given me an assignment to teach the Body of Christ about
prosperity. He wants His people to know that it is His will and
good pleasure to prosper them. And God wants the Body of Christ to
take back what the devil has stolen.

The Lord wants us to go in and possess the land of prosperity that
He has already provided for us in Christ. God wants His children to
have money, not to be broke and in poverty.

That is what I am going to talk about in this book: *money! Money
cometh to the Body of Christ!*

These two prophetic words "Money cometh" came to me from the
Lord for the Body of Christ. The Lord showed me that through these
two words, "Money cometh," the Body of Christ can come out of
certain situations, such as financial hardships and lack.

The power of the words "Money cometh" can carry out certain
results in your life. They can activate the power to cause money to
come to you.

If you're in the Body of Christ, say this out loud: "Money cometh
to the Body of Christ! That means money cometh to *me now!* God
wants me to have plenty of money so I can carry out His covenant.
Money cometh to me—today, tomorrow, the next day—*every* day.
Money cometh!"

God does not want you to barely get by, so don't accept barely getting by. Money *cometh!*

You've got to "speak it out" if you want it. Don't sit around and say nothing. Speak it out! Say, "Money cometh!"

Wealthy But Not Worldly

Money is not evil. But the devil has lied to us and has told us that money is evil. He has told us, "The more broke you are, the closer you are to God." Have you ever heard that? The devil has tricked people into believing that if you're godly and humble, you won't want much.

In this book, I want to teach you how to be wealthy and happy— in other words, how to be wealthy but not worldly. There is a way.

You see, the devil has told the Church that people who are wealthy are *worldly* because they have so much. Because people in the Church are prosperous and blessed, the devil labels them as worldly. He shows us the complete opposite of what the Lord sees and wants us to see.

How does the devil label wealthy people as worldly? *With church people's words!* The devil wants us to believe that they are after money and that's *all* they're after, because they have so much. But, no, most of the time, a wealthy Christian is a person the Lord is blessing, and we shouldn't call him worldly. We should call him *worthy* because he is in God's plan and will.

In prospering us, God is only doing what He wants to do for His children. He has been saying it down through the ages. It's *preachers* who have not been saying it! But God wants us out of debt, He wants us out of distress and He wants us out of discouragement. And the only way that can happen is not just by our singing, "Hallelujah," but by our *prospering.*

There's a Practical Side to Divine Prosperity

This book will give you some scriptures and some faith confessions to make in order to help you get your finances straight. But there are also some practical steps you need to take.

For example, if you don't have a savings account, open one. I don't know how much money it takes to open a savings account in your area. I opened mine years ago, but when those people at the bank first told me how much money it took to open a savings account, I didn't have enough to open one. (They don't do all that paperwork for two dollars!)

If you don't have a savings account, you don't have a storehouse for the Lord to put anything in! You don't have to have $1,500 or some large amount to have a savings account. Just find out what the minimum requirement is, and make sure you open an account so you can have a place where you can deposit money. Then, once you have a savings account, you need to train yourself to put money into your account, no matter how small the amount.

If you're married, start an account in both partners' names. I don't believe in all this "separate account" mess or "his and her" accounts! You made a vow when you were married. You said, "We're one." You can't confess, "Money cometh!" and then turn around and holler, "My money!" The Lord isn't going to give anybody money who's hollering, "This is *my* money!" No, money cometh to those who say, "Everything I have, use it, Lord; it's all Yours. I am what I am because You made me what I am. I'm not going to reserve and hoard this money just for my purposes. Lord, whatever You want to do with it is fine with me."

So get rid of those separate accounts. A house divided shall not stand (Matthew 12:25; Mark 3:25; Luke 11:17). When husbands and wives have "his and her" accounts, the devil has them split. God can't bless that. God is not going to give His money to a divided house.

Let me clarify something about having separate accounts, because there are some exceptions. Some people *have* to have a separate account. If you have a husband, for example, who's not doing what's right, you can't put all the money in one pot with him, because he's not going to act right. You have to hold a little something back for you and the children. If you don't, he might spend it all. He might give his gal or mistress all the money! (That's all that mistress wants anyway. She might be saying, "I love you," but she actually wants a new dress!)

Situations like this cause little children to go hungry. "Daddy" is out there good-timing and partying while his little children at home don't get anything for Christmas but a little truck with a wheel missing! The other children in the neighborhood are riding around on big toy tractors, but his children are doing without.

So sometimes a married person has to have a separate account at the bank.

Whatever your situation, you need to have a savings account so you can have a storehouse for God to bless. Another thing you need to do is stop buying things on credit you don't need just because you see them. Get out of debt. I'll talk more about that later.

God Wants You To Have Money!

I'm not preaching something I don't know about. I'm preaching "Money cometh" because it's working for me. Almost every four days, somebody gives me a check! My church is out of debt—*way* out of debt! And the same spirit that is upon our church should be on *you*.

One man from North Carolina recently gave me a check, crying, "'Money cometh' has changed my whole business! My wife and I are so blessed. Money 'cometh' to us from everywhere! So here, Brother Thompson," and he handed me a check. He said, "I want *you* to have some money!"

I said, "Thank you." (Don't get the money and then forget about the preacher. He may believe "money cometh" *too.* I know *I* believe it!)

God wants us to have money. To prove it by the Word, let's look again at our texts in Deuteronomy and Psalms.

> **All the commandments which I command thee this day shall ye observe to do, that ye may live, and multiply, and go in and possess the land which the Lord sware unto your fathers.**
>
> **Deuteronomy 8:1**

> **Let them shout for joy, and be glad, that favour my righteous cause: yea, let them say continually, Let the**

Lord be magnified, which hath pleasure in the prosperity
of his servant.

Psalm 35:27

We have to establish the fact that God wants money in the pocket,
in the savings account, in the house, in the checkbook of *every*
believer. He wants you to have it! And in this book, I'm going to tell
you *why* He wants you to have it and how to get "Money cometh"
working in your life.

Prosperity Begins With Obedience

Deuteronomy 8 gives us some specific direction for being in the
will of God. If you're in the will of God according to Deuteronomy
8:1, you'll be financially blessed. Notice the first part of that verse: **All
the commandments which I command thee this day shall ye
observe TO DO....** You have to be a doer of God's *commandments* to
receive God's *blessings.*

Oh, I like that, don't you! In other words, just what He tells you
to do about finances, you have to do. You have to make up your mind
that you're going to be a doer of God's commandments, or His Word,
on the subject of finances.

Money cometh to the Body of Christ! But before "money cometh"
to you, you are going to have to make up your mind, *I'm going to be a
doer of God's commandments for me concerning finances.*

Right now, you can think of what you need to do in your own life
concerning obedience. You can't get in on this thing without obeying
or being a doer of God's Word. There's no side door to God's blessings. In other words, you can't creep in a side door by *prayer* when He
told you to *give.* You can't pray past giving! If God said, "Here's what
you're to do. I want you to give," and you say, "No, I'm going to pray;
praying is really spiritual," then "Money cometh" won't work for you.

Yes, the Bible says the prayer of a righteous man availeth much
(James 5:16). But what is a righteous man? A righteous man is one
who favors God's righteous cause. In other words, God blesses those
who do what He tells them to do. So "Money cometh" to you will
mean that you are doing what God has told you to do in His Word.

Renew Your Mind and Expand Your Vision

The Church has been all messed up about what God thinks about money. To tell you the truth, in one sense, God doesn't even think about money—He has so much!

You see, when you have money, you don't have to think about it. The reason people are so money-minded is that they don't have it, and they have to think about where they are going to get it! But those who have money don't even think about it.

I heard the president of a large corporation say he never thinks about money. This man is a multimillionaire. Well, he doesn't *have* to think about money; he's *got* it! I think he has four or five houses in different states in this country. Most people have never thought about *two* houses in different states! Some Christians can't even get the *first* one, and they are in the Body of Christ!

If you don't already live in Florida, wouldn't it be wonderful to have a nice house there so that when it gets cold, you could "fly away" from the cold weather and sit on a beach somewhere? You could call back home to your state and ask your friends how they are doing back there. You could tell them, "I'm on vacation. I'll be back in three weeks!"

Some people get "holy" on you when you talk like that, and they look at you like you're strange. But, you see, that's what God expects for you! If anybody is supposed to be out there on the beach sucking pineapple juice with a soft straw, it ought to be us!

So don't put on a religious face. Get rid of that old stingy poverty spirit. Don't let the devil hold you back. No, we're not to be in *covetousness*, but we are in *covenant*. We are to be controlling this financial system instead of this financial system controlling *us*.

What has God said about prosperity? Do you believe God and what He has said in His Word? Do you believe that God is not a liar? Do you believe that what He said in His Word, He meant for us to have?

If you want what God wants you to have, then pay careful attention to what I'm about to show you in Psalm 35:27:

> Let them shout for JOY, and be GLAD, that favour my
> righteous cause: yea, let them say continually, Let the
> Lord be magnified, which hath pleasure in the prosperity
> of his servant.

Look at those two words: "joy" and "glad." I tell you, when you're in God's divine program financially, it brings joy and gladness!

For example, someone could say, "I want to go to Africa, but I need $40,000." Then the preacher could say, "I need eight people to give this person $5,000." And if you had $5,000 to give, you could jump up and say, "Hey, you've got your $5,000. I'll give the first $5,000."

Most people couldn't jump up and say that. They wouldn't be full of joy and gladness. No, they'd jump under their seats if the preacher looked at them seriously and asked them for $5,000, because they know they don't *have* $5,000! They might have a heart attack if he asked them that, and he'd have to raise them from the dead!

If that describes your situation, don't quit; just keep reading. I'm going to help you get out of that condition. But first, I have to help you cleanse your mind of wrong, messed-up thinking concerning money. The Bible said we're cleansed through the Word.

> Now ye are clean through the word which I have spoken
> unto you.
>
> John 15:3

I want to help you cleanse your mind because if you have a religious mindset, you are not going to hear what I'm saying. You are going to say, "All that man talks about is money." But I'm not just talking about money. I'm talking about God's *covenant.* I'm talking about what God wants to do for His sons and daughters!

What would you do for *your* son or daughter if you had plenty of money?

Suppose for a moment that you were a multimillionaire business-man, and your twenty-five-year-old son just found the girl of his dreams and married her. You and your wife like this girl. She's just the kind of girl you wanted your son to have.

Then, your son sees a house that he really likes. You need to spend some money because of taxes; *you've got too much money!*

The house your son likes costs no more than $175,000. You don't bat an eye. To you, $175,000 is like $1.75 because you have so much.

So you say to your sweet little daughter–in–law, "Do you like that house, Honey?" She says, "Yes." So you say, "Then call the realtor. Tell him you want it, and tell him I'm financing it. It's paid for in full. I'm going to pay for the furniture too!"

You don't even have to go into your savings account to buy that house; you've got that much in the checking account!

I'm trying to change your thinking—to raise your level of thinking. If you were a multimillionaire, wouldn't you do good things for your children? There's a scripture that says, **If ye then, being evil** [or natural], **know how to give good gifts unto your children, how much MORE shall your Father which is in heaven give good things to them that ask him?** (Matthew 7:11).

So if you would do that much for your son or daughter if you were a multimillionaire, how much more is God willing to do for His children? Do you believe God is *at least* a multimillionaire?

Let me help you cleanse your mind so you don't have any religious thinking left. How did I say you cleanse your mind? Through the Word. The Word gets all the religious, stingy, poverty, poor-mouthing spirits out of you and away from around you and away from around your house.

I tell you, you ought to think about prosperity all the time. You ought to think about abundance. You ought to picture people who are in debt and distress and then picture yourself helping them.

Keep a Right Attitude

You also have to have a right attitude to go with your clean mind. You can't be envious or jealous because somebody else gets blessed. You have to look with a right attitude at people who are "with it" when it comes to walking in God's prosperity.

If you don't have a good attitude toward those God is blessing, God isn't going to give prosperity to you, because He doesn't want you in the same restaurant with them! He wants them to enjoy their food, so He is going to have you going to the "broke" restaurant—the restaurant where broke people go—until you learn to look correctly at those who have money. Then you can go into the same restaurant they're in and be happy.

So when you see people with plenty of money (I'm not talking about the gangsters or rogues; I'm talking about those who got their prosperity *God's* way), just smile and be happy with them, and prosperity will rub off on *you!*

You Don't Have To Be Broke "No More"!

You have to have a right attitude if you want "Money cometh!" If you don't have a right attitude, then change it. Get your attitude straight about money. Get your attitude straight about God. Have the right attitude about those who are blessed. And then have the right attitude about those who are broke; give them something.

> **Give, and it shall be given unto you; GOOD MEASURE,
> PRESSED DOWN, and SHAKEN TOGETHER, and RUNNING OVER,
> shall men give into your bosom. For with the same measure
> that ye mete withal it shall be measured to you again.**
>
> Luke 6:38

Say this out loud: "I'll never be broke another day in my life. In the Name of Jesus, I plead the blood over my finances."

Some people act so "holy" when you talk about pleading the blood of Jesus over your finances. Somebody with a religious mind will say, "Don't talk about the blood and money at the same time. Get the blood away from that money!"

But, "good measure, pressed down and shaken together" is the blood covenant "running over!" It's part of the blood covenant. One of the reasons Jesus shed His blood was so that you could have "good measure."

You know, good measure is when the basket is full (Deuteronomy 28:5). "Pressed down" means that when you press something down and you want to add some more to it, you shake the basket a little so that if there's any little crack that's not full, the contents will get into that crack!

So the blood and money *do* go together! Somebody said, "Oh, no. Communion—the Lord's Supper—and being wealthy don't go together." But, yes, Jesus became poor and He died that you might become rich (2 Corinthians 8:9). We'll talk more about that in another chapter.

Don't get upset because I'm talking about money. That's the subject of this book: *Money!* I could talk about grace or prayer or any other Bible subject you want to mention. But God told me to write this book about *money.*

Now, having money is not the only way to be prosperous. There's such a thing as prosperity in the world, and there's such a thing as *successful* prosperity in the world. You could have money and not be successfully prosperous *God's* way if you're not walking in the light of His Word.

Having money is not the only way to be prosperous, but I'm talking about money because God told me to talk about it. Why? Because so many in the Body of Christ are broke. They've got their confessions and their smiles, but they need some money to back up those confessions and smiles!

That's why I'm talking about money and not grace or prayer. Some people will get ahold of this revelation of "Money cometh," and their "debt days" are going to be over.

Say it out loud again: "Money cometh!"

The Body of Christ needs this message. Too many in the Body are broke. Many have a false prosperity or a false front. In other words, they over-buy to try to prove they have money. But, really, they're broke.

Some people are able to buy a Mercedes Benz automobile, but they'd rather go all over the world with money in their pockets, preaching the Gospel and supporting and blessing others who preach the Gospel. But if some people bought a Mercedes, they wouldn't be able to support the Gospel at all because they don't have enough money to own *and* maintain a new Mercedes. You see, you have to have some *money* to drive a new Mercedes!

If you take a new Mercedes to the mechanic's shop, when you pick it up and those people say your bill is $800, you have to have the money to pay the bill. You may have taken the car in because it had a little rattle in it somewhere. But you can't crack or flinch when you get your bill. You can't be at the Mercedes shop crying, "Oh, I wish it could be $35." It's *never* going to be $35!

You have to be able to pay the price to drive a new Mercedes. Mercedes' mechanics are higher-priced than other mechanics. You can't go to the Mercedes shop with just $200 to have your new car worked on; it won't work.

I know a couple who recently bought a new Mercedes. But they bought it when they were *able* to buy it. They drove the car they had for so long, I thought they were never going to get rid of it! But they washed that other car and always kept it as clean as a brand-new car. Now they're financially able to have a Mercedes. And they're not broke; they're able to maintain that car. They're covenant people too. They tithe and always bless and take care of their pastor. They make sure he has some money too! So God lets them drive a Mercedes.

Do you believe that God wants *you* to have money? If you're broke, just laugh out loud right now. If you're in debt, laugh because you're coming out of debt! Then say this out loud: "I ain't going to be broke 'no more'!!!"

> Let them shout for joy, and be glad, THAT FAVOUR MY RIGHTEOUS CAUSE: yea, let them say continually, Let the Lord be magnified, which hath pleasure in the prosperity of his servant.
>
> **Psalm 35:27**

Let them shout for joy and be glad.... What type of people is God talking about here? Those who favor His righteous cause!

Psalm 35 is a psalm of David. David said, **Let them shout for joy, and be glad, THAT FAVOUR MY RIGHTEOUS CAUSE....** David was a covenant man, anointed by God. And David was a man after God's own heart (Acts 13:22). David's cause was *God's* cause.

What is God's righteous cause? It's the covenant. It's evangelism. It's going out to preach the Gospel. It's supporting people who preach the Gospel. I'm not just talking about supporting the local church; I'm talking about supporting people who go to the mission field too.

Look at the next part of that verse: **...Yea, let them say continually, Let the Lord be MAGNIFIED, which hath pleasure in the prosperity of his servant.**

God wants to be magnified in our lives. He gets magnified when we are prosperous according to His plan. The rest of that verse says, **which hath *pleasure* in the prosperity of his servant.** What does "pleasure" mean? It means *enjoyment, fulfillment, joy* or *satisfaction.*

God is pleased about our prosperity. We could say it this way: "Let the Lord be magnified, which hath *enjoyment, fulfillment, joy* and *satisfaction* in the prosperity of His servant!"

God is not satisfied with your being in debt. He is your Father, and He has provided for you to have prosperity.

We Have a Money Covenant With God

Now, we know from Deuteronomy 8:1 that if you want to be under God's covenant of blessing, you have to do what the Lord tells you to do. Then when "money cometh" to you, a son or daughter of God, for the purpose of covenant and evangelism, from the extra money that comes in, your "stuff"—your personal business—is going to be taken care of too!

You see, God is giving you plenty so *His* business can be taken care of. And it's an overflowing amount that God wants you to have. Yes, I'm talking about money! I'm not talking about grace or prayer. I'm talking about *money. Money cometh!*

We have a money covenant with God. There is a way to be money-minded *properly* without being covetous. We have a money covenant that God wants us to get into. He wants the Body of Christ to tap into this money covenant. He gave me the words "Money cometh" because He wants us to have it so He can spread this Gospel in every part of the earth!

God wants us to have money so we can spread the Gospel and bring Bibles to those who have never heard about Jesus. **For the Son of man is come to save that which was lost** (Matthew 18:11). That is our mission today—and we need money to do that. We need to build churches and send ministers out to preach the Gospel. We need millions of dollars to do that, and God is giving it to us!

Do *You* Favor God's Righteous Cause?

I have a question for you. How much do you favor God's righteous cause? Here's a scale to help you measure: Are you willing to give God ten cents out of every dollar you receive? The Body of Christ needs everyone who is in the Body to be a tither.

Some Christians are not tithing. But to get blessed by God, you have to favor His righteous cause. You have to obey Him, especially in the area of tithing and giving.

Another way to get blessed by God is to stay out of other people's business. If you want money to come to you, stay out of other people's affairs. Scripture instructs us to go about our own work and to leave other people's business alone. (See also 2 Thessalonians 3:11; 1 Timothy 5:13; 1 Peter 4:15.)

> **And that ye study to be quiet, and to do your own business, and to work with your own hands, as we commanded you.**
>
> **1 Thessalonians 4:11**

If you want money to come to you, stay out of other people's business. Stop criticizing people who buy a new car or get a new house. Stop criticizing others' blessings if you want to be blessed too. God doesn't give nosy people money. Nosy people are *supposed* to be broke!

All of us have been a little nosy at some time in our lives. But, boy, I'm not going to be nosy anymore, are you?

You may have even criticized someone who got a brand new Mercedes. But have you ever bought gas to put in that car? Have you ever made one payment on the note? Then leave that person alone. Let him drive his new car and enjoy it. He's putting the gas in it, and he's making the payments on it. Don't criticize others' blessings if you want to get blessed too.

Do you favor God's righteous cause? Do you believe that money cometh? "Money cometh" could begin happening in your life while you're reading this book! The Lord will bring you from one place to another place in your finances if you get ahold of this message.

Not everybody is going to understand this message. Some are going to criticize me because I drive a nice car and live in a big house. They'll say, "That man is just teaching on prosperity to get people to send him their money." But I'm trying to get money *in* your pocket, not *out of* your pocket!

And do you know something else? I'm not broke. "Money cometh" to me above and beyond my salary as a pastor. Last year, my wife and I received financial blessings beyond my salary. My church is not my source. *God* is my Source! And God is not going to give me the revelation of "Money cometh" to spread all over the world without money coming to me too!

I'm not a broke preacher. If you're looking for a broke preacher to give something to, don't give it to me. And I'm not covetous either; I'm a *covenant* man. When God tells me to do something, I do it.

I'm a covenant man, and my ministry is a covenant ministry. If you're looking for good ground to sow into, go ahead and give to my ministry when the Lord tells you to give. But I don't want anybody to give me money because they think we're broke and they feel sorry for us. People who feel sorry for you because you're broke will *keep* you broke!

You know, we need to live a lifestyle of prosperity so we don't cheat God. He's given us so much revelation so we'll know what His will is and we'll know what to do about it. We owe it to Him to walk in the light of prosperity.

I want to demonstrate that God is strong in my life. I don't care what people say about me. Do you know what to do with critics? First, don't give your critics any credit, because when you give them credit, you give them credentials to criticize you some more. In other words, *ignore* your critics. Don't even talk about them. Don't give them any credit.

If you are going to rise up in God's plan, you have to get ready for critics. The world will begin to say, "They are getting our money." When the world sees the Church rising up, they will work with the devil. They will stir themselves up and start saying bad things about you, because the more you get, the less they're going to have.

There will always be those who will criticize. They will try to critique the blessings of God. But who can critique what God has decided to do for someone? Who can critique God's blessing someone for his or her obedience? Who can critique Isaiah 1:19, **If ye be willing and obedient, ye shall eat the good of the land?**

I have dedicated my life to Kingdom business. I've been in the ministry more than twenty years. God would be a liar if I weren't blessed by this time. He'd be a lying God, and *He can't be a lying God!* If I weren't blessed and if He were a lying God, we'd be serving a lying Jesus, and we'd have a lying Holy Ghost!

But God is not a liar! I tell you, I love the Lord; I'm sold out to Him and His Word. That's why I'm blessed. And if you want money to come to you, you have to sell out to Him too. Jesus Christ Himself said, **But seek ye first the kingdom of God, and his righteousness; and all these things shall be added unto you** (Matthew 6:33).

God is giving me things all the time. I'm seeking Him, and the "things" just show up! Many people have it backwards. They're seeking the *things* when they should be seeking the *Kingdom.*

Robbed for a Dime

Do you favor God's righteous cause? Will you do what God has told you to do in His Word?

> **Will a man rob God? Yet ye have robbed me. But ye say, Wherein have we robbed thee? In TITHES and OFFERINGS. Ye are cursed with a curse: for ye have robbed me, even this whole nation. Bring ye all the tithes into the storehouse, that there may be meat in mine house, and prove me now herewith, saith the Lord of hosts, if I will not open you the**

windows of heaven, and pour you out a blessing, that there shall not be room enough to receive it.

Malachi 3:8-10

If you are not tithing or giving God ten cents out of every dollar you get, you are letting the devil rob you for a dime! You are selling yourself cheap! You are selling your prosperity for a dime! You are selling your whole financial package—your prosperity and your "Money cometh"—down the drain. For ten cents, you are selling your prosperity—your ability to pay your bills and to help pay your neighbor's bills!

Some people hear Malachi 3:10 preached, and they get happy. They say, "Okay, I'm going to tithe!" They tithe for two weeks. Then when they go to counting up their bills they say, "I just can't tithe anymore." For ten cents, they are holding back their promotion.

Robbed because of a dime! If that describes you, the devil is stealing from you. He has his hand in your pocket. While you're stealing ten cents from God, the devil is stealing *ninety* cents from you. Why? Because when you don't give God that ten cents, then that other ninety cents belongs to you *and* the devil.

Robbed because of a dime! If that describes you, just repent for holding God's tithe, that dime. You can't "figure out" how much you're going to tithe—it's already figured out! Tithe means a *tenth.* You can't recalculate God's tithe.

(Some people think they make too much to tithe. I'll pray for those people so that their paychecks be cut in size so they can go ahead and tithe!)

It doesn't matter how many or how few dollars you have, it's only a dime out of each dollar that belongs to God. I believe that if you haven't been tithing, you will begin to tithe if you're tired of being broke. Your car is breaking down before it's supposed to break down. It's the devil who's breaking it down because you've been in cahoots with him! He's been riding along in your car, and suddenly, he gets mad and says, *"Break!"* Then you cry to God and say, "God, pay for the devil's and my ride!"

You say, "Lord, You know I love You. Lord, You are my King and my Master. Lord, I need a water pump. Hallelujah. You are my God."

You see, as long as the water was flowing through the radiator, it was you and the devil. But when the water pump went out, it was you and God!

God Wants You To Have Financial *Power*, Not Financial *Pressure*

I was preaching on this subject of prosperity in a meeting, and the Lord told me to tell the people that instead of having financial *pressure*, He wants them to have financial *power*.

The Father told me in my spirit, "I want you to have financial power, for if you get financial power, the power of My Gospel will be able to go to the four ends of the earth because you are going to give."

God doesn't want you to have financial *pressure*. He wants you to have financial *power*. What's the difference between financial pressure and financial power? Financial pressure means you're in debt, in distress and you're discouraged. Financial power means you're free from debt. You've got a savings account, and you're looking for somebody to bless!

It's so good when the Lord tells you to give somebody $500, and you're able to just reach into your pocket and get it out without making a big "tah-dah" or big deal about it.

Do you know what I mean by *tah-dah?* I mean, you don't want everybody in the world to know you're giving somebody $500. You just kind of walk by the person, give him the $500 and just keep walking! The Bible says, **That thine alms may be in secret: and thy Father which seeth in secret himself shall reward thee openly** (Matthew 6:4).

God wants us to have financial power, not financial pressure. He has pleasure in the prosperity of His servants!

How God Gave Me the Revelation "Money Cometh!"

Now let me tell you how God taught me about "Money cometh!"

One day a couple of years ago, I went to the supermarket to buy some apples and oranges. I was in line at the supermarket behind a gentleman who had a six- or eight-pack of beer that he was buying.

This gentleman pulled out his wallet, and I saw that it was empty except for one bill that he used to pay for the beer. The checker gave him back a few dollars and some change. He put the change in his pocket and the dollars in his wallet. Then he looked back at me and said, "Money really goeth, doesn't it?"

I didn't know this man. I was just making small talk with him when I nodded and said, "Yeah, money really goes." I thought nothing of it. I paid for my apples and oranges and went to my car.

When I got in my car, the Spirit of God was strong in there, and He spoke to me! The Lord asked me sort of chidingly, *"Money really go...."*

He was starting to say, *"Money really goeth, does it?"* But I didn't let Him get "goeth" out. I'm telling you, when He said "go...," I heard down deep in my spirit two words that were breathed on and endorsed by heaven! Those two astounding words were, "Money *cometh!"*

When the Lord said, *"Money really goeth, does it?"* He was sort of repeating what that man had said to me in the supermarket. Actually, as I said, the Lord said it a little differently than that. (You know, God is not a "stuffed shirt"; He's comical sometimes, and He's cool. And He'll talk "cool" to you sometimes.)

The Lord *started* to say, *"Money really goeth, does it?"* I knew what He was going to say. But before He got out the word "goeth," I heard those words "Money cometh!" loud and clear and strong in my spirit, and I said them out loud.

I knew the Holy Ghost was moving in that car. I thought, *If saying those two words did this much good, I'm going to say them again.* So I said it out of my mouth the second time, "Money cometh!" And when I did, a prosperity anointing started rising up in that car! So I said it a third time, "Money *cometh!"* There's just something about saying it a third time, because the third time I said it, the revelation of those two words started rising up within my spirit, and I declared with boldness, "I'll never be broke another day in my life!"

Actually, I was being rebuked by the Lord. Out of my spirit, my innermost being, those words came up, correcting me. When I heard those two words in my spirit, "Money cometh!" it was something like what a woman who's eight months pregnant might feel when the baby inside her gives a good kick!

I know the voice of God. That voice that spoke "Money cometh" so loud and strong was the same voice that spoke to me and told me He brought me out of the kingdom of darkness and into the Kingdom of light when I got born again. It was the same God who, a year later, called me into the ministry and told me, "You're going to preach My Gospel to thousands of people." It was the same voice that later told me when I was on my job, where I'd worked for sixteen years, "Tomorrow is your day. Quit." And the voice that spoke to me in my car that day was the same voice that told me to stay in the church I was pastoring years ago when I had the opportunity to pastor a much larger church somewhere else.

"Money cometh" was nothing I thought up. Those two simple words in the natural shouldn't give such a thrill! But I knew those words were supernaturally spoken. They had a special, heavenly "perfume" on them that filled my car. The phrase "Money cometh" consists of two common words, but when God breathes on it, the common part is taken out. Any word that God breathes on is not common anymore!

You see, those two words "Money cometh" were God-breathed into my spirit. At first, I thought they were just words from the Lord to bless me and my family. I didn't know the far-reaching ramifications they would have on the Body of Christ. But then, God started dealing with me about those two words. He started telling me some more things about "Money cometh!" And He told me to share them with you.

Christ hath redeemed us from the curse of the law,
being made a curse for us: for it is written,
Cursed is every one that hangeth on a tree.
—GALATIANS 3:13

David therefore departed thence, and escaped to the cave Adullam:
and when his brethren and all his father's house heard it,
they went down thither to him. And every one that was
IN DISTRESS, and every one that was IN DEBT, and every one
that was DISCONTENTED, gathered themselves unto him;
and he became a captain over them: and there were
with him about four hundred men.
—1 SAMUEL 22:1,2

This situation in First Samuel 22 is the same situation that a great number of Christians are in today. They are in distress, in debt and they are discontented.

But the Lord wants to get them out of that because He wants them in His vineyard doing something special. God has a special mission for you who are in the Body of Christ, but you are going to need money to do it.

Debt, distress and discontentment are cousins. Have you ever wondered what causes just a few—a remnant—in the Body of Christ to break out and escape poverty and do pretty well, while the majority are still in debt, in distress and discontented?

This book answers that question and can help you come out of poverty and walk in the sunshine of divine prosperity. That is the will of God for you!

Our text, First Samuel 22:2, describes the condition of the average Christian and of the average church: **Every one that was IN DISTRESS, and every one that was IN DEBT, and every one that was**

DISCONTENTED.... This description has a sense of disturbance in it. In other words, the people were not happy.

And people in that condition today aren't happy either. They can't have joy, because they're constantly struggling in the area of finances.

The reason the Body of Christ is in this condition is they have not been taught prosperity, or they have not been taught prosperity *properly*—or they have simply turned down the truth they've heard and the benefits offered to them by God.

One of the greatest bondages that the Church has today is not having enough money to do what the Lord wants them to do. Christians overall have been broke, and there's distress, discouragement and discontentment in being broke.

You know, being broke has caused more divorces than anything else. It hasn't been "the other woman" or "the other man" as much as it's been simply being broke! Being broke has caused more fussing and fighting among husbands and wives than just about anything.

My wife, Carolyn, and I have had some of our biggest fusses over money. Of course, our fusses have only been from the neck up. In other words, we never let our fussing come between us or get down into our hearts.

When you don't have enough money to pay your bills, it seems as if some spirit gets in your house and causes tension and strife among family members. You want to act right and love your mate, but you're so broke, you end up fussing and fighting instead of loving! You can't even make love well when you're broke! You really can't, because after the lovemaking is over, you have to go back to reality and the land of "brokeness," because those bills are still there waiting for you!

Carolyn manages the bills at our house. And in times past, she'd get tired of trying to figure out how to pay all of our bills. She was under stress and pressure trying to pay bills without enough money to pay them. She was in distress and discontentment. You know what I'm talking about if you've been in the same condition.

Yet many people in that condition will go sit in those nice restaurants and order themselves a seafood platter or steak, knowing they're not really able to buy seafood or steak. They act as if they have money, but they're broke—they're in debt, distress and discontentment.

Many in the Body of Christ are broke and in debt and can't meet the needs of their family or church. As a result, the Church can't move out beyond its four walls with the Gospel like it's supposed to. That brings distress. Being broke and in debt—being in so much debt that you can hardly breathe or even think straight—is something that has to be dealt with. Poverty and debt simply cause problems in people's lives.

But I believe we're going to get that stopped! God wants you to rise up in your finances. And these words "Money cometh" are bringing on a prosperity revival, so to speak, that can change the circumstances of every believer who wants to come out of debt and walk in the prosperity of God!

You can't be happy and be broke—not for very long, anyway. My wife was distressed, trying to raise our children, run a household and also trying to figure out how to pay the bills.

Some husbands need to be more considerate of their wives. For example, you might go walking through the house, whistling and singing like you have a million dollars. You're just so glad it's Friday.

Then you say, "Hey, Honey, what's for dinner? Did you pay the bills?" You don't know that five or six creditors called her before you got home. She had to deal with those creditors, and now she has to deal with you too. And you wonder why she's so upset!

In debt, in distress and in discontentment. Did you ever wonder why those 400 men in First Samuel 22 gathered themselves around David? David had the anointing to destroy the yoke of poverty.

David had what we call the "spirit of faith." Second Corinthians 4:13 says, **We having the same SPIRIT OF FAITH, according as it is written, I BELIEVED, and therefore HAVE I SPOKEN; we also BELIEVE, and therefore SPEAK.**

Notice again those three words in First Samuel 22:2: *distress, debt* and *discontentment.* I submit to you that all of those conditions really come from debt. In other words, distress and discontentment are derived from debt! You see, debt that can't be paid will keep you in distress. And if you're broke, can't pay your bills, can't get your needs met and can't have a little something to enjoy life with, you are discontented.

David had the spirit of faith. And the spirit of faith can destroy any yoke, whether it be of sin, sickness, poverty or anything else that binds you. When a person is operating in the spirit of faith—believing and speaking according to the Word—distress, debt and discontentment will be destroyed.

Those men saw the lifestyle of faith and blessings that David had, and they gathered around him so he could train them and lead them out of distress, debt and discontentment.

The Bible talks about David's men becoming great in David's army and kingdom. (See 1 and 2 Samuel, 1 and 2 Kings and 1 Chronicles).

They were no longer in distress, in debt and in discontentment, because they stayed around this man David, who had the spirit of faith. He walked them out of distress, debt and discontentment with his experience and his example. They saw how he lived before the Lord.

David had the spirit of faith that says you *believe* and then you *speak.* That same spirit of faith is exactly what I used to destroy poverty in my life.

Don't feel badly if you're not there yet. Don't feel badly just because you don't have the money you'd like to have to give to the Gospel. Most people would give it; they just don't *have* it. We've got to get that changed!

The Children's Bread

I preached this same message in a particular meeting, and the following word came forth from the Lord:

> How sorrowful My heart has been to see My children begging for bread. I've provided for My children to have plenty, plenty, plenty of bread. My children are supposed to be in the baker's shop. My children have been eating crumbs from the Master's table when they are supposed to be eating at the table that I have prepared for them. Come up from the crumbs and get the bread!

Well, you've never heard of a baker's shop running out of bread, have you! No, and that's where God's children should be—in the baker's shop! Prosperity is the children's bread!

Do you remember the Canaanite woman in Matthew 15? She came to Jesus because she wanted to get somebody healed in her family.

> **Then Jesus went thence, and departed into the coasts of Tyre and Sidon. And, behold, A WOMAN OF CANAAN came out of the same coasts, and cried unto him, saying, Have mercy on me, O Lord, thou Son of David; my daughter is grievously vexed with a devil. But he answered her not a word. And his disciples came and besought him, saying, Send her away; for she crieth after us. But he answered and said, I am not sent but unto the lost sheep of the house of Israel. Then came she and worshipped him, saying, Lord, help me. But he answered and said, It is not meet to take the CHILDREN'S BREAD, and to cast it to dogs. And she said, Truth, Lord: YET THE DOGS EAT OF THE CRUMBS WHICH FALL FROM THEIR MASTERS' TABLE. Then Jesus answered and said unto her, O woman, great is thy faith: be it unto thee even as thou wilt. And her daughter was made whole from that very hour.**
>
> Matthew 15:21-28

In verse 26, Jesus was saying that healing was the children's bread. Well, prosperity, just like healing, is also the children's bread. And when you were born again, you entered into God's "baker shop" of prosperity! Now you are to eat at the Master's table of prosperity!

Say this out loud: "God wants me blessed. As a matter of fact, I *am* blessed. From now on, I'll speak words of prosperity. I won't speak *against* prosperity."

There is an anointing for prosperity. God told me, personally, "I have put a prosperity anointing on you." Some "holy," religious people might say, *"Prosperity* anointing? The anointing is just to get people *healed."*

But God's plan of redemption also includes our redemption from poverty. We are redeemed from the curse of the law (Galatians 3:13).

Poverty is a curse of the law just as sickness is a curse of the law. So prosperity is in our redemption, just as healing is in our redemption.

Let's look at our text again.

> **David therefore departed thence, and escaped to the cave Adullam: and when his brethren and all his father's house heard it, they went down thither to him. And every one that was in DISTRESS, and every one that was in DEBT, and every one that was DISCONTENTED, gathered themselves unto him; and he became a captain over them: and there were with him about four hundred men.**
>
> 1 Samuel 22:1,2

In this chapter, I am going to talk about debt, distress and discontentment *leaving* you! Make this confession: "Debt, get away from me. Distress, get away from me. Discontentment, get away from me, in Jesus' Name!"

When you're broke, you really are discontented. I've been broke, so I know what I'm talking about! I've been broke buying new cars, acting as if I had something. That's almost the worst kind of "broke" there is—buying new dresses, new suits and other things on credit when a person is as broke as can be.

My wife and I were buying new cars, new dresses and new suits because we wanted people to think we had plenty. But we were broke. That's not prosperity. That's just putting up a false front.

I used to tell my wife, "Honey, buy yourself a new dress. Take the credit card, but make sure nobody is around when you buy it because the charge might not be approved. Go to the store when it's empty. Wait till it's almost closed."

Credit cards can ruin some people if they don't know anything about a budget. If they don't know how much they've spent on their credit cards or whether they can pay the bills when they come, credit cards could ruin them and cause them distress and discontentment.

Some people put on those good dresses and those nice suits and neckties, and they think they're fooling somebody. But they're broke. I mean, they don't have a quarter!

They can come out of that. That's why the Lord told me to get this message into the hands of the Body of Christ. Money cometh!

Information That Can Change Your Situation!

If you're broke, you need to laugh. Just laugh out loud. Laugh at the devil. Why? *Because you are about to come upon some information that is going to change your situation!* The "broker" you are, the harder you should laugh. Why are you laughing? Because you are coming out of debt, distress and discontentment!

I don't care what demon in hell will get mad about the fact that I'm teaching the Body of Christ about money. And if you get mad about it, don't just put this book down. Keep reading because poverty is not the will of God for you! You've been redeemed from the curse of poverty!

> **Christ hath redeemed us from the curse of the law, being made a curse for us: for it is written, Cursed is every one that hangeth on a tree. That the blessing of Abraham might come on the Gentiles through Jesus Christ; that we might receive the promise of the Spirit through faith.**
>
> **Galatians 3:13,14**

Look at the first part of that thirteenth verse: **Christ hath redeemed us.** Christ has delivered us; He has set us free. Free from what? **From the curse of the law, being made a curse for us....**

Christ became poor that we might become rich (2 Corinthians 8:9). *Rich!* Somebody might say, "Well, I'm rich *spiritually;* I've got the Holy Ghost." Yes, but the Holy Ghost is rich with *finances* because He's got all the revelation!

Listen, Brother and Sister, every financial secret for prosperity there is, God knows it, and He wants to tell you. God doesn't want you in debt upon debt, always worried about money. Some of you have to squeeze your paycheck so tight, that little check is hollering, "You're choking me; I can't go any further!"

I'm not preaching some secret I don't know about. My wife and I and our family are blessed. God is running after us with blessings.

Everywhere we go, here comes God "running us down" and blessing us!

God has shown me how to prosper. I have an anointing for prosperity, and I'm tired of keeping it a secret and holding it in the closet. I'm bringing it out to the Body of Christ because I want you to have it. You don't have to always be worried with those little debts while those creditors are calling you and bothering you about paying them.

God has prospered me and my family, and He will do the same for you. This message is for Christians. And I'm telling you, Body of Christ, we're going places! My own ministry is going places. We are out of debt. We are building, and we are going to *continue* to build. An older minister once said, "Don't ever stop building. Always keep something in front of your people to do." So we are going to build and keep on building.

If you are broke and in debt, are you ready to come out of that condition? Are you ready to quit standing in line at stores with your credit card, wondering if it is going to "go through" and be approved?

That's not for the Body of Christ! That's poverty. But I'm sharing some things with you that you can put into practice, and eventually you'll get to the place where you can go into a store and buy anything you want. When you go somewhere to try on suits, for example, you're just going to say what size you want, go into the dressing room, put it on, come back out and lead the salesperson to the cash register—all without asking how much the suit costs—because you are part of the Body of Christ!

You need to get that old poverty spirit and poverty mentality out of you. But, as I said before, the first thing you need to do is to take some practical steps. And the first practical step you need to take is to open a savings account and then stop buying things with those credit cards that you're not able to pay for. Drive the automobile you have until you are able to drive a better one. Clean that car you have; shine the tires. Wear your woven necktie until you are able to wear a silk one.

Another practical step you need to take is to line your bills up from the smallest to the biggest. They may look like a giant, but they're no giant—they are just *Goliath!* (See 1 Samuel 17.) But you've got the sling-shot of faith, and you're going to shoot that "Goliath" down!

So pay off every bill you have. Pay your cars off. Pay your house off. You might say, "I can't pay my house off!" Yes, you can! Christ has redeemed us from the curse of the law!

The fact that Christ has redeemed you becomes more and more real with your confession. That's why you need to say over and over again: "Christ has redeemed me. I'll never be broke another day of my life. In the Name of Jesus, I plead the blood over my finances."

Somebody might say, "I still don't understand what the blood has to do with it."

Look at Galatians, chapter 3, again. The blood of Jesus does have something to do with your finances. You know, God didn't do much of a job of delivering us if He didn't deliver us from poverty. What kind of God would He be if He didn't deliver us from poverty? A broke God? Or a rich God who dearly loves His children but doesn't want them to be prosperous?

> **Christ hath redeemed us from the curse of the law,**
> **being made a curse for us: for it is written, Cursed is every**
> **one that hangeth on a tree.**
>
> **Galatians 3:13**

Study that verse. Can you believe Galatians 3:13? Does God lie? *No.* Is God broke? *No.* Is God your Daddy? Yes, He is if you are born again.

Christ has redeemed us. It was in God the Father's great plan to redeem us. Christ has paid the price for our financial debt. Christ made an expensive deposit in the bank of heaven on our behalf. And by making that deposit, He has set us free from poverty, lack, debt, distress and discontentment. He has blessed us with everything we need to live godly, holy lives *free* from the curse of the law, not bound by it.

God made a deposit in Christ so that none of His children would ever have to be broke. Religion and man's ideas have messed us up in this area. Preachers who don't know what to preach can mess you up. Those stingy little groups in a church can also mess you up. For example, when the Lord gives the pastor a vision of what He wants that pastor to do, those stingy, tight-fisted groups get together and think of all the reasons it can't be done!

Don't listen to people like that. If you do, they will keep you broke. They will keep those department stores calling you because you can't pay your bills!

You see, in order to get poverty to leave you, you have to change your way of thinking concerning money and prosperity.

God made a deposit in heaven for us, and because He made that deposit, He has blessed us with all spiritual blessings in heavenly places in Christ Jesus (Ephesians 1:3). But I'm not talking about just having spiritual blessings. As a matter of fact, you can't be too spiritual while you're broke and can't pay your bills, because there's a little fellow that goes along with "brokeness" called *worry*. Then another little fellow comes in, too, and his name is *fear*. Worry and fear run with broke folks!

We *have been* redeemed from poverty, and we are blessed *right now*. But we must get our minds cleansed from poverty so we can come into prosperity.

Many Christians t-h-i-n-k broke, and then they almost t-h-a-n-k the Lord that they're broke! They'll say, "Thank You, Lord. I don't have anything. I love You so much. I serve You because I'm broke. I don't have a fine car or a nice home like the man down the street. But I love You, Lord."

But if they really loved the Lord, they'd love and obey His Word, allowing Him to bless them according to His Word so people could see what a good Daddy our God is!

Take Off Those "Family Glasses"!

You see, some people think incorrectly about money. They think about how poor mama, daddy, grandma and grandpa were. They've got those "family glasses" on, and that's all they can see. "All Daddy had was an old truck; *I* have an old truck." They can't see the truth correctly.

You know, I always tell people it doesn't really matter what kind of automobile you have. Just drive it and be happy until you get something else. But whatever you do, take those "family glasses" off! Get your mind cleansed and renewed with the Word of God and begin to think like God thinks about prosperity.

I drive a big car. It's a nice car, a Mercedes Benz. That car draws people's attention, and God gets all the glory. I tell people what a good God I serve and what a good Daddy He is. I didn't always drive that kind of car, but I do now.

People sometimes judge me because I have nice things. But they don't know me, so they shouldn't judge me. Some of them try to put me in the same sack with all those preachers who aren't doing right. But I'm not in the same sack or category as those preachers. My Father has blessed me because I'm sold out to Him. I love Him, and I'm obedient to Him. (You know, people won't judge somebody or get mad at somebody for being poor, so why do they get mad at some-body for being blessed?)

> **If ye be willing and obedient, ye shall eat the good of the land.**
>
> **Isaiah 1:19**

Do you know why I'm blessed the way I am? Because if the Lord told me to go to Greece tomorrow, I'd go. He knows I'll do whatever He tells me to do. If He told me to whip two baboons, He knows I'd jump on them! He'd have to help me, but I'd jump on them!

I'm not bragging on *me;* I'm trying to show you how to get blessed and how to get the curse of poverty out of your life. Isaiah 1:19 says, **If ye be WILLING and OBEDIENT, ye shall eat the good of the land.** Willing to do what? Well, first, be willing to change your mind about finances. Your mind may be telling you, *You don't have to have all that prosperity. Just serve the Lord. You don't have to have all that.*

That's a demon telling you that. That's a devil trying to hold you back and keep you broke. It's harder to serve the Lord when you're broke.

The Body of Christ needs to be in the financial position to send people to preach the Gospel. I mean, we can't go down to "Joe Saloon" to get money for the ministry! The sinners aren't going to send people out to preach the Gospel!

For example, if you had $75,000 in the bank with all your bills paid, and the Lord told you to give $5,000, you'd probably gladly give $5,000 instantly.

That may stagger your mind right now, but I believe you're getting your mind cleansed and renewed with the Word of God so you can begin to think like God thinks concerning money.

Some people have a hard time accepting the fact that God doesn't want them broke. They need to enlarge their vision and their expectancy of what God wants to do in their lives and how God wants to bless them and use them to bless others!

God Is No Respecter of Persons—That Means He's No Respecter of Color

We are the Body of Christ. We are not white men, black men or any other color of men. Even though we all have different colors and cultures, we have a common denominator—His Name is Jesus! We have one Lord, one faith, one Holy Ghost and one Church!

The Lord told me to say that because this subject of race is an area that is keeping some people under the curse of poverty.

For example, some people think their lack of prosperity is due to their race or the color of their skin. But if you're black, for example, a lack of prosperity doesn't have anything to do with your being black.

So don't tell me, "Oh, we've been held back so long." *Nobody* can hold you back when you're walking in God's Word and you're obeying Him!

I don't like to hear excuses, such as, "We haven't been treated fairly." The Bible doesn't even talk about that. I know some of that goes on, but you, as a covenant child of God, don't have to be concerned about prejudice, regardless of your race or color. Just do something about it by obeying God and believing Him. Don't be crying, wanting somebody to give you some kind of little spoonful of charity.

And if you are on welfare and food stamps, I encourage you to get off them as soon as you can. Welfare is a poverty train that will keep you broke, because if you're always depending on somebody else to do something for you, you're going to stay in poverty. So rise up and do something for yourself.

I said this in a meeting once and started to say, "welfare and *Green Stamps*" instead of "welfare and *food* stamps"! But Green Stamps are almost as bad! My mama used to lick those Green Stamps and save books full of them. We'd go to the Green Stamps store with forty-five books, and those people at that Green Stamps store would give us two or three little ol' items in exchange for them! I'd been licking stamps for *months*—I thought we were going to bring the whole store back with those forty-five books!

I remember riding to that Green Stamps store in my daddy's Chevrolet. I'd say to myself, *I don't know what Mama's thinking—we aren't going to be able to bring all the stuff back in this Chevrolet!* I didn't know any better; I thought you could really buy some stuff with those Green Stamps!

Then they'd say, "Well, you need seven books for such and such." And I'd say, "Man, my tongue is sore, and you're talking about wanting seven books for this doggone little ol' thing!" I wasn't saved back then. I'd say, "After all the licking I did, I'll whip your tail for talking to me about seven books for this little thing!"

But if you had some money, partner, you wouldn't need Green Stamps or food stamps either! And, you see, if *I'd* had money—some of God's money—for all the licking I did, I could have bought that whole Green Stamps store!

You don't have to depend on Green Stamps or any other kind of stamps to make you prosperous. God wants to get some money into the hands of Christians. He doesn't want them broke, and He doesn't want them depending on some little check every month so they can get by.

You folks who are on welfare know what it took to get that check every month. You had to sit in a little office or booth and fill out about ninety-five sheets of paper! Then the people at the welfare office told you to go back outside and wait, and they told you that you might not get the welfare. They took you through the "wringer" for those few dollars!

But you're coming out of those booths and off welfare, because *money cometh!* I believe you're coming into your inheritance! You may not believe it right now, but keep reading. There's an anointing for prosperity, and what God says in His anointed Word is true.

A Word of Caution

Don't misunderstand me. If you're on welfare, stay on it until you can get off of it. Don't throw those food stamps away immediately; you may not be ready yet. One message on prosperity won't get you off welfare. But if you will continue to study God's Word on the subject of prosperity, a prosperity spirit will come upon you, and you won't even be able to *think* broke anymore!

Read Isaiah 1:19 again and read it out loud: **If ye be willing and obedient, ye shall eat the good of the land.**

What does the last part of that verse say? It says, **Ye shall eat the good of the land.** What does God mean by **the good of the land?** He means *the best.* He's not talking about having a good "church" service. He means having *the best the land has to offer!*

Don't Settle for Less Than God's Best

If ye be willing and obedient.... As I said before, you have to be willing to change your mind about how God thinks about money in order to get into His flow of prosperity.

Have you ever been in a religious church? Do you know what I mean by a "religious" church? I mean the preachers in religious churches will beg you for money all day long, but then they'll be quick to tell you that *you* shouldn't have any! They'll tell you, **The love of money is the root of all evil** (1 Timothy 6:10).

Well, it's true, the *love* of money *is* the root of all evil. But the *lack* of money could be the root of evil, too, because you could not have a dime and still be in love with money! So being broke can be evil too.

I don't love money, but I need it to operate. I need money to finish building our ministry. You need money too.

God is prospering His people so they can help ministers build buildings that will be used to get the Gospel out. If Christians are not giving to the work of God, but being tightfisted with God's money that He's given them, they ought to be "closed down," so to speak.

People like that are not going to do any more than hoard God's money to buy stuff only for themselves. Then they want to go to church and "ride for free" and try to make others look bad by flashing their diamond rings and showing off with God's money. Why did I say, *"God's* money"? Because when it comes to the tithe, they are holding back that dime.

But money cometh to those who will believe and obey God and be willing to do what He tells them to do.

Would you like to have plenty, plenty, plenty, *plenty of money?* I mean, how would you like to have enough money that, after you get your house built and buy that car you like (we're not just talking about getting things for yourself, but that's part of it), you can send some people overseas to preach the Gospel? You can sow finances into worthy ministries that are doing something for God.

A good friend of mine, who's a minister, gave $200,000 to a large ministry that's starting a church every two and a half days. That ministry is training people to go into all the world, behind every wall and curtain.

I watched my friend give that money in a certain meeting we were both in. He never batted an eye. I looked right at him because I like to watch people who give that kind of money. He wasn't in any kind of pride. He just sat there as calm as can be. He gave that money so that the Gospel could go further.

Our church gave a large offering to that same ministry that's starting a church every two and a half days. My wife and I also gave a large personal offering out of our own pocket. And God is blessing us for our giving. I can remember a day when my wife and I would give just $100 and then hurry back home and check every drawer in the house to see how many pennies we could find! We wanted to make sure we made that check good at the bank!

But when we gave that large offering recently, we didn't worry about when the check was going to go through our bank. It could have gone through at any time because we were ready for it. We got hold of what I'm preaching to you, and it got hold of us! It's working for us. *Money cometh!*

God Will Bless Your Storehouse

A poverty spirit has tried to latch itself onto the Body of Christ. It has caused Christians to think poor and not expect to have anything more than they already have.

That's why I told you to open a savings account if you don't have one. The Lord said He'd bless our storehouse (Deuteronomy 28:5), so you have to have a storehouse for God to bless! Then you can say, "Lord, I have a storehouse for You to bless. Thank You for my storehouse."

Some Christians say, "Well, we're going to be raptured; we're not going to be here all of our lives, so we don't need to save any money."

That's foolish! Put some money up in savings! Then if the Lord sends you to get some money out to give to a worthy cause, you'll be glad you did. If you had $75,000 in the bank, you could go to the bank and say, "Give me $5,000," and then give it to the Lord's work. That's how God wants to use you.

Three Things the Lord Told Me To Tell You

I shared in the first chapter how God gave me the revelation of "Money cometh!" After He gave me that revelation, He told me three things that He wanted me to tell the Body of Christ so they could make money start coming in their lives:

1. **"Tell My people that 'Money cometh' is not for covetous reasons."**

First, we need to know that "Money cometh" means a *continual process of money coming to you—a continual supply.* Then we need to know that this continual supply is not for covetousness. That means that "Money cometh" is not for "just me and my four and no more." It's not for *"my* car, *my* house, *my* things, *my* rings, *my* suits and *my* dresses." The Lord said to me, "Tell them that those things will come with 'Money cometh,' but it's not for those reasons."

Covetousness is one of the things that has kept money from people. Covetousness will cause a person not to be a tither. But that ten cents that he withholds from God will cause him to be broke. A dime will cause him to be in financial jeopardy.

Now covetousness means you want everything for yourself, and you're not planning to help anybody else. In other words, covetousness means you don't care about the preacher's heart to do something for God or his vision for the church. That doesn't make any difference to you—you're going to give your forty dollars and no more! That's covetousness, and if that's your attitude and motive, God isn't going to trust you with much.

Now the *devil* might give you some money, but you are going to catch "hell" with it! The devil might give you some money, but you're not going to be happy and full of joy. The devil will end up whipping you because if he gives you money—if you get money by being in cahoots with him—then he has a right to do whatever he wants with you.

The devil does give people money. Do you remember what he told Jesus when he took Him to a high mountain and showed Him all the kingdoms of the world? ...**All these things will I give thee, if thou wilt fall down and worship me** (Matthew 4:9). Jesus said, ...**Get thee hence, Satan: for it is written, Thou shalt worship the Lord thy God, and him only shalt thou serve** (v. 10).

So, you see, the devil can give you money, but he'll do it to buy your soul. For example, he'll see to it that you get some money, but then he'll come to your house and oppress your wife and family.

God wants to give you money, not for *covetousness*, but for *covenant*. He wants to establish a money covenant with you.

Many in the Body of Christ don't tithe. And God is saying, "All the silver and gold are Mine, and you're swapping all the silver and gold that's Mine for a dime."

Think about that! All the silver and gold belong to God (Haggai 2:8), and you know that if you belong to Him, He will give some to you. Yet many will swap that for a dime!

If you're not a tither, you can just keep on going down the same road after you read this, just doing the same thing you've been doing. But I know in my heart that some people are going to change. Some people are going to begin to tithe and come out of their old way of living—of living payday to payday, just trying to make ends meet.

2. "Tell My people that 'Money cometh' is for *covenant* reasons."

After the Lord gave me the words "Money cometh," He told me *why* He wanted the Body of Christ to have money. God said, "Tell the people that 'Money cometh' is not for *covetous* reasons but for *covenant* reasons."

Someone may ask, "What exactly does that mean?" The Lord said, "First, I want to fulfill My covenant and take care of My children well. Second, I want My Gospel to go to the four corners of the earth, and I want people to be in My churches and to be able to give unto the proclamation of the Gospel that the world might be evangelized."

Now what does "Money cometh" mean for you? "Money cometh" means that money is *constantly* coming to you! And it's coming to you for covenant reasons.

We have a money covenant with God so we can get His Gospel out to the ends of the earth. Our prosperity—our "Money cometh"—is not for covetousness, but it is for *covenant*.

I was talking to the Lord about this, and He said to me, "Why do you think Abraham was rich?"

I said, "Lord, I don't even have to think about it. He was rich because he was serving You."

"Well," the Lord said, "that's why I want the Body of Christ to be rich. I want their needs met. I want people to look at them and say, 'Oh, that's a person who's serving God!'"

You see, God made a covenant with Abraham and told him, "I'm going to bless you, and I'm going to give you all that you see" (Genesis 13:14-17; 15:5).

Now, we should have at least the same blessing that Abraham had. In other words, if we didn't have any *more* than Abraham had, we should *at least* have the *same kind* of blessing he had! Well, the

Bible says in Hebrews 8:6 that we have a new and *better* covenant established upon *better* promises!

Abraham was rich, but he wasn't what some people call "filthy" rich. Abraham was "clean" rich because Abraham honored God, and *God* gave Abraham his prosperity.

God will give you prosperity, but your prosperity is for covenant, not for covetousness. The devil will try to get you off track with covetousness. He will try to take you away from being willing and obedient, because he knows that if you're willing and obedient, you will eat the good of the land (Isaiah 1:19). As a matter of fact, you can't be willing and obedient and broke at the same time. Write that down and don't forget it. "Willing and obedient" and "broke" don't go together! Willingness and obedience run "broke" off!

3.   "Tell My people to say, 'I'll never be broke another day in my life!'"

God told me to tell you to confess, "I'll never be broke another day in my life!" And when you confess it, say it like you mean it. Don't just whisper it. Say it boldly and keep on saying it.

This is one part of the revelation: You have to say it if you want it. And this is what the Lord told me: "Tell My people to say, 'I'll never be broke another day in my life!'"

So to get "Money cometh" to work for you, you have to make the confession, "Money cometh to *me!* I'll never be broke another day in my life!"

Now don't start saying "Money cometh" just because you got happy when you heard somebody else saying it. You've got to actually see yourself not broke. You have to see yourself not living from paycheck to paycheck. You have to see yourself as a covenant man or woman who's walking in the inheritance your Father has provided for you.

You've got to say from your "guts" (you've heard the expression "*gut* instinct"), or from your spirit, "Money cometh! Money cometh! Money *cometh!* I'll never be broke another day in my life, in Jesus' Name!"

I want you to say that with all that is within your heart: "*Money cometh!*" It's not how *loudly* you say it, but it's how *deeply* you say it: It's how much you *believe* it that counts!

God gave me all of this for the Body of Christ. Well, are you part of the Body? If you are, that means money cometh to *you!* And it's not for covetous reasons, but it is for *covenant* reasons.

This prosperity message has gotten ahold of me. I can't even *think* broke! I can't even *think* of an empty wallet and an empty checking account. I tell you, 55,000 demons holding spiritual machine guns to my spirit couldn't make me think broke! I'd still holler out, "No!!! I'm not broke! I'll never be broke! I've got the revelation of prosperity in my heart, and I'm not covetous!"

God wants you to have plenty so He can get the Gospel out. So quit using all those credit cards. Have a storehouse for God to bless, and then don't be tight with the blessings He gives you. If it takes $50 or $100 to open the account, then you couldn't give $50 or $100 away, because you need that money to keep your account open. But after you get a little bit, say $200, God might tell you, "Go get $100 and plant it into so-and-so's ministry." You might think, *Oh, God, it took me three months to get that extra $100.* But, no. Go get it, because He wants to give you more. Hurry up and get that $100 out of there. If you don't, it will block your bigger blessing. Give when God tells you to give, because God just wants to give you more.

Your Father doesn't want you to be broke, and He has made a way for you not to be broke. But you have to do something for yourself. You have to be obedient to believe the Word and to do what the Lord tells you to do with your money. You also have to say something. You've got to speak up and mean what you say!

We are redeemed from the curse of the law! Poverty is a curse of the law, but God said Christ has redeemed us. And it's through preaching and teaching and cleansing your mind with the Word that the curse of poverty, which has bound you, will begin to fall by the wayside.

The Body of Christ is going to the top! We are rising above this world's system and entering into the land of prosperity that God has provided for us. We're in covenant with God, and we're financing the preaching of the Gospel to every creature. Money cometh to the Body of Christ!

Ye have sown much, and bring in little; ye eat, but ye have not enough; ye drink, but ye are not filled with drink; ye clothe you, but there is none warm; and he that earneth wages earneth wages to put it into a bag with holes.
—HAGGAI 1:6

In this chapter, I am going to talk more specifically about some things that cause money *not* to come. You need to know what those things are so you can stand strong against them and get in on what God wants for you—*prosperity.*

There's no shortage of money with God. But often there's something we're doing that's stopping God from giving it to us.

I am going to show you what may be blocking money from coming to you.

Failing To Tithe Will Cause
Money Not To Come

We already saw that if you are not a tither, the first blockage is that dime. That is the first thing that's causing money not to come to you.

A dime could be keeping you from your prosperity, because if you're not tithing and you're not obedient to God's Word concerning finances, then "Money cometh" will not work for you.

But just because you are tithing and are sold out to God doesn't mean the devil is just going to "roll over" and let you have some money! He will try to block it from coming to you.

The *devil* doesn't want you to have it, and the *world* doesn't want you to have it.

Get on God's Money System—
You Can't Outgive God!

Let's read the first part of our text: **Ye have sown MUCH, and bring in LITTLE...** (Haggai 1:6).

Pay careful attention to what I'm about to tell you: *That can never happen with God!* It is impossible for you to sow *much* into the Kingdom of God and come up with *little.* That would never happen with God. Luke 6:38 tells us why:

> **Give, and it SHALL be given unto you; good measure, pressed down, and shaken together, and running over, shall men give into your bosom. For with the same measure that ye mete withal it shall be measured to you again.**
>
> **Luke 6:38**

The Bible says that God loves a cheerful giver (2 Corinthians 9:7). Other translations say that He loves a "happy" or "hilarious" giver. In other words, if you say, "Well, I have my tithe ready, and I'm going to add $200 in offerings" and then do it, there's no way you will receive *little* in return.

No, that can't happen with my God. God is not cheap—He is not "tight." And God is not broke! The Bible says He gives seed to the sower and bread to the eater (Isaiah 55:10). And God intends for you to reap a harvest from your giving.

Now look at Luke 6:38 again. Look at it as you've never looked at it before. Listen as if Jesus Himself is talking to you, because He *is* talking to you through His Word. Don't have the attitude that makes you think, *Oh, I know what Luke 6:38 says.* If you have that attitude, you're not going to hear Jesus.

That "bringing in little" in Haggai 1:6 can never happen with your giving to God and the work of God, because Luke 6:38 says, **Give, and it *shall* be given unto you....** And Galatians 6:7 says, **Whatsoever a man soweth, that shall he also reap.** You see, money cometh by giving!

God works opposite this world's system. Money cometh through this world's system by stealing. To this world's system, "Money cometh" means cheating everybody you can. That's the way the world works.

But God's system of prosperity is opposite this world's system. Giving and being a tither get you in on God's system. God wants you to give, and He wants you to reap a harvest from your giving. He doesn't want you to sow *much* and bring in *little*.

Another Look at the Tithe

Let me tell you just how a person sows much and brings in little—by not tithing. If he doesn't tithe, he gets holes in his bag, and the devil steals from him because of a dime. He might be working two jobs, but he's putting his money in a bag—and out the bottom of the bag it goes! Why? Because he has the Lord's dime!

> **Ye have sown much, and bring in little; ye eat, but ye have not enough; ye drink, but ye are not filled with drink; ye clothe you, but there is none warm; and HE THAT EARNETH WAGES EARNETH WAGES TO PUT IT INTO A BAG WITH HOLES.**
>
> **Haggai 1:6**

If that applies to you, let's get those holes out of your bag! In fact, let's get you a *new bag!*

The tithe is the dime off every dollar that you're supposed to give to the Lord—10 percent of your income. Certainly, when you look at it as a dime off every dollar, the dimes add up to dollars. But just remember, it is God who has given you the money in the first place. And He will keep on giving it to you if you'll obey Him in faith.

But if you are not a tither, the devil is holding you back from real prosperity by fooling you into keeping a dime that's not yours. He's causing holes to be in your bag.

Most Christians who don't tithe have holes in their pocketbooks, holes in their checkbooks and holes in their savings accounts—because they're robbing God of a dime.

I'm not condemning you if you're not a tither, but I know there's going to be some conviction after you read this. There needs to be. I want to get some finances in your pocket, but it won't happen in God's system as long as you're not tithing.

Read Haggai 1:6 again: ...**Ye eat, but ye HAVE NOT ENOUGH; ye drink, but ye are NOT FILLED WITH DRINK; ye clothe you, but THERE IS NONE WARM....**

It says, "You eat, but you don't have enough." In other words, you're not satisfied.

Let me tell you why many Christians are not satisfied. They may have good jobs, but if they're not doing what God called them to do, they're never going to be satisfied.

Notice Haggai 1:6 *doesn't* say, "You're not eating, and that's why you don't have enough and are not satisfied." No, they were eating, all right, but they were not satisfied, because they weren't putting God and His Word first.

That applies to some Christians today. They're eating, all right. They're eating in nice restaurants! But they know their bills aren't paid at home, and they're using some of God's money and some of that "bill" money to eat at those fancy restaurants. So they're not satisfied.

If you are not a tither, you don't want to keep going down the same road you've gone down before. But the only way to keep from *repeating* history is by *repenting.*

If that describes you, pray this prayer: "Father, in the Name of Jesus, I repent. I don't want to go down this same road anymore, Lord. I repent of robbing You. In the Name of Jesus, help me, Lord, to do what I'm supposed to do."

We need to get rid of the bag with the holes in it! And what causes a person to have holes in his bag? *Robbing God.* So if you've been robbing God, get rid of that bag. Change bags!

Also, we need to change attitudes if our attitude isn't right. We must have a right attitude toward the Word of God, and we must have a right attitude toward the *work* of God. We have to have a giving attitude and a good attitude about tithing.

God wants you to enjoy the nine-tenths. He wants you to really enjoy it! You're not going to, though, if you don't give the Lord His tenth. You've got to give Him His dime. He wants to get you out of debt. He wants you to have plenty of money in the bank and be ready to evangelize the world. But He can't do it if you don't have a right attitude, a willing attitude, toward Him and what He wants you to do.

I realize that you may be a tither today. And yet some who are tithers are still broke or are facing financial hardship and difficulty. They may simply need to learn how to release their faith concerning the tithe. God has made certain promises for those who are tithers. (See Malachi 3:10.)

Others who are tithers aren't broke at all, but they might not be where they want to be financially. They need to know that God wants to bless and prosper them even more so they can do more for Him.

Now let's read something in Malachi 3 that addresses the issue of tithing.

> **Even from the days of your fathers ye are gone away from mine ordinances, and have not kept them. Return unto me, and I will return unto you, saith the Lord of hosts. But ye said, Wherein shall we return? Will a man rob God? Yet ye have robbed me. But ye say, Wherein have we robbed thee? In tithes and offerings. Ye are cursed with a curse: for ye have robbed me, even this whole nation.**
>
> **Malachi 3:7-9**

Notice in verse 7, God said, "Return to Me, and I will return to you." God was saying, "Return to Me and do what I tell you to do, and I'm going to return to you and make you like Abraham."

In Christ, you are Abraham's seed (Galatians 3:29). That means that Abraham's blessings are yours. The Bible says about Lot and Abraham that they couldn't even stay in the same area of the country together because they had so many possessions (Genesis 13:6)!

Today, many Christians in one local church could probably move into the same *neighborhood* and that wouldn't be a problem! And without all the things they bought with their credit cards, they might be able to move into the same *house!*

Let's keep reading in Malachi 3: **Even from the days of your fathers ye are gone away from mine ordinances, and have not kept them. Return unto me, and I will return unto you, saith the Lord of hosts. But ye said, WHEREIN SHALL WE RETURN?** (v. 7).

The Lord wants to make sure you know what He's talking about, because look at His answer in verse 8: **Will a man rob God? Yet ye have robbed me. But ye say, Wherein have we robbed thee? In TITHES and OFFERINGS.**

Then look at what He says in verse 9: **Ye are cursed with a curse: for ye have robbed me, even this whole nation.**

Then look at what God says to do about it! Verse 10 says, **Bring ye all the tithes into the storehouse, that there may be meat in mine house, and prove me now herewith, saith the Lord of hosts, if I will not open you the windows of heaven, and pour you out a blessing, that there shall not be room enough to receive it!**

Now this is what happens: Some don't believe the part of God's Word that says, **There shall not be room enough to receive it.** They may be tithers, all right. But they don't believe what God says about it, so they receive little in return because of their lack of faith, and "Money cometh" doesn't work for them.

Verse 11 gives some more of the promise for you to take hold of. God said, "And I will stop the devil in your life!"

> **And I will rebuke the devourer for your sakes, and he shall not destroy the fruits of your ground; neither shall your vine cast her fruit before the time in the field, saith the Lord of hosts.**
>
> Malachi 3:11

If you think *that's* good, the Lord is still not finished! He said in verse 12, **And ALL NATIONS shall call you BLESSED: for ye shall be a DELIGHTSOME LAND, saith the Lord of hosts.**

God wants people to see you! He wants them to see you blessed. Say this if you need to: "Lord, I'm returning to Your will right now!"

Can a Man Really Rob God?

Look at Malachi 3:8 again: **Will a man ROB GOD? Yet YE HAVE ROBBED ME. But ye say, Wherein have we robbed thee? In TITHES and OFFERINGS.**

I have a question for you. Can you really rob God? I mean, when it comes to money, can you really rob Him? Since God has all the silver and gold and all the cattle on a thousand hills, you can't rob Him of money.

That verse is not talking about robbing God of money. Do you remember in Matthew 17:24-27 when the disciples needed to pay their taxes? Jesus told Peter to go catch a certain fish, and that fish had the money they needed in its mouth! So, you see, money is no problem with God!

Then, how can you rob God? When you hold back that dime, the tithe, *you rob God of His holy desire to bless you and His pleasure in making you the most prosperous person He can see!* You rob the Father of the opportunity to give His child whatever he or she wants, because you went astray from Him and didn't do what He told you to do.

It's the same way in the natural. Remember the question I asked in chapter 1: "What would you do for your son or daughter if you were a multimillionaire?" Remember how I talked about your buying a house for your son and daughter-in-law?

Now suppose your *daughter* who just got married has been "in good" with Daddy and Mama. She's acted right and she's been obedient.

So she takes you to a particular house she likes and says, "Oh, Daddy, I'd really like to have this house."

You're a multimillionaire. You say, "Okay, you've got it, Baby."

But your daughter doesn't seem to hear you. She is still talking: "Daddy, you don't understand. The finance company doesn't want to lend us the money because we don't have much credit yet."

You say, "No, Baby, *you* don't understand. You don't need that finance company. You've got the house. Daddy's going to buy it for you."

As I said before, the price of that house doesn't even bother you, because you're a multimillionaire. Well, I wonder if God the Father has any money! Certainly, He does! And He wants you to say, "Money cometh to *me!*" and then do what He told you to do in His Word so He can make it start coming to you.

Small Thinking Will Cause
Money Not To Come

Money cometh to the Body of Christ, but in this chapter, we're talking about what causes money *not* to come. Christians need to find out why they don't have the money. The Lord says He wants them to have it. He says He's a prosperous God. Yet in churches all over the land, people are broke. There's only a remnant of them who have some money.

There's a poverty spirit that has gotten into the Body of Christ, and it's been living there. It's an old stingy, "tight" spirit, and it has affected people's thinking. That's one of the things that's causing money not to come to them. But the Word of God is driving that spirit and that attitude *out!*

> **Now unto him that is able to do EXCEEDING ABUN-DANTLY ABOVE all that we ask or think, according to the power that worketh in us.**
>
> **Ephesians 3:20**

I want you to read this verse of Scripture as if you didn't know anything about the Bible. The Holy Ghost uses all kinds of good words in this verse—*exceeding, abundantly, above*—to describe what God will do for His children. I don't see "beneath" in that verse anywhere! I don't see the word "under" in there anywhere!

It says, **Now unto him that is ABLE....** God is *able!* Able to do what? **EXCEEDING ABUNDANTLY ABOVE all that we ask or think, according to the power that worketh in us.**

I want you to get a blank sheet of paper. Write, in big letters, the word "EXCEEDING." Then, directly beneath that, write "ABUNDANTLY."

Then write down the word "ABOVE." You need to get a revelation of prosperity in your spirit if you want money to start coming to you!

Exceeding Abundantly Above!

Exceeding. Abundantly. Above. This is what God wants for you—*exceeding abundantly above* in every area of your life! Exceeding abundantly above what? Above your paycheck, for one!

That job of yours is not your source. Don't let that job and your paycheck become your source. *God wants to send you some more money from somewhere else—through somebody else—in addition to your paycheck.* And God is *able!* God can cause birds to fly over your driveway and drop hundred dollar bills on you if He wants to. *God is your Source!*

Let's continue looking at Ephesians 3:20. There's another word we need to look at. **Now unto him that is able to do exceeding abundantly above ALL....**

What does *all* mean? All means *all* your bills paid; *all* your debt, distress and discontentment gone; and *all* your heart's desires fulfilled!

You see, all that your little heart ever desires, God wants you to have. You wouldn't even make a dent in what God has to make you so happy. God will make you happy and bless you so much more than you could ask or think or imagine!

You know, the world wants to keep you on its system of having just enough to get by. Two paychecks, two cars, a nice house, and that's it. That's the world's system. But the world doesn't want you to have enough money to give "big" to the Gospel.

If you wanted to give $5,000 today for the Gospel, could you do it? I'm talking about a "free five"—$5,000, free and clear. In other words, could you do it without it hurting you and setting you back financially? Could you do it without having to eat beans and corn bread for the next five years while you try to catch up? I mean, could you give $5,000 and still eat the same way you've been eating, drive the same car and dress up to go out with your family? I'm not talking about giving $5,000 and then struggling for five years to catch up!

Look at Ephesians 3:20 again: **Now unto him that is able to do exceeding abundantly above all that we ask or think, according to the power that worketh in us.**

Are you living that verse? I'm not talking about living that verse "by faith." I know we have to live by faith, but too many just stay in that "by faith" mode when, really, faith is just passing them by!

Why do I say that? Because if it were real faith, their faith would bring in the answer. After a while—after a certain period of time— they should be able to say, "It's here; I've got it!"

We know everything works by faith. In other words, everything we get from God, we get by faith. But some people use that phrase "by faith" as a scapegoat so they don't have to admit and attest to the fact that they're missing it somewhere in their faith. They're missing God somewhere.

If you've been serving God for fifteen years, living "by faith" and you're still broke, you've missed God somewhere. At one of those turns in the road somewhere, you turned the wrong way. You might as well face it if it's true. That's the only way you're going to come out of the situation you're in. God doesn't want you broke!

I love the Body of Christ—God's people, His children. I would never put one of God's children down or look down on him. I'm preaching and teaching strongly about "Money cometh," not to make people feel badly because they don't have it, but because I want them to have it!

Listening to "False Prophets"
Causes Money Not To Come

Some preachers are always talking about money, but they're talking money out of your pocket! Certainly, you should give to churches and ministries. In fact, you can't receive without giving. But some preachers are not teaching this message of prosperity correctly.

I'm not preaching about the tithe for the sake of my church— you're supposed to tithe to *your* local church, the place where you are spiritually fed. I'm not preaching this message to get money into my church. I'm preaching this message to help the Body of Christ. I could just be at home, resting, enjoying the blessings God has given me and my family. But the Lord told me to tell His people about this prosperity and to tell them how to get it.

Certainly, there are false prophets out there. They're out there, and they'll try to "prophesy" to you, saying, "If you give $300, such and such is going to happen in your life." But don't let false prophets keep you from listening to God and His Word concerning money and financial prosperity.

Don't Throw Out the True With the False

You're always going to have the false out there along with the true. But what is false shouldn't stand in your way of the revelation of "Money cometh!" Money "cometh" into your life so that God can use you as a reservoir and an agent to get His Word out and to bless you "real good" at the same time! While the money is passing through your hands, God is going to let you keep some of it!

So get all of these false prophets out of your mind. Some of them have your money because you put your faith in them rather than in God and His Word.

Experiences like that could cause you not to believe a real prophet or a real pastor, teacher or apostle. When the real thing comes along, you're leery. You're thinking about all the tricks you've heard in the past. You've mailed your money to different preachers all over the country who claimed they had a message from God for you, but a lot of it was false. A lot of it was just a trick to get your money.

I want to show you some of the things that cause money not to come, so you can do the right things according to the Word of God and get in on what He wants you to have.

My Own Story

We're going to take a little "side trip" together as I tell you the story of my coming into prosperity. I may say some things that will make you laugh, but God wants to say some things to you through my testimony that will help you so you won't make some of the mistakes about money that I have made.

I was tired of being in debt and broke all the time. I was tired of hearing the preachers ask, "Who will give $500?" and then having to hide behind somebody because I didn't have $500!

An extra $500—are you kidding me! Man, if I would have given $500 not too many years ago, it would have taken me months or *years* to catch up again because the credit card company would have gotten me! I wouldn't have been able to keep up with my credit card payment and give $500 too! And when you don't send those credit card companies their money, they slap the *big* interest payments and late fees on you! Some of those companies charge up to 22 percent!

Now I didn't have any money back then, but I always had a front. In other words, I always had a new car, but I was just as broke as I could be. You see, cars don't mean you have money. Everybody you see driving a new car isn't rich. He may be broke, trying to pay for that car! That's the way it was in my case.

Years ago my wife and I were getting two paychecks, and when we'd get paid, we'd sit at our kitchen table and figure and figure and figure. We were figuring out how to pay all our bills! We couldn't even go out and get ice cream after paying the bills.

We didn't have any extra money to go get ice cream or anything beyond just what we needed. Sometimes I would just cheat. I'd say, "I'm not paying this bill; I'm going to get me some ice cream!"

I heard a minister tell the story one time about a certain man who had an over-abundance of bills. A creditor wrote to the man and talked to him kind of "rough" in the letter and harassed him about the money he owed.

The man wrote back to the creditor and said, "I've got so many bills that here's how I've decided to pay them: I put them all on the table and shuffle them, and the three I pick out are the ones I pay." Then the man said to the creditor, "If you write me another letter like the one you wrote me, I'm not even going to put you in the *shuffle!*"

That sounds funny, but if you've ever been in a situation like that, you know the frustration of having more bills than you can pay.

I'm so glad I got hold of the message I'm giving to you, because faith in God's Word on the subject of money and financial prosperity has changed my situation. The revelation of "Money cometh" has brought me and my family to another level in our finances.

Many people—really "spiritual" folks—think they have to be crying and rolling on the floor to get a revelation from God. No! A thousand times, no! If you keep listening, God is speaking to you right now.

God wants you to have joy. He wants you to be jolly. And this revelation knowledge from God that you're seeking can come through smiles just like it comes through tears. We don't have to be serious and sad and dressed in black to be spiritual and hear from God. The Spirit of God doesn't work like that. The Bible says, **Let them shout for JOY, and be GLAD, THAT FAVOUR MY RIGHTEOUS CAUSE: yea, let them say continually, Let the Lord be magnified, which hath pleasure in the prosperity of his servant** (Psalm 35:27). God wants us to be glad!

Gladness and joy are the result of favoring God's righteous cause. How do you favor God's righteous cause? By being open to what the Lord tells you to do with your money. In other words, your checking and savings accounts are available to God when He speaks to you to give.

Remember I said that when I first tried to open a savings account years ago, I didn't even have enough money to open one. We didn't start out in life prosperous. My wife and I had good jobs, yet we were broke. But not anymore! That's why I encouraged you to have a savings account. God can't bless your storehouse if you don't have one for Him to bless! And He can't bless you like He wants to if you're buying stuff on credit that you don't need. In other words, you need to get out of debt.

I also encouraged you to stop trying to buy big cars to impress somebody if you can't afford them. Those big cars could keep you broke! Just buy yourself a basic car, stripped down with no extras in it if you have to, until you get further up in faith.

In my own case, I remember when I was still driving an old Corvair (no, not _Corvette_—_Corvair!_). I'd shift gears in that thing, and smoke would come in through every window! That was all I had to drive.

And there was a time when my wife sewed her own clothes. Sometimes she'd be putting her last stitch in right before church. She did that for years.

We were broke at that time, but we didn't ask anybody for anything. (By the way, my wife looked better in those "stitched" dresses than some of the women who bought their clothes, because God's aroma and blessing were on them!) We were broke, but we didn't stay broke. We began to take certain steps, and we began to rise up in our finances.

Prosperity doesn't come to a person overnight just because he's heard one teaching. You have to walk in what you know for a period of time to rise up in the things of God.

You know, God will test you. He doesn't tempt you with evil, but He will test you to know if you're serious about His business. The main way God knows if you're serious about His business is how you operate in your finances. If you can give up your money, God knows there's a chance you love Him. But if you hold on to that money, and you don't care how the Church makes it, God knows He can't trust you with much.

For example, if you're making $2,500 a month, and you give $5 to the church like you think you turned the world over with that five, chances are you won't pass God's test! God will know you're not serious about His business.

Having that kind of attitude would be like your going to a nice restaurant, eating about $140 in food and then saying, "I'm paying $40 and no more." The waiter says, "No, sir, your bill is $140." And you say, "I'm only paying forty!"

Some Christians have been *tipping* the Lord and *paying* the world! They've been giving the Lord their leftovers. But the Lord doesn't take scraps, and He doesn't play the tipping game.

So give the Lord His tenth! Don't tip Him. Churches ought to put up a big sign that says, "No Tipping!"

Impatience Will Cause Money Not To Come

Now let me show you some more things that cause money *not* to come to you.

> Ye have sown much, and bring in little; ye eat, but ye
> have not enough; ye drink, but ye are not filled with drink;
> ye clothe you, but there is none warm; and he that earneth
> wages earneth wages to put it into a bag with holes.
>
> Haggai 1:6

Something else that causes money not to come to Christians is impatience. For example, people may get ahold of the message "Money cometh," but when their circumstances don't begin to change immediately, they give up.

But if you're broke, it's going to take you a little while to get to that place of prosperity. In the natural, once you're in a deep hole, it takes you a while to climb out of it. You don't just come out of that hole instantly!

So if you're in a big "dirt hole" of debt, you didn't get there overnight. But you can come out of that hole if you will be patient and continue in the Word of God.

You Can Come Out of the "Hole" of Debt!

You may be down in that "debt hole," but you've got some revelation now. You have the Word of God, the sword of the Spirit, that you can use to dig into the side of the cave. You can make your own steps to climb out.

That's how you're going to come out of debt—step by step. You're not going to jump out of there like Superman! You're not going to get out of debt tomorrow; you didn't get deep into debt just yesterday.

I'm telling you how to come out of debt the *right* way—*God's* way. You take your little prosperity shovel and chip your way out! You chip your way to one level and walk around on that level. Then you chip your way to another level. You're coming out of that hole of debt! You may have been down deep in the hole of debt, distress and discontentment, but you're coming out!

The Holy Ghost gave me that illustration because often people will hear teaching on prosperity, and they'll go out tomorrow and get crazy and start buying all kinds of stuff. Then they believe they're just going to pay all those bills off, along with the bills they already have and just get out of debt instantly.

The blessings of God don't just fall on you all at once. You have to get ahold of the truth and walk in it consistently, day by day, for it to work for you.

It's something like one minister's testimony of how he lost a lot of weight. This minister was a big old dude at one time. He was *fat!* But God helped him lose weight. This minister just kept confessing the Word concerning keeping his flesh under, and he lost all the weight he needed to lose. People think he did that overnight, but it took him months and years to get to the weight he wanted to be.

So, you see, you're going to have to be consistent in digging your way out of debt. And while you're doing it, put away those credit cards I sometimes call "demons." They *are* "demons" if you don't know how to handle them! A credit card is good if you know how to use it. But if you don't know how to use it, that credit card is using *you!*

Overspending on Credit
Will Cause Money Not To Come

That's exactly what happened to me—my credit cards were using me. I overcharged on my credit cards. It's so easy to use a credit card, because you don't actually see your money going. But then the following month when you look in your mailbox and see that bill, you don't like that old thing bought on credit nearly as much!

A credit card is a good thing to have if you pay your balance every month. But some people overcharge on credit cards. They can't pay their balances. If that describes you, quit using those cards and begin chipping your way out of debt with the Word of God.

You see, many of those credit card companies are designed to keep you broke. If you can't pay your balance on a credit card each month, you may never pay it off! You might send a credit card company a minimum payment due of $35, and they will take a large portion of that just for interest! You have to send more than the minimum payment due each month if you want to chip away at your balance. Otherwise, as I said, you might never pay that account off.

I paid all my credit card balances off. I paid those turkeys off, and then I got a big pair of scissors and starting cutting! I cut my credit cards up, one by one. I said, "You credit card, you kept me broke because I bought things with you that I didn't need! But now I'm getting rid of you!"

I always tell people to cut their credit cards up if they can't discipline themselves to pay their balances in full at the end of the month.

Some people are so in debt to credit card companies that they take the Lord's tithe to send to the creditors. That's one of the things that's keeping them broke. They take the very thing that will bring them prosperity and mail it to the credit card companies.

Now you might ask me, "Reverend, what would you do right now if you were in my shoes—if you were in debt up to your neck—and the Lord started talking to you about tithing?"

I'm glad you asked that, because that's the very position I was in at one time! And here's my answer: I'd start tithing *today!*

I can say that boldly, because I did it! And I owed everybody! But the Lord starting dealing with me about tithing. He talked to me three times about it in just a short period of time—the first time through a radio preacher, the second time through another preacher and the third time through a bug exterminator who came to spray the church for bugs!

The "bug man" sprayed the church, and when it was time for me to pay the bill, he told me, "Here's the price, less 10 percent."

I looked at him and said, "Less 10 percent? What for?"

He said, "Oh, I tithe off the bill at every church I spray."

I was a pastor, and here was the roach man telling the pastor to tithe!

After he left, I said, "That's enough, Lord. You don't have to send anybody else." Then I went home and told my wife, "Every dollar that we've got coming into this house, 10 percent of it is going to the Lord."

My wife didn't argue with me. She said, "All right, let's do it." My wife has always been a good wife—a real woman. She has always submitted to me. I've always tried to do the right thing even if I didn't always *end up* doing the right thing, but my wife always stood by me.

We started to tithe, and because we didn't know too much about faith, for quite some time, we gave our tithe and didn't receive anything in return.

You see, you have to tithe in *faith.* You have to remind God of what He said in His Word. In time, my wife and I began to see some things in the Word, and when we started mixing our faith with that, we began to rise to the top financially.

As I said, there are some practical steps to walking in divine prosperity. We believed God for finances; we used our faith. But we took those natural steps too. The first thing we did to start coming out of debt and into financial prosperity was to start tithing. The second thing we did was to start paying off our debts and stop buying things we didn't need.

We wrote out a list of all our bills from the smallest to the biggest and began to talk to our bills. We got out the smallest bill. It was for about $200, and, boy, I had some fun! I said, "You're gone!" and I put $50 toward that bill. Then later I put another $50 on it—and, finally, I paid the rest of the balance and got rid of that bill. I scratched that bill off the list, just shouting! You see, we were coming out of that hole!

Then I went to the next bill and said, "You're next!" Pay attention to what I'm saying, because this is how we did it, and it worked. We believed God would help us come out of debt, and He brought us out supernaturally. But we weren't buying new suits and dresses; we just pressed the suits and dresses we had!

While we were doing all this, credit card companies would write to us and tell us we could buy something else—that they were raising our credit limit. They'd say, "Mr. Thompson, you're a good customer. We're extending your line of credit."

I said to myself, *Oh, no, you don't, credit card! You're not extending anything for me! I've cut you up!* I knew they wanted me to go buy another suit, but I was pressing the one I had!

I never said it was going to be easy to come out of debt. It's not going to be easy. But, you see, people get in debt by not listening to the Lord—by just buying a lot of stuff on the world's system. To get out of debt, they have to listen to what God says.

You may think that what I'm saying sounds unspiritual and fleshly, but I'm telling you the truth! My wife will tell you, when we first decided to come out of debt, I cut our credit cards up. Now some of you may be stronger than I was. You might be able to put your cards in a drawer somewhere and quit using them until you come out of debt. But I couldn't have trusted in the drawer. It would have been too easy to go back into that drawer and get those cards out fast!

Then I got one of those cards that you use just for convenience and pay off in full every month. That company doesn't play that "interest and carrying charge" game.

I have a friend who got one of those cards once. He liked the fact that there was no credit limit. So he got one, and he took his family shopping. He also bought a nice suit and a new pair of shoes for himself. He said, "Man, I like this card!"

Then the bill came. I think it was for a couple thousand dollars, and that company wanted their money! My friend didn't know you had to pay the balance in full every month. He said to his wife, "Honey, I don't want this kind of card!" He wanted the kind of card for which you could pay $15 a month for the rest of your life!

When you have to pay your balance in full every month, that tells you if you can pass the test or not. What is the test? The test is to determine whether you can afford the things you're buying.

To some of you, your credit cards are your favorite friends. But you need to "crucify" those credit cards for the Lord Jesus Christ and be resurrected to the financial stability that the Father wants for you! God doesn't want you in debt, in distress and discontented. He wants you to prosper!

Making Excuses Will Cause Money Not To Come

Sometimes people make excuses for not prospering. They'll hear that it's the Father's will to prosper them, but they make excuses, such as, "Well, I come from such and such a family."

But none of that can stop you! Your circumstances can't stop you. *God* says that no weapon formed against you shall prosper (Isaiah 54:17)! *God* says that if He is for you, who can be against you (Romans 8:31)! *He* says that all things work together for good for those who love Him (Romans 8:28)! *God* says, "In all these things, we are more than conquerors through Him who loved us" (Romans 8:37)!

So don't make excuses. Making excuses will cause money not to come to you. You'll just stay in the same condition you're in now if you make excuses for not prospering. God is on your side! And "Money cometh" belongs to you!

Disobedience Will Cause Money Not To Come

Now I want you to always remember this revelation of how a person robs God when he keeps the Lord's tithe. You can't rob God, *per se,* by keeping money from Him. You can't rob Him of money, but by keeping money from Him—in keeping the tithe—you are robbing God of the opportunity of giving you what you want and even more above that. God can't bless disobedience.

Disobedience will keep money out of your house and out of your pocket. God can't bless you while you are disobeying what He told you to do.

Some people say, "Well, tithing was only for the Old Testament. We're not under the law." But let's not use that as an excuse. Some people just want to "ride" that excuse. They want to coast along on that excuse so they don't have to pay their tithes.

But the tithe was instituted 400 years before the law. Four hundred years before God even gave the law to Moses, the tithe was there! Look at Abraham and those boys living back during that time before the law. Those boys were tithers, and God had no problem giving them exceeding abundantly above all they could ask or think!

The Body of Christ is going places! Promotions and businesses are going to rise up in the Body of Christ! The Bible says the wealth of the wicked is laid up for the just (Proverbs 13:22). The wicked have had all the money, but we're getting hold of this revelation, and we're taking back what's ours. We're not going to be broke anymore!

Friend, I want you to get what belongs to you in Christ! You can have it; it's yours! The wealth of the wicked is laid up for the *informed* just!

Here's what I want you to do: Say, "Lord, I want what is mine, and I'm going to give You what's Yours—tithes and offerings."

Then, after you say that, get all your bills out. Write down everything you owe and then say, "Look, bills, I'm talking to you. I'm calling you paid. You're paid in full in Jesus' Name!"

Some people don't want to speak to their bills. But Jesus spoke to the fig tree! (See Matthew 21:19 and Mark 11:13.) If you don't want to speak to your situation, then forget about "Money cometh," because you're going to have to do some talking to get this to work for you.

But if you are willing to do what God tells you to do, God can help you get out of debt. He will give you divine, supernatural strategies to pay off all your bills.

I remember one time I had two cars, and the notes on both of those cars were just riding me and weighing me down. God showed me how to finance both of them and pay for them faster and with less interest.

God will show *you* things too. He'll get you out of debt. And it doesn't always have to be with more money. Sometimes He'll give you divine strategies and show you how to do it with what you have.

Dishonesty Will Cause Money Not To Come

But hear me now: God is going to show you how to do it *honestly*. Whatever God shows you is going to be honest. For example, if somebody gives you fifty dollars too much in change, that's not God paying your bill! Go back and give that person the fifty dollars if that happens to you. That's the devil trying to keep you from coming out of debt by getting you to steal.

Someone gave my wife and me plenty of money in change one time—$200 over what it was supposed to be. When we realized what happened, we said, "No, we don't want this money." Then the person almost fainted when we went back to return it. We said, "We came back because you gave us too much money." That person had given us $700 in change, and it was only supposed to be $500. We didn't want that extra $200. It would have been dishonest money.

You can't shout for joy, talking about what the Lord gave you, when you get too much change somewhere! You might cause someone to lose his job. That's the devil tricking you, trying to get you to take that extra money.

But you don't have to fall for that trick, because you know that God is going to bring prosperity to you the *honest* way.

Shout for Joy From a Good and Honest Heart, for Money *Cometh!*

People shout and dance and praise God when He blesses them with prosperity or some other blessing. And they *should* dance and praise God. But they also shouldn't forget to praise God *before* the blessing comes.

I praised God and danced and shouted for joy when I was still broke! My wife can tell you, sometimes I broke out dancing in the bedroom, or I'd come out of the bathroom dancing and shouting, "I'm free!"

You see, when you get the revelation of "Money cometh" down in your spirit, you have enough. You don't need anything else. Really, you're already out of debt. You're prosperous. Nobody can talk you out of it and tell you that you're not prosperous. No bill or bill collector can tell you you're not prosperous. Those bills of yours may be telling you you're not rich, but you know you are because you have the revelation down in your spirit.

Giving Offerings Beyond Your Tithes

As I said earlier, money cometh to you through *giving*—by being a faithful tither and by giving finances to God's work that the Gospel may go further.

The Bible talks about tithes *and* offerings. But some people aren't able to give big offerings beyond their tithes. If that describes your situation, don't come under condemnation about it. Don't even bother about it. That's why I'm writing this book—to help you get out from under being broke and in poverty. Broke folks can't support the preaching of the Gospel beyond their tithes. They need everything they have.

But when money cometh to you, you need to be obedient to God with what He has given you. Don't be greedy and stingy.

Did you know that Jesus watches your giving?

And Jesus sat over against the treasury, and beheld how the people cast money into the treasury: and many that were rich cast in much. And there came a certain poor widow, and she threw in two mites, which make a farthing. And he called unto him his disciples, and saith unto them, Verily I say unto you, That this poor widow hath cast more in, than all they which have cast into the treasury.

Mark 12:41-43

Jesus is watching everything you give, and if He sees that you're not going to give as He tells you to give, you will be keeping money out of your house. If He sees that you have the money to give, but you're not giving it when He tells you to, He won't be able to prosper you like He wants to.

Verse 41 says that the Lord Jesus went to a certain place near the treasury and sat down. He didn't watch who was acting spiritually; He watched who was putting money into the treasury.

Imagine Jesus watching some people today when the offering bucket goes by them in church! All morning for an hour and a half, they're telling the Lord, "I love You. Glory to God." But then their giving isn't in line with what their mouths are speaking! Their giving is saying less than what they're speaking.

Don't get upset with me if I've stepped on your toes, so to speak. This is the way I minister and teach. I believe in telling the truth. I am prosperous, and I'm telling you how to become prosperous too.

Look at verse 41 again: **And Jesus sat over against the treasury....** Now you'd think Jesus ought to be more spiritual than that! I mean, He came to the earth to save us, and there He was sitting by the treasury where the money was being given!

Now don't tear that page out of your Bible. Look at what Jesus was doing there. He was beholding **how the people cast money into the treasury: and many that were rich cast in much** (v. 41). Jesus was looking at how the people cast money into the treasury. In other words, He was looking at how much they gave!

As I said, Jesus knows how much you love Him and how much you love God by watching what you do with your money. It's not by your prayers or by your testimony or by your raising your hands in church to praise Him. One of your "tests" is what you do with your money.

God wants you to give so He can get some money back to you *so you can get some money back to Him* so He can get some money back to you *so you can get some money back to Him and His work!* And He's watching your money, not so much your prayers. Actually, your prayers are cheap without your obedience to the Word concerning tithes and offerings.

Many preachers don't have the nerve to say that and to give people the truth, because they can get criticized for preaching like that, especially in the area of money. But people are going to criticize me and put all kinds of names and labels on me anyway. So when I'm criticized, I just laugh with the Lord and go on about my business. I'm in the divine, perfect will of God, and if I start to go a wrong way, God tells me, and I get right back on the right road. So I don't worry about my critics. I've got the King of kings and the Lord of lords on my side!

Looking again at Jesus sitting near the temple treasury, we could ask why Jesus was watching the money that went into the treasury. As I said, it could have been so He'd know who loved Him so He could bless them "real good!"

> **And Jesus sat over against the treasury, and beheld how the people cast money into the treasury: and MANY THAT WERE RICH cast in MUCH.**
>
> Mark 12:41

Some people are waiting until they have some large amount of money before they'll give to the Lord. They say, "If I had $3,000 more, I would really give." But, no, they wouldn't. If they won't start right now where they're at, they won't give when they get the $3,000.

Jesus explained why the widow cast more money into the treasury than the others: **For all they did cast in of their abundance; but she of her want did cast in all that she had, even all her living** (Mark 12:44). She started giving to God right where she was in her finances. She didn't wait until her financial picture was better. She just gave what she could give.

I'm telling you how I know to get out of debt faster. Money cometh by your being obedient to God's Word concerning tithes and offerings.

Now, people are going to criticize you for prospering. As the Body of Christ rises up in this area, people may say, "What do they think they're doing?"

Well, what do those critics *think* we're doing? We're doing the *Bible!* People may be criticizing and gossiping, cutting their blessings off and shortening their lives. But *we're* doing the Bible. We're doing what Jesus said to do!

You see, prosperity doesn't just have to do with money. I mean, there are people with plenty of money, and they're still not prosperous. But as for the people with plenty of money who know and are in the will of God—*they* are prosperous!

My wife will tell you, I go to bed at night and go to sleep. I don't worry about anything. I'm prosperous naturally, or financially, and I'm prosperous spiritually too.

Do you believe God can do that for you? Are you going to let Him do it? He will prosper you and cause money to come to you if you'll cooperate with Him. You have to be willing and obedient to God and His Word. You have to be a tither and a cheerful giver. Don't wait until you get all your bills straight to start tithing. Tithe the next time the church doors open.

The devil is going to talk to you when you first begin to tithe. He'll say, "You fool! Don't do this!" You see, the devil will try to talk you out of doing what's right, because he knows that when you start doing what's right, you're going to get on the right track and catch on to all of his tricks. Then his days of dominating you will be over.

If you're not tithing, you need to begin tithing right now. When I made the decision to start tithing, my attitude was, *Boom—here's the truth: I'm supposed to be giving the Lord a dime off every dollar I get. So I'm going to start tithing immediately!*

I was cursed because I hadn't been giving a dime! I was robbing God! So I decided I was going to give it to Him. When the "bug man" talked to me, that was it! The "bug man" had more understanding about God than I did. The man who went around killing bugs was paying God, and I wasn't!

Have a Giving Attitude, Because God Looks on the Heart

I remember hearing a story about a man out on the mission field who wanted so badly to give to God, but he didn't have anything to give. The offering basket was being passed during a meeting, and as it passed him, he caught the usher by the arm and started to climb into the basket!

You see, this man didn't have anything else to give, but he was so strong in his conviction about giving to God that he said, "I want the Lord! I'm getting in the basket. I don't have anything else, but I'm giving the Lord all I've got. I'm giving Him myself!"

That's the kind of dedication it takes to be obedient to God's will and to prosper as He wants you to prosper. You have to start giving to God right where you are now. Your confession and your giving to God are your faith in action. So give. Then say out loud: "Satan, take your hands off my finances. I'm not going to cooperate with you. Prosperity is mine, and I'm going to receive what's mine in the Name of Jesus. Money cometh to *me!*"

Right and Wrong Thinking About Money   4

All the commandments which I command thee this day shall ye observe to do, that ye may live, and multiply, and go in and POSSESS the land which the Lord sware unto your fathers. And thou shalt remember all the way which the Lord thy God led thee these forty years in the wilderness, to humble thee, and to prove thee, to know what was in thine heart, whether thou wouldest keep his commandments, or no.
—DEUTERONOMY 8:1,2

As I discussed earlier, wrong thinking in the area of prosperity will cause money not to come to you. It will cause prosperity not to be real to you in your spirit or heart. So if you want "Money cometh," you're going to have to get your thinking straightened out about money.

Look at that word "possess" in our text, Deuteronomy 8:1. It actually says, **Go in and possess.** That's what God wants us to do. What does He want us to go in and possess? Our finances. We are to go in and possess the financial prosperity God intends for us to have.

Deuteronomy 8:2 says, **And thou shalt remember all the way which the Lord thy God led thee these forty years in the wilderness, TO HUMBLE thee, and TO PROVE thee, TO KNOW WHAT WAS IN THINE HEART, WHETHER THOU WOULDEST KEEP HIS COMMANDMENTS, OR NO.**

There are four main points I want to make from this verse concerning right and wrong thinking about money.

God led His people through the wilderness for forty years to do four things: (1) to *humble* them; (2) to *prove* them; (3) to *know them*— to *know what was in their hearts*; and (4) to *know whether or not they would keep His Word.*

You see, all of these things are qualifiers for divine prosperity.

Really, Deuteronomy 8, is a qualifying chapter written when the Lord was bringing the children of Israel into their Promised Land. There were some qualifications they had to meet, because God didn't want them to miss out on the blessings by turning away from Him once they arrived in that good land.

The Lord is saying something to us today from this chapter. There are some qualifications for walking in divine prosperity.

As I said before, the Lord's primary method of testing you is with your money. In other words, He knows whether or not He's first in your life by how you handle your money. I know you thought it was through prayer. But, no, anybody can pray, because prayer means getting an answer! Everybody likes to do that—pray and get an answer!

But at one time or another, most of us have failed God's primary method of testing us. We failed the test because we didn't put God first in our finances. Or we failed because we listened to religion and tradition, and we believed that poverty was a mark of holiness. Therefore, we wouldn't let God bless us and use our finances to bless others like He wanted to.

Let's look again at Deuteronomy 8:2:

> **And thou shalt remember all the way which the Lord thy God led thee these forty years in the wilderness, to humble thee, and to prove thee, to know what was in thine heart, whether thou wouldest keep his commandments, or no.**

If God is going to trust you with prosperity, you have to qualify according to the conditions in this verse in Deuteronomy 8. In other words, if you're going to come into the land of prosperity, you have to have a certain attitude so that prosperity does not throw you and cause you to miss the mark. So for you to come into prosperity, you have to meet certain qualifications. You have to think correctly about money.

Now when I say "prosperity," I'm talking about money. I know we talk about healing in connection with prosperity. And we can also talk about the joy of the Lord and other blessings of the Lord in connection with prosperity. But the Lord wants me to talk about money!

The Body of Christ is not having problems having joy and dancing and shouting. But many of them are broke and living from paycheck to paycheck. And many are deep in debt to credit card companies. But it shouldn't be that way.

Now let me clarify something about debt. I'm not against borrowing money. It's incorrect thinking to believe that it's always wrong to borrow money.

No, I'm only against borrowing money you can't pay back! And I'm against having those high-interest credit card accounts where you owe so much money on them that, without God's help, you might *never* be able to pay them off! Borrowing or buying on credit like that causes you to get further and further and deeper and deeper into debt.

I heard one minister say this about borrowing: "You don't really owe somebody if you're paying your bills on time."

In other words, if I have a contract that says I owe such and such amount on the fifteenth every month, then if I pay that note by the fifteenth every month, that creditor will never bother me.

Why do creditors write and call and bother people who owe them money? Because those people aren't paying what they owe on time. Those creditors write those little letters to see if the people have forgotten to pay their bills!

Creditors don't bother people who pay what they owe on time. It's a rare occasion that a creditor will ask for money from someone who's paying on time and keeping his end of the contract. I've borrowed money before and never heard from my creditor until they sent me a document verifying that I'd paid the last payment on the note.

I'm not teaching that you should pay cash for everything, because most people would have to wait a long time to get some of the things they want if they have to pay cash for all of them.

Some people refuse any kind of borrowing. They pay for everything with cash. Well, that's fine. There's nothing wrong with that. But on the other hand, you can't condemn somebody for borrowing, because the Bible talks about borrowing.

If you want to pay cash for everything right off the start, you can. It can be done. But doing that is going to take more faith than the average person has.

So understand what I'm saying. I'm not against borrowing money, but I am against borrowing money that causes you distress and discontentment because you can't pay it back.

God doesn't want His people to be deep in debt. He wants us to prosper and have plenty of money. But as I said, there are some requirements to fulfill to walk in divine prosperity.

Humble, Not Haughty

First, before God will trust you with prosperity, you have to be humble. Humility is a part of "right thinking" about money.

That's why God led the children of Israel through the wilderness—to humble them. They couldn't go into the Promised Land, that land flowing with milk and honey, at first.

You see, you won't know how to act when you get into the "land flowing with milk and honey" if you don't know how to humble yourself. You would become high-minded instead of humble-minded.

The Bible says, HUMBLE **yourselves therefore under the mighty hand of God, that he may exalt you in** DUE TIME (1 Peter 5:6). That due time won't come until God knows you can hold your place in humility. He does not dare to lift you up in finances and let you go your own way in arrogance and high-mindedness. God is not going to help you lose out with Him. The Father is not going to lift you up with finances, and then have the very finances He blesses you with cause you to stumble and fall.

You see, God is not going to bless you for you to be cursed. If He lifts you up, He wants you to stay humble and blessed. Then He can continue to lift you up. But if He lifted you up in a certain bracket or category and you weren't ready for it yet, it would cause you to stumble and fall away from Him. There are brackets and categories with God, and everybody has to move up in his or her own due season.

Now *you* determine how fast your season comes due. How fast your season comes due depends on your consistently obeying God and His Word, including First Peter 5:6: **Humble yourselves therefore under the mighty hand of God, that he may exalt you in due time.**

Get Pride Out!

According to First Peter 5:6, you must humble yourself under the mighty hand of God and get every ounce of pride out of you. It doesn't matter if you have to pray it out or speak it out—just get it out and keep it out! Get pride out, because you can't prosper with pride in your heart. Pride and divine prosperity cannot stay in the same house.

I'm talking about right and wrong thinking concerning money. You have to know how to think about money before God will trust you with a lot of it. That's because if you're not properly trained, instead of being humble, you will be high-minded. And a high-minded attitude toward money is as dangerous as cancer in a person's body.

You don't want to be high-minded; you want to be humble. When God blesses you, don't put your nose up in the air. Stay sturdy and steady and strong in Him.

So what is one qualification for going in and possessing the land of financial prosperity? Being humble instead of haughty and high-minded.

Be Willing To Be Proved

Notice it says in Deuteronomy 8:2, ...**to humble thee, and to PROVE thee....**

What does that word "prove" mean? Well, suppose God said to you: *"Prove* that you love Me. Don't just keep telling Me that you love Me. Separate yourself from that money. Separate yourself from that dime and prove that you love Me. Am I worth a dime to you?"

You can't just answer yes. You've got to *prove* it! And one of the main ways to prove that you love God is to give up that dime, the tithe. Separate from it. Let it leave your hand. Put God first—*that's* how you prove that you love Him. Pay your tithes and give offerings. Stop just tipping the Lord while you're paying the world. Instead, pay God and tip the world! God is not the server at your table; He is the *Giver* of the table!

You see, the time you go through prior to entering into prosperity is a proving time. God wants to know what you really want. In other words, do you just want what He *has,* or do you want *Him?*

Most people fail during the testing time. They get impatient and say, "Oh, this prosperity stuff doesn't work." But they need to realize they are in their trying period. God is proving them. He wants to see if they can believe Him for a *slice* of bread before He will give them the whole loaf.

The Lord wants to see if they will stay with Him when they get the slice. If they will run off with the slice of bread, He knows they will run off if they get the whole loaf. God knows that if you can believe Him for a slice of bread and be happy and full of joy, then He can trust you with the loaf. He knows that if He can trust you with $50, He can trust you with $1,000.

God will use the way you honor Him with your finances right now to prove how much money you can handle in the future. The amount of money you can handle is measured according to what you are doing *right now* with your money!

Recently, a young lady came to our church who had come into a great inheritance of thousands of dollars. But she blew it all. I mean, she didn't have a quarter! She said to me, "Brother Thompson, if only I'd heard this message earlier. I'd have money today."

This lady didn't know anything about tithing when she blew her inheritance. She told me, "I came into a great inheritance, but now they're about to take my house that I inherited. I'm broke! The only thing I have to show for my inheritance is my car. But I would still have the money if I'd heard this message sooner." She stood before me and just wept.

I've had church members who have come into large amounts of money, and they have tithed from what they've received. They've given 10 percent of it to the church. They've just put it in the offering basket and have never complained or hesitated or disobeyed. And they've continued to be blessed as a result!

But there are some people who will not do that. They're not ready to walk in divine prosperity yet. How do I know that? Because they get twenty-five dollars and aren't giving the two dollars and fifty cents!

That's easy enough to judge, isn't it? If someone is making $500 a week, and he is not giving $50, he wouldn't tithe if he made $5,000. He might *say* he would, but he is lying to his own heart.

God is not holding anything back from you. You need to get that established in your thinking. Everything that is held back from you is a result of what *you're* doing and the decisions *you've* made. Everything that your little heart desires may be held back from you, and it is really your own fault!

I know that's "heavy," but it's the truth. I'm not talking down to you; I'm just telling it to you like it is so you can get in on what God wants for you—so you can get in on "Money cometh!"

You know, we like to put the blame on the devil when we're not being blessed as we should be. But, really, the devil can't hold up the money or stop it from coming to us if we're in the will of God, trusting and obeying God and thinking correctly about money.

I'm about to make another heavy statement: Since walking in prosperity is the will of God, then every Christian who is living from paycheck to paycheck, barely getting by, is not living in the will of God! That doesn't mean he has to *stay* in that condition. It just means that, at this time, he is not living in the will of God for him in the area of finances.

Don't become offended at that statement. Some Christians pride themselves in their spiritual walks with God. They don't want to hear that they may be missing it in a certain area. But if you want to walk in God's financial plan for you, you are going to have to know that prosperity is the will of God for you and poverty is *not* the will of God for you! If you are broke and barely getting along, the fault is not with God. It just means that you might have to make some kind of an adjustment in your life to get prosperity coming your way.

It is the Father's will that you have a sufficient and abundant supply. That means you have more than enough so that your life can be taken care of, God's business can be taken care of and your neighbor can be taken care of!

We have to learn how to think properly about money. We have to find out how God sees money and begin to see it as He sees it.

We also have to learn how to be humble and willing to let God prove us and train us in the area of money. Sometimes people get discouraged when they go through certain tests and trials. I'm sure you've gone through certain "wildernesses" in your own life. But God led you through those times. He saw you through them; He didn't let you go under.

God will never let you go under if you're trusting Him. So when you go through certain things, learn to see them as training periods. Those tests and trials are training periods to teach you how to come out of the condition you've been in!

Honor God With Your Finances and Move Up to Higher Ground!

You see, you're supposed to learn from all the experiences you have in life concerning finances. Each experience is a training ground to move you to the next stage. Don't ever be satisfied with what you have. Desire more so you can help more people.

Let's look again at Deuteronomy 8:

> **And he humbled thee, and suffered thee to hunger, and fed thee with manna, which thou knewest not, neither did thy fathers know; that he might make thee know that man doth not live by bread only, but by every word that proceedeth out of the mouth of the Lord doth man live. Thy raiment waxed not old upon thee, neither did thy foot swell, these forty years. Thou shalt also consider in thine heart, that, as a man chasteneth his son, so the Lord thy God chasteneth thee. Therefore thou shalt keep the commandments of the Lord thy God, to walk in his ways, and to fear him.**
>
> **Deuteronomy 8:3-6**

Verse 6 says, **Thou shalt keep the commandments of the Lord thy God, to walk in his ways, and to fear him.** Now "the commandments of the Lord thy God" aren't just the Ten Commandments. They are the entire Word of God.

We are to keep God's Word and fear Him. That word "fear" is talking about *reverential* fear, not the ungodly kind of fear that we've been delivered from (2 Timothy 1:7). We are to reverence and respect the Lord by keeping His Word.

Now notice verse 7:

> **For the Lord thy God bringeth thee into a GOOD LAND,**
> **a land of brooks of water, of fountains and depths that**
> **spring out of valleys and hills.**
>
> **Deuteronomy 8:7**

Say that out loud: "The Lord is bringing me into a good land!" What is the opposite of a good land? A *bad* land! A bad land is a poverty land. But God is not bringing you into poverty; He's bringing you into a good land!

Actually, verse 7 is talking about God's chosen people, Israel. But we are God's people if we are in Christ. And we have a *better* covenant with God (Hebrews 8:6). If God wanted to bring Israel, His *servants,* into a good land, how much more does He want to bring His *sons and daughters* into a good land!

A good land is not a land of living paycheck to paycheck. And it's not a good land you're living in when you're trying to figure out how to pay all those folks you owe. It's not a good land when you've bought too much, and creditors are calling you and writing you threatening letters.

What is a good land? Well, for one, it's a land of financial prosperity!

God describes what a good land is in Deuteronomy 8:

> **...a land of brooks of water, of fountains and depths**
> **that spring out of valleys and hills; A land of wheat, and**
> **barley, and vines, and fig trees, and pomegranates; a land**
> **of oil olive, and honey; A land wherein thou shalt eat bread**
> **without scarceness, thou shalt not lack any thing in it; a**
> **land whose stones are iron, and out of whose hills thou**
> **mayest dig brass.**
>
> **Deuteronomy 8:7-9**

Notice how God describes this type of land: **A land of wheat, and barley, and vines, and fig trees, and pomegranates; a land of oil olive, and honey** (v. 8). All of these things represent prosperity. God is actually saying that this good land is a land of everything you need to be prosperous!

It's so wonderful to be prosperous and have all your bills paid. It's so much better to have them all paid in full than it is to owe everybody you know! And you can have that—you can have your bills paid in full! You just have to get your thinking straight. You have to meditate on the fact that you're serving a big God. You have to believe that "Money cometh to the Body of Christ!" That means money cometh to *you!*

I don't know why it is that, while most of God's people in the Old Testament were rich, most Christians today seem to be broke! We read that we have a *better* covenant than they had, established upon *better* promises (Hebrews 8:6)!

Some people want to blame the preachers for the fact that many Christians are broke. They blame preachers for not teaching the truth about prosperity. Certainly, some preachers don't preach the Word concerning prosperity, and others aren't practicing God's principles in the area of money. But we can't put all the blame on preachers. We can do better than to blame someone else. The Bible says we have an anointing that abides in us that teaches us all things (1 John 2:20,27).

So let's look for ourselves to see what the Word says about that "good land" God wants to bring us into.

Look again at verse 9: **A land wherein thou shalt eat bread WITHOUT SCARCENESS....** What does that mean? *It means, it's a land where there's no scraping by!*

You know, there are married couples in the Body of Christ who have two good jobs and still can't even buy the house they want. It seems that one of the marks of the entire Body of Christ in this generation is being broke.

But we've got the answer! The answer is in the Book, the Bible! All we have to do is read it and believe it and act on it. God says in the Book that He wants to bring you into a good land—a land where you shall eat bread without scarceness and lack no good thing!

What does that word "scarceness" mean? Well, think about your checkbook. Think about your savings account. When you think about your bank accounts, do you think *scarceness* or *plenty?*

Some people think that if they have $5,000 in the bank, they have a lot of money. But that's not a lot of money. That $5,000 could be the cost of one hospital bill. Even $15,000 or $20,000 is not really a lot of money. But most people don't even have $5,000 in the bank.

You know I'm telling the truth! I lived from paycheck to paycheck for years, so I know what I'm talking about. I was making good money when my wife and I got married, but we didn't have a quarter! My wife was making good money too. She'd had a good job for many years, but when we got married, we only had $100 between the two of us. We couldn't go on a honeymoon any farther than Baton Rouge! We got to Baton Rouge, and I told my wife, "Honey, this is the farthest our money will take us."

So, please, don't even *think* about saying, "Well, Reverend Thompson can talk all of this 'Money cometh' talk because he's a preacher." I can take you down "Preachers' Row" and show you thousands of broke preachers! Most of them are broke because their congregations keep them broke. And because the congregations keep them broke, the congregations are broke themselves. So "broke" is following "broke," heading toward the "broke" ditch! *Everybody* is broke while they're carrying around the Bible of prosperity in their hands!

Let God Bring You Into a Good Land!

God promised the children of Israel that they would eat bread without scarceness in the land He was bringing them to (Deuteronomy 8:9). We, as the Body of Christ, need to be in that land. We don't need to be scraping by, just barely making it day after day.

Now look at the next statement in Deuteronomy 8:9: **THOU SHALT NOT LACK ANY THING in it; a land whose stones are iron, and out of whose hills thou mayest dig brass.**

Thou shalt not lack anything! Is that in your Bible? Mark that in your Bible so you'll be sure to read it over and over again. It says, **Thou shalt not lack ANY THING....** How much does that cover? *Everything.*

If you are not already living that verse, how would you like to live that lifestyle? You know, the "lifestyles of the rich and famous" shouldn't be for the world. The world has hoodwinked the Church, and the world is living our lifestyle! The world has tricked the Church into thinking the Church is supposed to be broke and in poverty. But the Word says, **Thou shalt not lack any thing!**

> **When thou hast eaten and art full, then thou shalt bless the Lord thy God for the good land which he hath given thee.**
>
> Deuteronomy 8:10

Now notice this verse: **When thou hast eaten and art full....** In other words, when all your bills are paid and you have a pocketful of money, you shall say, "Bless the Lord."

Don't ever forget to bless the Lord; don't forget God in all your prosperity.

Let me ask you a question: If God paid all of your bills within the next six months and got you to the place where you could just relax a little bit and enjoy the prosperity He's given you, would you still bless Him or would you get in your boat on Sunday morning and go take a little boat ride instead of going to church?

If the Lord got you to a place of prosperity where you became the biggest giver in your church, would you still submit to the pastor, or would you want to run the church?

You see, God wants you to remember Him after He blesses you. In other words, God is not going to help you to get away from Him. So if He sees that prosperity is going to change your love for Him and your submission to His will, He will not permit you to have it.

God is not going to pay you to get out of His will! A person who does not obey God in his finances is hooked on money like a person might be hooked on drugs. Money has become a drug to that person. God can't trust a person like that.

Let's continue looking at God's good land of prosperity and how He views money and financial prosperity so we will know how to think correctly about money.

> **Beware that thou forget not the Lord thy God, in not keeping his commandments, and his judgments, and his statutes, which I command thee this day: Lest when thou**

hast eaten and art full, and hast built goodly houses, and
dwelt therein; And when thy herds and thy flocks multiply, and thy silver and thy gold is multiplied, and all
that thou hast is multiplied; Then thine heart be lifted up,
and thou FORGET the Lord thy God, which brought thee
forth out of the land of Egypt, from the house of bondage;
Who led thee through that great and terrible wilderness,
wherein were fiery serpents, and scorpions, and drought,
where there was no water; who brought thee forth water out
of the rock of flint; Who fed thee in the wilderness with
manna, which thy fathers knew not, that he might humble
thee, and that he might prove thee, to do thee good at thy
latter end; And thou say in thine heart, My power and the
might of mine hand hath gotten me this wealth.

Deuteronomy 8:11-17

This passage of Scripture is warning us about becoming proud or
arrogant and forgetting God after He's prospered us.

Verse 15 says, **Who led thee through that great and terrible
wilderness, wherein were fiery serpents, and scorpions, and
drought, where there was no water; who brought thee forth water
out of the rock of flint.** You see, when God leads you out of debt, He's
leading you through that "great and terrible wilderness wherein are
fiery serpents, scorpions and drought." You could paraphrase verse 15
like this: "God is leading me out of debt, distress and discontentment!"

Now look at verse 12 where it talks about "goodly houses."

You know, some people will get blessed with just one of those
portable or mobile homes, and you can't even talk to them anymore
after that—they've become so arrogant! They're not humble before the
Lord. (And if that mobile home is two different colors with a double
carport or garage they're *really* arrogant!)

I'm just telling you the truth. I'm going to have to tell the truth as
much as I can without offending you, because the Lord is trying to say
something that will help us in these verses.

God wants us to remain humble no matter how much He's prospered us. Really, it doesn't matter how big a house you build; that house
doesn't mean anything. The house doesn't make *you; you* make the *house!*

So, you see, you have to stay the same no matter how much God blesses you. You have to stay humble, **Lest when thou hast eaten and art full, and hast built goodly houses, and dwelt therein; and when thy herds and thy flocks multiply, and thy silver and thy gold is multiplied, and all that thou hast is multiplied; Then THINE HEART BE LIFTED UP, and THOU FORGET THE LORD THY GOD...** (Deuteronomy 8:12-14).

Multiplied, Multiplied, Multiplied Blessings!

These verses in Deuteronomy 8 are not just a warning. They are telling us how the Lord wants to prosper us! For example, notice how many times "multiply" or some form of that word is used in Deuteronomy 8:13:

And when thy herds and thy flocks MULTIPLY, and thy silver and thy gold is MULTIPLIED, and all that thou hast is MULTIPLIED.

God said through Moses, "When your herds and flocks *multiply.*" Then He said, "When your silver and gold are *multiplied.*" Then He said, "And when all that you have is *multiplied!*"

Multiplied, multiplied, multiplied. That's what God is saying about you and your finances!

Make this confession: "Beginning now, my income is multiplying. Satan, take your hands off my finances. I will not believe your lies anymore. God does not want me, His child, in poverty. Poverty is a lie from you, Satan, and from religion and tradition. God wants me to prosper, and I'm in agreement with God from this time forward. Hallelujah!"

Multiplied Finances, But Not for a Rainy Day

Have you ever heard the statement "I'm saving money for a rainy day"? First of all, you shouldn't be looking for any rainy day! Do you know what a rainy day is? A rainy day is when something comes up in your life that's bad. But we don't have a covenant of curses; we have a covenant of blessings! So we need to get rid of the mentality of saving for a rainy day.

Now, don't misunderstand me. I didn't say it was wrong to save. In fact, I believe in savings accounts. (You know I do, because I encouraged you to open one if you didn't have one!) Some people want to spend everything they have. They think, *Well, we only have one life; we're not going to live any more than one round, so let's spend it!*

There are actually people who live like that. They live "crazy." They're never going to get what God wants them to have living that way.

Most people who spend money like that don't tithe. They'd rather buy dresses and shoes; they're not thinking about the Lord and His work. They come to church and give a "proud five"—a five-dollar offering! Then they tell the Lord how much they love Him.

I'm saving my money, not for a rainy day, but for the time when God might want to do something with it. I'm saving money to fulfill His plan and purpose. When the Lord tells me, "Leroy, go get some of that money and give it to Sister so-and-so," with gladness I will go get it and give it to that sister.

Christians who say they don't need money aren't aware of our money covenant with God. You see, you need to have some money to fulfill the Gospel. You need money to walk in divine prosperity like God wants you to and to help send men and women around the world to spread the good news of the Gospel.

Some Christians say, "Well, I've got the Holy Ghost; I don't need any money." But if they don't have any money, all their singing, shouting, falling out on the floor and rolling isn't going to help them when their bills come due or when the missionary needs some money to go preach the Gospel!

What if a man came to collect the utility payment for my church, but instead of giving him money, I just rolled on the floor and told him, "I've got the Holy Ghost!" My congregation wouldn't have heating or air conditioning come Sunday if I did that!

If it were summertime, they wouldn't have any air conditioning. Then instead of having a good time in the Holy Ghost, they'd have a *hot* time, because it gets hot in Louisiana in the summertime!

I'm talking about right and wrong thinking about money. We have to get our thinking straightened out about money and meet God's qualifications for prosperity if we want "Money cometh" to work for us.

Deuteronomy 8:13 says, **When thy herds and thy flocks multiply, and thy silver and thy gold is multiplied, and all that thou hast is multiplied.** The first and second qualifications for that kind of divine prosperity are *humility* and *the willingness to be proven in the area of finances.*

Now let's talk about the third and fourth qualifications for walking in the prosperity of God. Third, before God can trust you with prosperity, *He has to know what's in your heart.* And the fourth qualification is that *God has to know whether or not you will keep His Word.*

> **Then thine heart be lifted up, and thou forget the Lord thy God, which brought thee forth out of the land of Egypt, from the house of bondage; Who led thee through that great and terrible wilderness, wherein were fiery serpents, and scorpions, and drought, where there was no water; who brought thee forth water out of the rock of flint; Who fed thee in the wilderness with manna, which thy fathers knew not, that he might humble thee, and that he might prove thee, to do thee good at thy latter end; And thou say in thine heart, My power and the might of mine hand hath gotten me this wealth.**
>
> **Deuteronomy 8:14-17**

We all want to be in the category described in Deuteronomy 8:7-9 in which God would bring us into the good land. But let's stay out of this category described in Deuteronomy 8:11-17 in which we would forget the Lord and think that our own power has gotten us all of our wealth.

Here is where many people miss it. They might go from a $500-a-month job to a $2,000-a-month job, and they'll begin to say in their hearts, *My own hand has gotten this for me.*

The Lord doesn't want that to happen. That kind of attitude is why He can't give many in the Body of Christ what He wants to give them.

So, third, before God can trust you with prosperity, *He has to know what's in your heart.* And the fourth qualification is closely connected with the third: *God has to know whether or not you will keep His Word.*

When Prosperity Comes, Don't Forget the God of Prosperity!

Many times when people begin to prosper, they forget God. Not only do they say in their hearts, *My own hand has gotten this for me,* but they forget to keep God's Word. After they become prosperous, they don't do what the Word says to do concerning finances. They don't tithe and give to the Gospel like they're supposed to. The Word of God is not in their hearts anymore as it should be. Instead, disobedience is in their hearts.

But what does the Lord want us to do? He wants us to trust and obey Him. He wants us to think correctly about money. He wants us to stay humble and to always obey His Word. And He wants us to prosper!

> **But thou shalt remember the Lord thy God: for it is he that giveth thee power to get wealth, that he may establish his covenant which he sware unto thy fathers, as it is this day.**
>
> **Deuteronomy 8:18**

You see, you have to be humble and not arrogant if you want the Lord's blessings. You can't forget the Lord. Remember, one time Abraham wouldn't take the spoils of war because, as he said, "I want it said of me that the *Lord* has made me rich" (Genesis 14:23). Abraham didn't forget the Lord, and we can't forget Him either if we want to walk in Abraham's blessings.

Another Aspect of Right and Wrong Thinking About Money

I said that staying humble before the Lord is one way to think correctly about money. But there is another aspect of right and wrong thinking about money that I want to discuss further.

To walk in God's kind of prosperity, you have to stop thinking *poor*, and you have to begin thinking *rich!*

You see, money cometh to those who think in line with God's Word. What does God's Word say? It says, **Let them shout for joy, and be glad, that favour my righteous cause: yea, let them say continually, Let the Lord be magnified, which hath pleasure in the prosperity of his servant** (Psalm 35:27). We need this scripture and others like it to have faith for prosperity, because how does faith come? Faith comes by hearing, and hearing by the Word of God (Romans 10:17).

Some people have been taught that prosperity is only for the "sweet by-and-by" or only for when they get to heaven and go through those pearly gates. But pay close attention to my next statement: All that the Bible says about money is for *now!*

What the Bible has to say about financial prosperity is for this life, not for when we get to heaven. There will be no need for money or any other type of prosperity in heaven because heaven is prosperity itself!

People have also been taught that it's wrong to prosper financially. In other words, those people believe it's worldly to have money.

But if you're going to rise up in the prosperity of God, you should not feel guilty about your prosperity when God gives it to you. Feeling guilty about prosperity is wrong thinking. It's incorrect according to the Word of God. You're going to have to forget the idea that money is sinful and that you have to feel guilty if you're prosperous and not broke or just barely getting by.

The idea has been passed on that you can have money, all right, but only enough to get by on. If you have plenty of money, you're sinful. I'm showing you through the Scriptures that that kind of thinking is wrong.

When God starts blessing a person, the devil tries to put a "guilt trip" on him, and the blessed person may try to hide his blessings. He wants to be humble, but really he's being stupid. He tries to act as if he thinks, *I don't want much. I love the Lord.*

But Jesus is in heaven looking down at that person and probably saying something such as, "Don't talk about Me like that! Don't call on My Name in connection with that poverty attitude! I want to help you get out of that condition."

If God can get money into your hands, you can help others who are in poverty. For example, James talks about the fellow who comes to a person and says, "I'm hungry and cold," but that person just pats him on the back and says, "Well, just have faith" (James 2:15,16).

In modern language, that hungry man could say, "Don't pat me on the back and tell me to have faith. I don't have *faith*; I have *'hunger'!* And I need some *money!*"

You see, some people want those who are destitute just to pray, obey God and have faith to get out of the condition they're in.

But those poor people are starving *right now*. They could die before they get to God! We should have some money to give them so they can be filled up right then. *Then* they could learn to pray correctly.

Yes, I know there are con artists out there. But the Spirit of God will help you try the spirits and know who's fake and who's real.

One time a man who was barefooted and had several little children came to my church, and he was asking for money. We found out later that they were playing the con game. They were going to every church in the area with the same sad story, asking for money. They got about $150 from us.

That was the last time I got hoodwinked! After that, I began checking up on everybody who came to us for help. Now when people come to our church asking for money, I ask them, "What church are you from? Who's your pastor?" I do a little checking up before I start giving them money.

Once a so-called preacher came to my church to hoodwink me. I asked him, "Who's your pastor?" He gave me a name, but I couldn't get in contact with the pastor; he was nowhere to be found. Then I caught the man in a few more lies, and I finally said to him, "Get out of my office." There were two fellows with me in my office, and, boy, they got nervous when I said that! They felt sorry for that man. I said, "Get up. You're sitting in my office, lying to me. I'm not giving you a quarter! Get your truck and get away from here!"

The two fellows in my office looked at me as if to say, *Man, Pastor, you treated that man unjustly.* But two days later we found out that "preacher" was a charlatan—a rogue. I didn't get hoodwinked that time, because I was more careful. (A dog might bite me once, and it's the *dog's* fault. But if that dog bites me twice, it's *my* fault!)

Faith Activates the Power
for Receiving the Blessings of God

In the area of right and wrong thinking about money, you have to believe correctly for prosperity to start coming your way. Remember, you have to see money as God sees it, and you have to think as He thinks about it.

You see, you have to check yourself when you're making your faith confessions. For example, you might say halfheartedly, "Well, money is coming." But, having the attitude that money *might* come at some future time means you're still waiting for it.

Money *cometh!* That means it is continually coming in. Say it out loud: "Money *cometh!*"

You might not believe it yet, but keep saying it until you believe it: "Money cometh!"

It's not "Money *goeth*" or "Money *might come.*" It's "Money *cometh!*"

In the natural, you don't write a contract if you don't mean what you say in the contract. Well, God is not a man that He should lie (Numbers 23:19). You know, God is an honest "businessman." So He can't put it in the contract, His Word, if He doesn't mean for us to have it! And this is what He put in the contract: **Now unto him that is able to do exceeding abundantly above all that we ask or think, according to the power that worketh in us** (Ephesians 3:20).

How is God able to do exceeding abundantly above all that we ask or think? According to the power that worketh in us!

Well, how do you get that "power that worketh in you" activated? By believing that the "exceeding abundantly above" is no problem with God. In fact, He's got "exceeding abundantly above" waiting for you!

You have to believe God can get the money to you in order to get it. That gets the power activated in you. When that power gets activated in you, you'll think rich. You'll think in line with prosperity. You'll think of yourself as someone who's able to support the Gospel. When they call for tithes, you'll say, "Wow! Bring me the bucket! I'm going to be the first one to put my tithes in, because when I put this in, God is going to give me a whole lot more!"

My job is to help you get "the switch" turned on. The switch of prosperity is in your heart. Just flip that switch and say, "I ain't going to be broke no more!!!"

My wife and I got the switch of prosperity turned on in our hearts and lives, and we have never been the same since! I'm not merely telling you about what I read in the Bible; I'm telling you what I'm living—what I'm giving, what I'm driving and what I'm living and sleeping in every night.

Don't Limit God and Lose Out on His Best

People have been looking down on the Lord, so to speak, for too long. They believe it's all right for the bank presidents and the politicians to have big houses. But they don't think having a nice big house is right for the average Christian. And they sure don't think having a nice house is right for the preacher! The devil has gotten people to stand against the preacher, especially when he's receiving God's blessings.

Don't you ever do that. Don't try to hold back a man of God. You'll just end up holding yourself back if you do.

God isn't going to let a congregation rise above the preacher financially when they are trying to hold him back. Some people have their nice big houses, but they want to leave the preacher in the junkyard. They want him to drive across the country in an old, beat up car, while they fly first class! Then, when he finally arrives on the other side of the country, they want to talk to him all night.

"Hey, Rev," they'll say, "let's talk." But the "Rev" might not want to talk. He might be too tired after driving across the country in that old car!

Do you get the picture? Don't hold your pastor back. Let him or her go up financially too. Bless him or her. There's a lot of work that goes along with the ministry. It's not all just shouting hallelujah in church.

There's a scripture that says, **Believe in the Lord your God, so shall ye be ESTABLISHED; believe his prophets, so shall ye PROSPER** (2 Chronicles 20:20). The first part of that verse says, **Believe in the Lord your God, so shall ye be established.**

Some Christians are established, but they're not really prospering. But the last part of that verse says, **Believe his prophets, so shall ye PROSPER!** I believe that means to believe the pastor too. I believe that's talking about the fivefold ministry gifts. Believe the *evangelist;* so shall you prosper. Believe the *teacher;* so shall you prosper. And so on.

You see, a lot of people don't believe. Some people are just established, and they can get a few dollars and prosper *to a certain degree.* But if they want to go all the way with God in the area of prosperity, they will have to believe the prophets.

There are a lot of false prophets in the world today. But the only purpose for *false* prophets is to get you not to believe the *real* prophets! The devil sends the false to look just like the real. The false prophet will say some of the same things the real prophet says so you will get confused about prophets. But you need to believe those ministers who are proclaiming the Word, because God wants you to prosper.

Beloved, I wish above all things that thou mayest prosper and be in health, even as thy soul prospereth.

3 John 2

Prosperity in your spirit, soul and body is the will of God for you. But men and religion and the devil will try to keep you from it. For example, concerning financial prosperity, some will say, "Money is the root of all evil," and they'll think they're quoting the Bible.

But what does the Bible really say?

> For the LOVE OF MONEY is the root of all evil: which
> while some coveted after, they have erred from the faith,
> and pierced themselves through with many sorrows.
>
> 1 Timothy 6:10

Money is not the root of all evil. It's the *love* of money that's evil. But, as I said before, the *lack* of money causes evil, too, because you can love money and be in sin and not even have a quarter!

Rightly Dividing the Word of Truth

The lack of money creates evil every day. We know that's true because if a man is stealing, it usually means he doesn't have money. A man whose needs are met doesn't usually rob a store. However, I'm not saying that being broke is an excuse to rob a store, because it's not.

Read carefully the verses before First Timothy 6:10. We need to look at that verse in its context.

> ...they that have believing masters, let them not despise
> them, because they are brethren; but rather do them
> service, because they are faithful and beloved, partakers of
> the benefit. These things teach and exhort. If any man
> teach otherwise, and consent not to wholesome words,
> even the words of our Lord Jesus Christ, and to the
> doctrine which is according to godliness; He is proud,
> knowing nothing, but doting about questions and strifes
> of words, whereof cometh envy, strife, railings, evil surmis-
> ings. Perverse disputings of men of CORRUPT MINDS, and
> destitute of the truth, supposing that gain is godliness:
> from such withdraw thyself.
>
> 1 Timothy 6:2-5

Paul is talking to Timothy about men with corrupt minds. Men with corrupt minds don't need to be blessed with a lot of money, because they're not going to use it for the Lord! Men with corrupt minds love money, and they're going to run with women and have "concubines" with their money! If you give some money to a man with a corrupt mind he'll buy his wife a car—and buy his gal or mistress a car too!

You think I'm kidding, but sometimes a man will buy his wife a car, and then the "other woman" gets mad, so he has to buy her a new car too! Most of the time such a corrupt man will buy his girlfriend a better car than he buys his wife! And then all three of them come to the same church—the man, his wife and his girlfriend! That is happening in the Body of Christ!

But if they want to prosper and have God's blessings, they are going to have to stop all of that. A married woman doesn't need a boyfriend on the side, and a married man doesn't need a girlfriend on the side! Those things shouldn't be happening in the Body of Christ.

Those married men with sweethearts on the side aren't as "hot" as they think they are anyhow! They are not nearly as great as they think they are. All they're doing is sweating and worrying themselves silly trying to handle two women. They might end up killing themselves with all that worrying! They can't handle two women! God made one woman for one man and one man for one woman. The devil is fooling them, getting them to believe otherwise. God is not going to give His money to somebody who acts like that.

I believe *that* kind of person is one example of someone who loves money and has a corrupt mind. People have been wrongly dividing the Word of truth by using this verse to tell us that money in itself is evil. They didn't tell us the *love* of money was evil. They just said *money* was evil. Therefore, they believe that if you confess, "Money cometh," *you're* evil too.

They'll say, "You love money because you're confessing for money. Why do you want money to come? You're starting to get evil." They will think you're in some kind of cult if you believe in prosperity and confess, "Money cometh!"

You can't share this message with just anybody. These words "Money cometh" came from God into my heart, but some people who don't know how to rightly divide the Word of truth will say you love money if you confess, "Money cometh!"

But here is the whole truth about the matter: **Beloved, I wish above all things that thou mayest prosper and be in health, even as thy soul prospereth** (3 John 2). As your soul prospers, you will prosper, because you will know from God's Word what He thinks about money, and you will know how to think correctly about money too.

For example, the Word says, **Bring ye all the tithes into the storehouse, that there may be meat in mine house, and prove me now herewith, saith the Lord of hosts, if I will not open you the windows of heaven, and pour you out a blessing, that there shall not be room enough to receive it** (Malachi 3:10).

The Father says, "Prove Me herewith to see if I will not open the windows of heaven." Somebody once said that those windows are the same windows God opened to let the flood down in Noah's day. Boy, it rained some water down on the earth then, didn't it! Well, God will open those same windows and rain down blessings on those who bring their tithes and offerings into the storehouse!

Gain Is Not Godliness, But Godliness Will Bring You Gain!

Look again at First Timothy 6:5, **Perverse disputings of men of corrupt minds, and destitute of the truth, supposing that gain is godliness: from such withdraw thyself."** Look at that phrase: "supposing that gain is godliness." Some people use that verse and say, "See, those men of corrupt minds think that gain is godliness. But gain is not godliness."

Yes, that verse says, **Supposing that gain is godliness....** But that verse didn't say that being broke was godliness either!

Paul was talking about men who are of a corrupt mind—men who use money improperly. But God wants His covenant people to have gain because we are going to use money properly. We are going to evangelize the world and get the Gospel out to the four corners of the earth. And we are going to bring our tithes into the local churches that feed us spiritually.

Now some people aren't getting fed and they aren't satisfied spiritually in the churches they're in. But they feel they can't leave, because their grandma is a member there and another relative is an usher, and their relatives are trying to run their lives.

Some people who are in a dying church can't even hear the Spirit of God telling them to "get out of Egypt," so to speak. So they just stay in a church where they're not satisfied. The preacher there never preaches on prosperity, because he doesn't *know* anything about prosperity. He doesn't have it, and he might never have it. He's just thinking about the little purse his congregation is going to give him, but they're not going to give him as much as he thinks they're going to give him! And they'll want him to march around the church for that!

Then if they give that preacher a little *extra*—look out! They might tell him to find the altar and get on his knees for that! Then the deacon will bring him the money in a sack and say, "Reverend, we're blessing you 'real good!'" And the deacon is the one who's running the whole church.

It used to make me angry to see the congregation use the pastor in the church we attended years ago. They would let him feed them and counsel them, and they would just "ride" him for everything he had. Then, every so often, they'd come up and give him $1,000 from the whole church and want him to practically get on the floor and roll for it!

That church was always in debt up to its neck. And do you know why? They didn't have God's system of finances working for them. They weren't doing what God told them to do. They didn't know anything about the good life. They couldn't travel anywhere, because it takes money to travel. They didn't honor the Lord with their finances. And they didn't honor their pastor either.

The Lord can't bless a church like that. You need to love your pastor. If you can't love your pastor, get out of that church and find a pastor you can love. And then, make sure you stay out of all those little gossip committees in your church. God can't prosper you if you're gossiping.

We need to think in line with the Word if we want to prosper. We know the Word says that the love of money is the root of all evil. But men with corrupt minds *love* money. You don't have a corrupt mind if you're doing what the Bible says to do with money.

Notice that First Timothy 6:5 didn't say that gain wasn't a *part* of godliness. It said that these men of corrupt minds suppose that gain *is* godliness. In other words, these kinds of people will do anything for money and think that they are godly just because they have a little something. The Bible says, **From such withdraw thyself.**

The next verse says, **But godliness with contentment is great gain** (v. 6). That means that if you have godliness and contentment, that's great gain because God is going to bless you. He's going to bless you spiritually, but He's going to bless you with finances too!

You see, you have to judge something you read in the Bible by all the rest of the Bible. You can't just take one scripture out of context to try to prove something. For example, if somebody wanted to prove that he should be broke in life, he might take this text in First Timothy 6:6 and say, "See, I'm godly and I'm contented. And I don't have anything."

Are you kidding me! A person can't be too contented if he has bills stacked up on his table that he can't pay.

Sometimes people who are broke will use the next verse: **For we brought nothing into this world, and it is certain we can carry nothing out** (1 Timothy 6:7). They'll say, "Well, I guess you can't carry anything out of this world, so it's all right that I'm broke." But with that attitude, they're not going to leave anything for anybody else to enjoy either!

Here's another scripture people will use to try to prove we should be broke: **And having food and raiment let us be therewith content** (1 Timothy 6:8). It gets even better for them because the next verse says, **But they that will be rich fall into temptation and a snare, and into many foolish and hurtful lusts, which drown men in destruction and perdition** (v. 9).

But that's still talking about those men with corrupt minds! Men with corrupt minds will fall into temptation and a snare, and into many foolish and hurtful lusts. Why? The very next verse tells us why: **For the love of money is the root of all evil: which while some coveted after, they have erred from the faith, and pierced themselves through with many sorrows** (v. 10).

Those corrupt-minded men will do anything for money. They are destitute of the truth. What does that mean? That means they are void of the truth; they have no truth in them.

But saved people aren't destitute of the truth, and they don't love money. But they still need money! A saved person can't go into a store to shop, and, when the cashier adds up the total, instead of handing him the money, just say, "Well, I'm saved!"

We're not erring from the faith. We don't have corrupt minds. We're not destitute of the truth. Verse 11 says, **But thou, O man of God, flee these things; and FOLLOW AFTER RIGHTEOUSNESS, GODLI-NESS, FAITH, LOVE, PATIENCE, MEEKNESS.**

That's us! We're following after righteousness, godliness, faith, love, patience and meekness. Those things are characteristics of the Body of Christ. They are the fruit of the Spirit (Galatians 5:22).

Let's continue reading that passage in First Timothy 6.

> **Fight the good fight of faith, lay hold on eternal life, whereunto thou art also called, and hast professed a good profession before many witnesses. I give thee charge in the sight of God, who quickeneth all things, and before Christ Jesus, who before Pontius Pilate witnessed a good confession; That thou keep this commandment without spot, unrebukeable, until the appearing of our Lord Jesus Christ: Which in his times he shall shew, who is the blessed and only Potentate, the King of kings, and Lord of lords; Who only hath immortality, dwelling in the light which no man can approach unto; whom no man hath seen, nor can see: to whom be honour and power everlasting. Amen. Charge them that are rich in this world, that they be not high-minded, nor trust in uncertain riches, but in the LIVING GOD, who giveth us RICHLY ALL THINGS TO ENJOY.**
>
> **1 Timothy 6:12-17**

God doesn't want you to trust in *riches,* but in *Him,* the Living God. That's a part of thinking properly about money. And the end of verse 17 gives us just a thought on what the living God thinks about finances: He gives us richly all things to enjoy!

This passage in Proverbs gives us another picture of what God thinks about finances.

> **Honour the Lord with thy substance, and with the first-fruits of all thine increase. So shall thy barns be filled with plenty, and thy presses shall burst out with new wine.**
>
> **Proverbs 3:9,10**

Now, if you're a farmer, you might have a barn, but most people don't. Verse 10 is not talking about a literal barn. It's talking about the place where you put your money. God has already said that He wants to put plenty of money in your pocket, in your savings account and in your storehouses. These verses are saying the same thing. God is saying that if a person honors Him, He will see to it that he doesn't go broke!

God is saying to the one who honors Him, "I am the Lord thy God. I am Jehovah Jireh. I am the Lord who provides."

You can't honor God and be broke! If you continually honor God, the day is going to come when, after He's proven you, He will open those windows! After He's humbled you so you won't be high-minded, those windows are going to fly open!

I remember when those windows first started to crack open a little bit for me. Boy, I thought I was in heaven then! But God did that for me because I learned how to think correctly about money. And He will do the same for you!

Seed, Power and Increase

But thou shalt remember the Lord thy God: for it is he that giveth thee POWER to get wealth, that he may establish his covenant which he sware unto thy fathers, as it is this day.
—DEUTERONOMY 8:18

God gives the seed, the power and the increase for you to get wealth. And God will see to it that if you handle the seed and the power properly, you will have the increase!

You need to recognize that God has given us everything we need to be prosperous. But the problem is that the Body of Christ has not known how to use the tools the Father has provided for them to attain financial stability and prosperity.

We're going to look at some of the things God has given us so we can prosper. He's given us *seed, power* and *increase.* In other words, there's a part we have to play and a part God has to play. God knows how to do His part, but the Church has not fully been taught her part.

We already talked about some of the parts we have to play in receiving God's prosperity. First, we have to trust and obey God and His Word and pay our tithes and give offerings. Then we have to think correctly about money and be humble before the Lord. The Lord wants to know what is in your heart before He trusts you with His prosperity.

God is saying, "Listen, children. The money is no problem; I've got it. I'll give you the seed to plant, the power to get wealth and the increase to cause it to come to pass in your life, but the seed, power and increase won't work if you don't let Me know what you're going to do with the prosperity when you get it."

God doesn't want you to hoard money selfishly and to be unconcerned about getting the Gospel out. He can't prosper you if you're not going to be concerned about building churches and supporting ministers.

You know, that's been one of the Church's unspoken mottos through ages past: "Keep the preacher broke!" But keeping God's ministers broke is one of the craziest things you can do, because it's not in line with the Word of God.

Another part we have to play to get "seed, power and increase" working in our lives is to have that same spirit of faith that King David had—the spirit of faith that *believes* and *speaks* (2 Corinthians 4:13).

I told poverty in my own life, "Get out of here!" And it did! I won't let any poverty tell me what I can't have. You see, I have a little "man" down in my spirit, just jumping for joy. It's called revelation knowledge, and it says to me, "You're rich!"

Do you know what "rich" means? It means having an abundant supply. You don't have to have a million dollars in the bank to be rich. If you can eat what you want, wear what you want, stay in the house you want and put plenty of money into sending out the Gospel, then you're rich!

Now let that settle in your spirit. If that truth rises up in your spirit (and if you say it enough, it will begin rising in your spirit), you'll look at poverty with such an eye of faith and with such tenacity, confidence and boldness that poverty won't want to be around you!

Have Respect for God's Word

God wants to do even more for you than that. If a person gave the Father as much respect as he gave his employer for forty years, when the end of his journey came on that job, he wouldn't have to worry about what his *employer* was giving him as a retirement benefit. The Father would see to it that he had a good retirement account and a comfortable bed on which to lay his head.

But most people like to see everything before they'll believe it. They like to stay in the natural, but we have to walk by faith and not by sight concerning the things God has promised us in His Word. As I said, real faith always turns to sight!

We know that God gives seed, power and increase. Let's look briefly at some things we need to do *after* the power of the seed of God's Word has produced increase in our lives!

> **When thou hast eaten and art full, then thou shalt bless**
> **the Lord thy God for the good land which he hath given thee.**
> **Deuteronomy 8:10**

Verse 10 talks about blessing the Lord for the good land that He gives you. Well, what about your paycheck and your job?

What should you do for the Lord with your paycheck and your job? You should bless Him—honor Him. Blessing the Lord doesn't just mean saying, "I bless You, Lord. Bless You! Hallelujah!" The Lord might say to you, "Then get your wallet out and show Me you love Me. Support My work and My Kingdom."

You see, to really bless the Lord, you have to separate from, or turn loose of, something you've sweated for. You're not doing any sweating by saying, "Hallelujah." I'm talking about giving *money*.

The Seed System

I want you to understand God's seed system in finances, so let's look at the following scriptures:

> **I have PLANTED, Apollos watered; but God gave the increase.**
> **1 Corinthians 3:6**

> **For as the rain cometh down, and the snow from**
> **heaven, and returneth not thither, but watereth the earth,**
> **and maketh it bring forth and bud, that it may give SEED to**
> **the sower, and bread to the eater.**
> **Isaiah 55:10**

We know that God gives the seed. Now the Word is called a seed in Luke 8:11, but God also gives us *financial* seed.

Many people eat up their seed. Instead of planting it or sowing it, they eat it up. Or they sow it in the wrong place. They sow it at one of those department stores, and, as a result, they're always broke or barely getting by.

That's why the Lord said to tell the people to continually say, "I'll never be broke another day in my life!" We need to say that and keep on saying it. We need to plant that seed of the revelation that "Money cometh" and yield to the power that will bring the increase by *continuing* to say it. Confession has a great deal to do with seed, power and increase.

Now, you might not believe money cometh when you first start confessing—especially if you've been broke a long time. But keep saying it. Don't say, "Money *is* coming." That means you're broke while you're waiting for it to get there! "Money cometh" is a continual process. Money *cometh!*

God told me, "Tell My people that I want them to have an abundant supply, and I've provided a way for them to have it."

If you will pay close attention to what I'm teaching and will act on what you learn, you will learn how to *receive* that abundant supply. You'll come out of debt. You'll come out of certain situations, such as having to work two and three jobs just to make ends meet.

I don't believe man was made to work two full-time jobs—not a married man, anyway. He needs to be at home with his wife and children. There's something wrong if you have to work night and day. Some men do that. They work all the time. Their wives don't even know them, because they're gone so much, and they're too tired to be husbands when they get home.

You see, it's an abundant supply that God wants to give you, and I don't believe you have to work so hard that you sacrifice time with your family in order to get it.

Don't Fall Into the Trap of Leaning to Your Own Understanding

One of the greatest handicaps to getting into God's system of seed, power and increase is trying to figure out *how* He's going to do it. Underline this statement or write it down somewhere and don't let it get away from you, because it's very important. The Holy Ghost told me to tell this to you: "Don't fall into the trap of trying to figure out *how* God is going to get money to you!"

You see, you're not to look to your job as your source. In my own personal experience, I have received money from some of the most unlikely sources. You know, you can get your eyes on the wrong person and it can hurt your faith. Just keep your eyes on God.

One day a particular woman gave me a check for $500. It almost knocked me off my feet because I never thought that woman would have $500 to give.

The Bible says, **Give, and it shall be given unto you; good measure, pressed down, and shaken together, and running over, shall men give into your bosom. For with the same measure that ye mete withal it shall be measured to you again** (Luke 6:38). God moved on this woman, and she gave "into my bosom." And it was a good measure!

When I got into my office with that check, I had to read the name on the check again. I just said, "Goodness!" Then I saw that there was another envelope on my desk. I looked at it and realized that it contained another check from the same woman for $500 more! Here was $1,000 from an unlikely source. (And both of those checks were good at the bank!)

You know, you can trust God in this area of seed, power and increase. But you have to get your eyes off how you think it's going to happen. When you are in God's will and you are doing what He tells you to do, just let it happen. Get in on His program and then stick with it.

You have to be persistent when you want to receive something from God. You can't just say "Money cometh" one or two times. You can't just tithe and give offerings once or twice and expect your situation to be turned around. Remember the illustration of the deep dirt hole of debt. If you're in that hole, you didn't just fall in last night! No, it may have even taken you *years* to dig that deep.

Some people are in a thirty year hole. Now if you really get ahold of this revelation, it won't take you that long to get out of that hole. If it did, you wouldn't have much time left after you got out to really enjoy your prosperity!

God doesn't think about money in terms of addition and subtraction. He thinks about money in terms of *multiplication!* And He can move on your behalf and turn your situation around much faster than you could turn it around yourself.

Let's look at Deuteronomy 8 again concerning seed, power and the multiplied, increased blessings of God.

> **And when thy herds and thy flocks MULTIPLY, and thy silver and thy gold IS MULTIPLIED, and all that thou hast IS MULTIPLIED.**
>
> **Deuteronomy 8:13**

Now think about your finances. If you yield to the Spirit of God—if you yield to the will of God with willingness and obedience to the divine financial system that He has set up for you—then you can claim the multiplied blessings of Deuteronomy 8:13.

That's what you can expect! And God never stops multiplying blessings to you once He starts. For example, I could say, "Oh, Lord, You have really blessed me." That's talking about blessings *having been* multiplied. But God would say to me, "That's past tense, Son. I'm still blessing you. I'm *still* multiplying blessings to you!"

You see, when you get in that right channel, or vein—with the right frame of mind and heart set toward God—then you can claim and confess and expect multiplied blessings to continually come to you.

God doesn't just want you to look at what He did for you yesterday. He is saying, "I want you to look ahead now." You can come from "multiplied" (what He has already done for you) to "multiply" (what He is doing now). As I said, once you get into that flow, God continually multiplies His blessings!

Now the world's system doesn't want you to get in that channel of blessings, so it tries to pull you in all kinds of different directions and put you in bondage. But you don't have to succumb to that. Lock into God's program. You don't have to figure out how it's going to happen—how your prosperity is going to come.

And you don't have to have a false prosperity, buying things on credit you don't need and buying a bigger house and better car than your neighbors'. The neighbors you've been trying to keep up with could be going bankrupt!

Don't try to keep up with other people. You'll stay in debt if you do. If you don't know how to use them, credit cards are the biggest "demons" there are to hold you back in your finances. Credit cards are here for *you* to use, not for the merchants and credit card companies to use *you*.

Sometimes when I shop in a store and the cashier asks me, "How will you be paying for this?" and I say, "Cash," he or she will look surprised.

Sometimes those cashiers act as if they don't know what to do with cash! Do you know why that is? Because we've gotten off the cash system and onto the card system. And it's been keeping many of us in debt after debt after debt.

Do you like that word "multiply"? Can you think about yourself as being out of debt? Can you picture yourself prosperous?

Just think about it! Think about getting your paycheck from your job and not owing anybody.

Some people are so deeply in debt that they've never even been able to imagine what it would be like not to owe anybody. But if they will get ahold of this message that "Money cometh," they can come out of that.

Being in debt is not a lifetime condition you should be in. Get out of the world's system and get on God's system, starting right now, because money cometh to the Body of Christ!

God Gives the Power, But *We* Have a Part To Play

Let's look at a verse in Deuteronomy 8 to see how God's system of seed, power and increase works.

> **But thou shalt remember the Lord thy God: for it is he that giveth thee POWER to get wealth, that he may establish his covenant which he sware unto thy fathers, as it is this day.**
> **Deuteronomy 8:18**

God is the One who gives you power to get wealth! He gives the seed (Isaiah 55:11). He gives the power (Deuteronomy 8:18). And He gives the increase (1 Corinthians 3:7)! *You*—through your faith, actually cause the prosperity, the increase, to come in with the power He gives you, but the power to increase still comes from God.

One of the powers God gave you was the 10 percent, the tithe. He gave you the power to separate yourself from that dime that made some of you broke because you held onto it!

The Lord gives us power to get wealth. That verse does not say He gives us the wealth. Some people are just sitting around, waiting for God to give them wealth, and He's not going to do it. He gives you the power to get that wealth, but you're going to have to do the getting.

That word "power"can also mean *ability.* God gives you the *ability* to get wealth. He gives you the means whereby you can get wealth.

Let's look again at a certain New Testament scripture that is closely connected with Deuteronomy 8:18.

> **Now unto him that is able to do exceeding abundantly above all that we ask or think, according to the POWER that worketh in us.**
>
> Ephesians 3:20

Now don't look at this verse as being familiar to you. Look at it in the context of what the Holy Ghost is talking about. The Old Testament text said, **But thou shalt remember the Lord thy God: for it is he that giveth thee power to get wealth, that he may establish his covenant which he sware unto thy fathers, as it is this day** (Deuteronomy 8:18).

God gives us power to get wealth. Now, do you think that a person who is activating the power that God gives is a person who is scraping by, just barely getting along? No, of course not! Why does God give us power? One reason He gives us power is to get wealth. Why does He give us the power to get wealth? First, the Bible says, it is to establish His covenant.

Look at the connection between these two verses, Deuteronomy 8:18 and Ephesians 3:20. It's the Lord thy God who gives you the *power* to get wealth that He may establish His covenant on earth. He gives you power to get wealth, but if you have not used the power—if the power is not activated and at work in your life—it is not God's fault that you are broke today.

Now if you were using the power, and God did not come through for you, you could look Him in the face and say, "You told me that if I use this power, I would get wealth!"

But not one of us can point our bony finger at God and say we've used that power and He has not given us wealth. No, if we have not received wealth, the problem is that we have not used the power! We may have *thought* we were using that power, but just making a confession once or twice is not enough.

As I said, confession has a great deal to do with seed, power and increase. But obedience has a great deal to do with it too.

When charismatic Christians first found out about the subject of confession, it seemed everybody was confessing for something. But not everybody was *"fessin' up!"* Those who weren't obeying what the Bible says about finances weren't confessing their wrongdoing of not paying tithes, giving offerings and looking after the poor.

I'm concerned about the poor, and our church takes care of the poor. We help out. We have sown money, and we give money to ministries that are feeding the poor and giving them the Gospel.

I would never belittle the poor, but I request the freedom to say this: the Body of Christ—or any member of the Body of Christ—doesn't have any business being poor!

You don't have any business licking Green Stamps and depending on food stamps. That's a form of bondage. Anybody who can put you in a long line and make you wait there for a handout has you in bondage.

Thank God we have such things as welfare, because some of us would be dead without it. And if you're on the welfare system now, don't just get off it immediately. But you don't have to *stay* on welfare. Money cometh!

Look again at Ephesians 3:20: **Now unto him that is able to do exceeding abundantly above all that we ask or think, ACCORDING TO the power that worketh IN us.**

You see, that power works in us!

Now who is in control of the power? Who is in control of how much power to prosper works in a person's life? In other words, who is in control of whether or not you prosper? Is it God? Or is it the devil?

Some people think the devil is holding them back from prosperity. They think it's the devil that's keeping them broke. They say, "That devil is dirty. He steals, kills and destroys" (John 10:10).

But, no, the devil can't steal from, kill or destroy you if you are an informed, inspired and illuminated, Spirit-filled, Word-believing, Word-speaking Christian! The devil is no match for you! You are the devil's master!

God set it up for us to be the devil's masters. When demons see one of us informed, blessed Christians coming down the street, those demons say, "Look, here he comes. Let's go to the other side of the street. We're going to wait for the joker who doesn't know anything. He won't put up a hard fight with us because he doesn't have any revelation. We'll wait for him and strip him of every dollar we can. We want him broke so he will misrepresent God."

Power! God gives us power to get wealth that He may establish His covenant on the earth. And He doesn't care how high you go—"exceeding abundantly above all you ask or think" is all right with Him!

Some people miss out on exceeding abundantly above because they are in a "comfort zone"—they're not really struggling with bills. They've got a few dollars in the bank, and they think, *Well, the preacher's not talking about me; this doesn't apply to me.*

A person may have $5,000 or even $15,000 in the bank, but that's not really a lot of money. With one hospital bill, he could end up broke. Then his little power would be gone. But God wants people to trust in the power that He gives. He wants to prosper them more than they're prospering now.

Getting In On God's System of Seed, Power and Increase

How can we prosper the way God wants us to prosper? By knowing what to do with the seed—by getting in on the system of "seed, power and increase!"

> I have planted, Apollos watered; BUT GOD GAVE THE INCREASE.
>
> 1 Corinthians 3:6

Now, actually, Paul is talking about preaching in this verse, but I see something else too. This scripture is talking about winning souls to the Kingdom, but you can also apply it to prosperity because it illustrates the increasing of the seed.

> The Lord shall increase you more and more, you and your children.
>
> Psalm 115:14

I like that. The Lord is in the increasing business! He wants increase, not decrease, to come into your life! But, remember, I said one of the traps you need to avoid is trying to figure out how your prosperity is going to come. You don't have to have a promotion on your job for it to come. You don't even have to get a better job for it to come. It's *God* who gives the increase as you yield to His power!

Actually, God told us that prosperity *does* comes from men. The Bible says men and women are going to give into your bosom (Luke 6:38). But it is still God who gives the increase.

I remember when I quit my job to be in the ministry full time. I didn't have any money, but God told me to quit that job, so I quit. There was an older gentleman in my church who was concerned about me. At times I used to sit outside my house in a rocker, reading the Bible, and this man would stop by to see me.

Once he said to me, "You're a nice young man. Why did you quit your job?"

I told him, "I'm out of that job because God told me to get out of it. I'm preaching now; that's all I'm doing."

He said, "Man, I don't see how you're going to make it."

I knew this man was a good man, and he was just concerned about me. But holy indignation rose up in me when he said that. I stood up and said, "Brother, if the Lord has to get a pack of quails to pass over this driveway and cause every one of them to have a heart attack when they get over my front door, my family and I are going to eat! God will see to it!"

When I said that, this brother just looked at me, kind of stupefied. He shook his head as if he was thinking, *That boy is past help.* He kind of shook my hand and left.

About a year later, this man came back to see me. He drove up to my house with a smile on his face. He said, "I know what you mean now. I see now that you're going to make it." He saw how the Lord was taking care of me. And he was really happy for me.

God gives us the seed for us to use to bring increase into our lives.

> **For as the rain cometh down, and the snow from heaven, and returneth not thither, but watereth the earth, and maketh it bring forth and bud, that it may give seed to the sower, and bread to the eater.**
>
> **Isaiah 55:10**

Now let's look at this scripture in its context to see what the Lord is saying to us about the seed.

> **Let the wicked forsake his way, and the unrighteous man his thoughts: and let him return unto the Lord, and he will have mercy upon him; and to our God, for he will abundantly pardon. For my thoughts are not your thoughts, neither are your ways my ways, saith the Lord. For as the heavens are higher than the earth, so are my ways higher than your ways, and my thoughts than your thoughts. For as the rain cometh down, and the snow from heaven, and returneth not thither, but watereth the earth, and maketh it bring forth and bud, that it may give SEED to the sower, and bread to the eater.**
>
> **Isaiah 55:7-10**

God is talking about wicked men here, but we Christians are not always in the Spirit! Any thinking that is not in line with the Word and the way God thinks is wicked thinking!

We don't always think like God thinks. Many Christians believe that just because they have been filled with the Holy Ghost, they always think like God thinks. But that's not true, because we're not always in the Spirit. A lot of times we're in the flesh.

God stays in the Spirit. God's ways stay high. Our ways are "up there" *sometimes!*

For example, when the glory of God and the power come upon you, you believe you can leap over tall buildings and that you're more powerful than a locomotive! You become a "superman" or a "superwoman"!

When *the* "Superman"—the Spirit of the living God—rises up inside of you, man, you don't care how many devils are against you. You're ready to jump on the first devil that raises his head! You'll think, *Let some hard case show up so I can deal with it.* That's what happens when the power or anointing of God comes on you. You turn into a "superman." But you're not always in the Spirit. Sometimes you're just "Clark Kent"!

God says, **For my thoughts are not your thoughts, neither are your ways my ways, saith the Lord. For as the heavens are higher than the earth, so are my ways higher than your ways, and my thoughts than your thoughts** (vv. 8,9).

God's thoughts are not your thoughts; neither are God's ways your ways. So don't think about how God is going to prosper you. God says, **For as the rain cometh down, and the snow from heaven, and returneth not thither, but watereth the earth, and maketh it bring forth and bud, that it may give SEED TO THE SOWER, and bread to the eater** (v. 10).

Don't Hold on Too Tight— ## That Seed Is for Sowing!

You see, God gives seed to the sower. You have to have seed in order to sow. God gives the financial seed, but, as I said, most of the time people eat their seed. Instead of sowing or planting their seed into the Gospel or somebody's life, they eat it.

Sometimes when money hits my hand, it never gets cold there because as soon as I get it, I hear the Holy Ghost saying, "Give that to so-and-so." It's as if that money is saying to me, "Gotta' go—can't stay long! Good-bye!"

You have to ask yourself the question, *Can God use me as a channel?* I've had money pass through my hands so quickly that as soon as I got it, I gave it to somebody else.

I may have even needed the money at the time, but I did what God told me to do. I knew the money wasn't for me. God was just using me. Maybe the person who gave it to me would never have given it to the other person whose name God called out to me. God wanted the person to whom I gave it to have it. So God used me as a financial channel.

The problem with many people, and the reason why God can't use them as a channel of His blessings is because when they get money, they hold on to it tightly! The Lord will tell them to give it, and they'll say, "The devil is speaking to me!" They just received that money, and they're not ready to let go of it yet!

Have you ever heard a minister preach about giving out of your need? They're preaching about giving, and there you are with needs too!

But you might not have enough to do what you need to do anyway, so you might as well plant what you have! Plant it and expect a crop to come up to help you and your situation.

Say to yourself, *Why should I mess around with these few dollars? I don't have enough anyway; I'm just going to put it into good soil and look up to heaven and praise God.* Then expect God to move on your behalf to get you out of whatever situation you're in!

Don't Sow Into Dead Ground

Let me tell you something else about giving, or sowing. There's an old spirit that tries to come in along with the message of giving, and you may end up giving to the wrong person as a result. I did that at one time. I got crazy—excited and exuberant about what I was learning about giving and prosperity—so I just started giving money away.

Once I said to my wife, "Give so-and-so fifty dollars." Then after we gave it, the Lord said to me, "That's dead ground you just planted in."

I said, "But, Lord, I *believe!*" He said, "Nothing is going to come up as a harvest. That was *you* who decided to give that; that wasn't Me."

You see, God will tell you to whom to give. God has even told me to give to wealthy people, so I just went ahead and gave them something in obedience to the Lord.

We have a habit of going around looking for somebody who's broke to give to. We look for the "brokest" preacher we can find whose tires are bald or threadbare and who has that same shiny suit on every time you see him. (He's ironed that thing so many times, it's full of starch and looks shiny!)

We think, *There's the reverend; I want to give to him because he's so broke, and I want to help the Lord.*

But that's not necessarily helping the Lord. If the Lord tells you to give to the broke preacher, then you go ahead and give. But, really, that preacher shouldn't have those bald tires if he's serving the same God I'm serving. He shouldn't be broke. Even if he started out broke, after about five years he shouldn't be broke anymore. (I was broke for about *fifteen* years. I was a really stupid preacher, but not anymore!)

Getting the Weeds Out of Your Harvest

God wants you to plant, water and weed your finances—your financial crop. You have to plant where He leads you to plant, water that seed and then keep the weeds out.

You might ask, "How do I do that?" Well, you plant and water by continuing to give. Then, keep the weeds out by holding your confession fast before the Lord. Tell Him, "Lord, I have done what You told me to do. I'm holding You to Your Word, and I'm expecting You to do what You said in Your Word You would do. I'm expecting You to show Yourself strong in my life."

You know, God is not a man that He should lie (Numbers 23:19). If He said it, He'll make it good!

Say this, "Money cometh unto me because my Father said so. Therefore, there will be no lack for preaching the Gospel, nor in my personal affairs. I am not covetous with the Lord's blessings, but I am a covenant partner with the plan, purpose and will of God.

"God is my Source. God is my supplier. Therefore, I will always have more than enough. Money is not my master. *Jesus* is my Master. I master and manage my money according to the will of God. And money cometh to *me!*"

By making these kinds of confessions, you are watering the seed of God's Word sown, and you are enabling God to bring increase into your life.

Apply the Power With Full Force

Once you know how to plant the seed, you need to understand how to yield to and work with the power so you can receive the increase. God gives you the power, the ability, to get wealth. So apply the power with full force. How do you do that? Well, first of all, you apply the power by tithing. Second, every time God tells you to give an offering, give it. Planting on a continual basis, not just once or twice, is how you give place to the power on your behalf.

Then, while you're expecting your increase, you need to practice thinking the thoughts of God and speaking the Word of God about wealth.

> **Praise ye the Lord. Blessed is the man that feareth the Lord, that delighteth greatly in his commandments. His seed** [children] **shall be mighty upon earth: the generation of the upright shall be blessed. Wealth and riches shall be in his house: and his righteousness endureth for ever.**
>
> **Psalm 112:1-3**

Now notice that there's a qualifier there: **Blessed is the man that feareth the Lord, THAT DELIGHTETH GREATLY IN HIS COMMANDMENTS.** What is the result? His seed shall be mighty upon the earth; the generation of the upright shall be blessed.

That verse is not talking about the generation of the upright just being blessed spiritually. That verse is not talking about prayer. It's talking about money!

Look at verse 3: **Wealth and riches shall be in his house: and his righteousness endureth for ever.** So we know that's not talking about prayer. We know how to pray, but we don't know how to give and to receive increase like God wants us to.

We have to think the thoughts of God about wealth. We have to cooperate with the power of God to get wealth by sowing or planting seed and then by speaking His Word over our finances. That's how we yield to the power.

Another way to yield to the power is to resist poverty, doubt and any suggestion of failure.

It's Possible!

You need to get this message inside you—in your spirit. Faith comes by hearing (Romans 10:17), so as you hear and ponder the Word concerning prosperity, you will begin to *think* of yourself as blessed. You will see yourself out of poverty and debt.

And God *will* bless you exceeding abundantly above all you ask or think according to the power that worketh in you. But you have to get your thinking straightened out to activate that power.

In other words, when the devil tells you, "It's impossible," you say, "It's *possible.*" When the devil says, "You're never going to get out of debt; it's impossible," you say, "It's *possible.*"

When the devil says, "I'm going to keep you broke," you say, "No, I'll never be broke another day in my life! It's *possible!*" When he says, "Your grandfather was broke, your father was broke and *you're* broke!" you say, "No! Money cometh to the Body of Christ! Money cometh to *me!* It's *possible!*"

Now, what word should you be thinking of when you think of yourself as free of debt? *Possible!* What should you say when you think of yourself as strong in finances? *Possible!*

What about your being a great supporter of your local church? *Possible!* What about when the pastor says he needs someone to give $5,000 to send out a missionary, and the pastor's looking right at you when he says it? *Possible!*

What would you say if somebody said, "Yes, I know money cometh, but what if I'm black?" *Possible!* What if somebody said, "I'm white"? *Possible!* "Indian"? *Possible!* "Chinese"? *Possible!* Your race doesn't make any difference then, does it! No, it doesn't. Money *cometh!* What would you think about getting your paycheck and then asking your wife, "Honey, who do we owe?" and her saying, "Nobody"? *Possible!*

God wants His children to enjoy prosperity. Those nice restaurants were built for us! If anybody ought to be eating that steak and lobster, it ought to be the Lord's children! The devil's children have been in those nice places too long. It's time for God's children to be there.

Once I was preaching to my congregation on this subject, and I told them, "I don't see enough of you eating out and enjoying yourselves. You don't ever go anywhere. Start showing up at some of those restaurants!" Then, speaking to some of the men in that service, I said, "That wife of yours doesn't want to be cooking all the time, you tight thing, you! Take her out somewhere!"

Some men will say, "Well, I like to eat at my house." But, no, most of the time, they just don't want to spend the money! They will say to their wives, "I like the way you cook, Honey." But some of those women are tired of sweating over that stove every night.

I told the men of my church to take their wives out to eat from time to time. (Say it out loud: *"Possible!"*) I told them to let their wives dress up and then leave the children at home sometimes. I told them, "Find a baby sitter. But to get a baby sitter, you have to have money to pay the baby sitter well so he or she can baby sit really well! Then you won't have to be concerned about the children when you get to the restaurant!" Then after I said all that, I said, "And get your wife a portable phone to put in her purse so she can call back home and check on the kids if she wants!" *Possible!*

What's your Daddy's Name? My Daddy's Name is El Shaddai. He's the God who's more than enough! His Name is Jehovah Jireh; He is my provider!

You know, because I'm a child of God, I couldn't feel inferior and in lack if I wanted to. I'm too "drunk" on being superior *in Christ.*

I'm complete in Him. Are you? You are if you're in Him—if you're a child of God.

We need to keep the power operating in our lives if we want "Money cometh" to work for us. We talked about the confession of your faith as one way to do that.

Getting Others To Confess Your Prosperity!

Now I'm going to teach you how to get *others* to confess for you that money cometh to you!

On the checks you write, just above the place where you sign your name, write "Money cometh!" Write it out in your own handwriting because something about doing that will help your faith.

Then the bank tellers and all the creditors you owe will be confessing, "Money cometh" for you!

Now this is how every creditor and bank teller who handles your check is going to confess "Money cometh" for you: They will say, for example, "John Doe—Money cometh! I wonder what that means?" Then they might show it to another teller: "Look at this check from John Doe. It says, 'John Doe—Money cometh!'"

They are confessing for you, "Money cometh!"

There is power in those two anointed words "Money cometh!" I preached a certain message on "Money cometh," and the following word from the Lord came to me for the people:

> *If you stay in the groove and continue to move in the vein in which I have placed you this night—yea, yield not only to the words of a man, but hear My Word that I speak to you—I will take you into prosperity.*
>
> *I know you may have been fooled before. But understand that every false thing must have a real thing. Yield to My Spirit, and I'll take you into real prosperity. I'll help you get out of the situation you are in. For you are My child, and I have good pleasure in your prosperity. So yield to My plan, yield to My way, and finally, it will come—that glorious day when you'll walk away from that table that has kept you puzzled and 'fuzzy.' That same table that*

day after day after day you've been dealing with—a table of bills and debt.

But, yea, you have gathered around My anointing, and I'm taking you out of debt, distress and discontentment. I'm taking you into the land that I promised your father Abraham and then paid in full to [the Seed] Jesus Christ, so that you may walk in prosperity for the rest of your life.

Hold Fast to Your Confession of Faith

You need to constantly make the confession that money cometh to you. That's how you keep the power working in your life so God can give the increase.

Make this confession right now: "Father, my mind is made up. I'm free from poverty. I'm redeemed from poverty.

"Wallet, you are full of money, in Jesus' Name! I am going to help get the Gospel preached with my finances. Devil, you're a liar. You've been lying to me. My Father wants me to have abundance. I *have* abundance. I don't care what anybody else says about it—I only care what my Father says. And I'm not going to feel guilty for having plenty. Money cometh to *me!*"

And when thy herds and thy flocks MULTIPLY, and thy silver and
thy gold is MULTIPLIED, and all that thou hast is MULTIPLIED.
—DEUTERONOMY 8:13

God wants you to live the life of abundance that He has provided
for you through the Lord Jesus Christ.

In the last chapter, we talked about seed, power and increase.
That's the system by which God multiplies His blessings in your life.
But, first, you've got to plant the seed—not just the seed of your faith
and your confession, but also the seed of money. You have to yield
what you have to God so He can multiply it. You don't have to have a
lot of money to get the blessings multiplied to you. You just have to
start where you are, yielding what you have to God.

For example, someone who's concerned about the fact that he
hasn't tithed in the past might say, "What do I do now?"

Start where you are. Forget about the past. You've missed it, but
now, go on from where you are, and God will work with you. But start
tithing now because if you don't tithe, you're under the world's
system, and you're going to suffer; you're not going to be blessed.

There's Freedom in Obeying God!

I tell you, a freedom came to me when I started to tithe—when I
started to give God the money that already belonged to Him. I had a
certain joy and a happiness in obeying Him. I always knew I was
going to make it. I could never even *think* of going under, because I
had backup from the Scriptures saying that God would supply my
need. I entered into a new realm in my finances when I began to yield
what I had to God!

By yielding what you have to God, you can get in on God's financial
program that will take you out of poverty and into divine prosperity. But

if you *don't* yield what you have to God and you just throw your finances into the world's system, you won't have any seed in the ground for God to multiply.

God wants to give you "divine" finances. He wants to work on your financial portfolio. He wants you to be in the black every payday with more than enough left over. That's called a Holy Ghost portfolio! And He wants to show you how to get in position to receive this financial prosperity.

> **Now therefore thus saith the Lord of hosts; CONSIDER YOUR WAYS. Ye have sown much, and bring in little; ye eat, but ye have not enough; ye drink, but ye are not filled with drink; ye clothe you, but there is none warm; and he that earneth wages earneth wages to put it into a bag with holes. Thus saith the Lord of hosts; CONSIDER YOUR WAYS.**
>
> **Haggai 1:5-7**

Notice in verses 5 and 7, God said, **Consider your ways.**

Verse 6 says, **Ye have sown much, and bring in little; ye eat, but ye have not enough; ye drink, but ye are not filled with drink; ye clothe you, but there is none warm; and he that earneth wages earneth wages to put it into a bag with holes.**

On both sides of verse 6, God said, **Consider your ways.** In other words, God is saying, "Consider how much time you're wasting with the world's system."

It doesn't matter if you have four jobs, you're still wasting your time if you're not a tither and on God's system of prosperity. You're never, ever going to get ahead while you're robbing God! Even if you do *seem* to get ahead, the enemy will try to put sickness or some other calamity on you.

You see, not tithing can open the door to the enemy because tithing is the will of God. Therefore, if you're not tithing, you are not in the will of God. It will be difficult for you to claim your full healing if you're not a tither. Why? Because you can't have a claim to God's best when you're not trusting Him. And you're not trusting Him if you're not obeying His Word.

Now that may hang a little heavy over our heads, but it's the truth.

Someone will ask, "What does tithing have to do with my healing?"

Well, being in the will of God will enable you to shake your finger in Satan's face and tell him, "Satan, I'm in the complete will of God. You take your stinky hands off of me. I'm walking with God, and my body is the temple of the Holy Ghost!"

There's *Confidence* in Obeying God!

Now, you can't do that with full confidence if you're not in complete obedience to the Word and will of God. You see, Satan likes to have something hanging over your head.

In the natural, sometimes someone who knows something about a person will try to hang that over his head and control him. Satan is like that. When you ask God for something, Satan likes to clear his throat to get God's attention so he can accuse you before Him. He likes to accuse you to God.

For example, if you're not a tither, he will say to God, "You can't do that for him because he's not a tither." And it's true. Even though God wants to bless you, His hands are tied. You are robbing God of the pleasure of blessing you.

So learn how to get in on God's system by tithing and yielding what you have to God so He can multiply it.

The most detrimental thing to the believer's prosperity is failing to yield everything he has to God. Let's look at the illustration of Elijah and the widow to see just how we can yield what we have to God. This illustration also shows how God will deal with your creditors for you when you get into His divine plan!

> **Now there cried a certain woman of the wives of the sons of the prophets unto Elisha, saying, Thy servant my husband is dead; and thou knowest that thy servant did fear the Lord: and the creditor is come to take unto him my two sons to be bondmen. And Elisha said unto her, What shall I do for thee? tell me, what hast thou in the house? And she said, Thine handmaid hath not any thing in the**

house, save a pot of oil. Then he said, Go, borrow thee vessels abroad of all thy neighbours, even empty vessels; borrow not a few. And when thou art come in, thou shalt shut the door upon thee and upon thy sons, and shalt pour out into all those vessels, and thou shalt set aside that which is full. So she went from him, and shut the door upon her and upon her sons, who brought the vessels to her; and she poured out. And it came to pass, when the vessels were full, that she said unto her son, Bring me yet a vessel. And he said unto her, There is not a vessel more. And the oil stayed. Then she came and told the man of God. And he said, Go, sell the oil, and pay thy debt, and live thou and thy children of the rest.

2 Kings 4:1-7

Once you get into God's divine plan for your finances, just let God deal with your creditors, and you go ahead and do what you're supposed to do. God will give you wisdom and show you how to approach your creditors. But first, you have to surrender to Him and obey Him and yield what you have to Him so He can multiply it.

First, let's define the word "creditor." A creditor is simply *someone to whom you owe something*. Second Kings 4:1 says, **Now there cried a certain woman of the wives of the sons of the prophets unto Elisha, saying, Thy servant my husband is dead; and thou knowest that thy servant did fear the Lord: and the CREDITOR is come to take unto him my two sons to be bondmen.**

Now the only reason that creditor came was that this widow wasn't able to pay what she owed to him. **And Elisha said unto her, What shall I do for thee?...** (v. 2). Elijah asked her, "What do you want me to do about it? How can I help you? Tell me, what do you have in your house?"

Now this widow was asking Elijah for help. Why do you suppose he wanted to know what she had in her house? Because she had to yield something to God so He could multiply it! She had to give God something to work with.

You see, it's not how much you do or don't have that counts. It's yielding to God what you do have that counts. You may not have been obedient to God in your finances in the past. But if you turn your heart to God and say, "This is where I am now; I want to do what's right," God will forgive and help you. He is such a good, gracious, forgiving, loving, merciful Father that He will take you from where you are and carry you as high as you want to go with Him!

God is not out to get you or punish you. The only thing God is out to do to you is *to bless you!* He wants to get you out of that hole of poverty and lack that you've fallen into. He wants to get you on top of your situation. So yield whatever you have to God, and He will multiply it!

A Pot of Oil Is Enough!

Notice that God never says how much you have to yield. He just says to yield what you have. What did the widow have in her house to yield to God? She told Elijah, **Thine handmaid hath not any thing in the house, save A POT OF OIL** (v. 2).

But, you see, with God, a pot of oil is enough! This is the revelation I want you to see: You just need something to start off with. The process has to be initiated on earth so heaven can come in and intervene on your behalf. Any little step you take, God will use it to pour out a blessing on your life.

In the case of this widow, it wasn't that she had a big pot of oil or an abundance to give to God. She only had a little bit of oil. She couldn't have had very much oil because she didn't have enough to pay her creditors. The prophet said, in essence, "Listen, just give me something to argue your case with."

When some of my church members talk to me about financial problems, I want to say, "Is there anything I can argue your case with? In other words, what have you been doing with Kingdom business? When was the last time you gave a gift toward the Lord's work? Let me argue your case for you."

If one of my members says, "Well, I'm a tither," then I have a right as his pastor to look God in the face, so to speak, and say, "What are You doing up there? What kind of assignment have You given me down here? You told me to be a shepherd to this local body of believers; and here this person is, doing what You told him to do and what I taught him from Your Word, yet it looks like You're letting him down!"

You see, I can help argue that church member's case. But your case can't be argued if you're robbing God. If you're not in the will of God, Satan is going to make some noise! He's going to say, "Look, God, this person doesn't obey Your Word." And God cannot violate His covenant. Whatever He said in His Word, He will abide by. So if you abide by it, too, God will work with you and bring you out of your situation. But if you *don't* obey the Word, you tie the hands of God to work on your behalf.

Let's look at something else concerning this widow and her pot of oil. She borrowed those vessels, or pots, from her neighbors because the prophet Elijah told her to do it (2 Kings 4:3). She believed the prophet.

Many people today don't believe the prophets, but Second Chronicles 20:20 says, **Believe in the Lord your God, so shall ye be established; believe his prophets, so shall ye prosper.**

As I said before, I don't believe that verse is only talking about the prophet. I believe God is talking about the fivefold ministry gifts. Many people don't believe in pastors; they don't trust their pastors. If they trusted their pastors and the Word of God that their pastors ministered to them, most of the Body of Christ would start tithing today!

People say, "Well, I believe in the Lord." But Second Chronicles 20:20 says, **Believe in the Lord your God, so shall ye be established; believe his prophets, so shall ye prosper.**

If they were really believing God and His Word, they would be established and they would *prosper.*

Believe and Prosper!

I can prove from the Bible that people who believe the Lord are established and prosperous and that people who *don't* believe the Lord are *not* established or prosperous. For example, the rich man in Luke 16 was rich financially, but he was not rich in the things of God.

In other words, he didn't prosper God's way. Well, this man died and went to hell. And hell was so hot, he started thinking about his five brothers who were still living on the earth. They were living the same wicked life he had lived. (See verses 19-31.)

So this rich man who was in hell cried out to Abraham in heaven, asking him to send Lazarus, who'd also died, to talk to his brothers. You see, Lazarus died and went to Abraham's bosom, or Paradise. The rich man wanted Abraham to send Lazarus back from the dead to tell his brothers, "Don't come here. Hell is a hot place!"

Abraham said to the rich man, "If they will not believe the prophets, they will not believe though one is raised from the dead" (Luke 16:31).

So, you see, you can't prosper if you're not believing God and His Word *or* if you're not believing God's prophets or ministers.

Honor the Ministry Gifts and Prosper

Not only has the enemy succeeded in influencing some Christians not to believe the ministers, but he has also gotten them to be irreverent and disrespectful toward God's ministers. But when people act disrespectful toward God's ministers, He won't let them receive anything from those men and women of God.

You can't receive from somebody you don't respect. Remember the widow in Second Kings 4. Look at the confidence this widow had in the man of God. She told him all of her business. She didn't put on a false front. She said, "I have nothing but a little oil." Then this man of God gave her certain instructions, and the woman obeyed him.

Sometimes instructions will embarrass you if you're not really submitted. But we see in Second Kings chapter 4 that this widow obeyed the man of God. He told her, "Go borrow some vessels." That's why borrowing can't be completely wrong. God wouldn't have told the prophet to tell the woman to borrow if it were wrong.

That widow could have said, "I don't need any vessels; I need *oil!* Those old preachers are always telling people to do silly things. I'm not going to get any vessels. I'm my own woman. I'm not going to borrow anything."

But what did this widow do? She did what the man of God said to do—and, boy, her obedience made a connection with heaven!

> Then he said, Go, borrow thee vessels abroad of all thy neighbours, even empty vessels; borrow not a few. And when thou art come in, thou shalt shut the door upon thee and upon thy sons, and shalt pour out into all those vessels, and thou shalt set aside that which is full. So she went from him, and shut the door upon her and upon her sons, who brought the vessels to her; and she poured out. And it came to pass, when the vessels were full, that she said unto her son, Bring me yet a vessel. And he said unto her, There is not a vessel more. And the oil stayed.
>
> 2 Kings 4:3-6

God filled all those vessels up with oil! Well, what does Isaiah 1:19 say? **If ye be willing and obedient, ye shall eat the good of the land.** She was willing and obedient. She believed the prophet and she ate the good of the land! The blessing was poured out on her.

I'm telling you, if you tithe and give finances to the Kingdom of God so the Gospel can be preached to evangelize this world, there is no way God will *not* pour out His blessings on you too!

But, on the other hand, you can't have prosperity without following the guidelines. You can't just do what you want to do if you want God to bless you. You have to follow His plan.

Notice in verse 6 what happened after the widow obeyed the man of God. AND IT CAME TO PASS.... Something came to pass! She made a connection with heaven! It says, **And it came to pass,** WHEN THE VESSELS WERE FULL....

Let's go back to verse 1. That widow told Elisha, **The creditor is come to take unto him my two sons to be bondmen.** She went from being broke and in poverty to having those vessels full!

Why? She yielded what she had to God, and He multiplied it!

Then, when the woman went back to the man of God, he said, **Go, sell the oil, and pay thy debt, and live thou and thy children of the rest** (2 Kings 4:7).

You just need to yield what you have to God, and He will multiply it. God will fix it so you can "sell the oil and pay your debts." He wants to get you in the position where you can get out of debt. He wants you to be happy and free and **live thou and thy children of the rest** (v. 7)!

You see, once you've followed God's instructions in His Word and you've made your connection with heaven, God will bring you out of debt and into prosperity just like He did for that widow. She paid her debts and had some money left over—enough for her and her children to live on.

So in your own life, be faithful with what you have. Yield it to God, and He will turn it into much. You can have the blessing this widow woman received, but you have to yield what you have in obedience to God. You have to get in on God's divine program.

Has the Lord ever told you to give something to someone, but you didn't obey right away? I mean, you knew it was the Lord telling you to give it, but you disobeyed. And you became so mixed up and unhappy, you couldn't figure out which way was up!

If God told you to give something to someone else, then whatever He told you to give doesn't belong to you; it belongs to that other person. And you can never be happy until you give it. So when God gives you an assignment, do it. You'll be blessed in your obedience.

This message of prosperity is for *every* child of God, not just a few. In the world, there are certain clubs that will make you pay a certain amount just to get in the door. You might have to have $1,000 to get in. It might be called the thousand dollar club. Or you might have to have $1,500 just to get in. That one's called the fifteen hundred dollar club!

But this Gospel and the message of prosperity is not a club. You can get in with what you have. And if you'll believe Him, He'll bring you to a solid place financially.

Your Prosperity Glorifies God

God wants you to be blessed. You're supposed to have people wondering what you're doing. If you don't have them wondering, you're not blessed yet! Others are supposed to say, "I wonder what in the world they're doing; they're so prosperous." You're prosperous because you have inside information!

All of God's children should have the world's children wondering and being tempted to cross over to the Kingdom of God. The world should say, "Man, if their God is that good, I want Him too."

The devil has lied to us—to the Church—long enough. He has lied to the preacher about God. But God is a good God. He's not different than any natural father who wants good things for his children. In fact, He's *better* than a natural father! He's better than me, and He's better than you. And He will "let loose" in your life with His blessings when you get in His will.

When my own son cuts the grass, washes my car, irons my suit or obeys what his mother and I tell him to do, then when he gets ready to take a girl out or do something he wants to do, I give him whatever he needs. I'll ask him, "Son, how much do you need?"

Well, what will God do for you if you follow His orders? When you honor God and His Word and do what He tells you to do, He says, "That's My son. Let him have whatever he's asking for," or He'll say, "That's My daughter. Let her have the blessing."

I *dare* you to try to think of something too big for God to give you!

I have simply *thought* about certain things as I was going about my business, working for the Lord, and He has brought them to pass in my life. For instance, once I thought about having a particular kind of watch. I never even mentioned it to anybody, and I received it! It was the top of the line for that particular brand of watch. God put it on another man's heart, and he said to me, "I believe you need to have a such and such kind of watch."

Understand me, now. You can't be covetous and expect God to bless you. You can't just be after things. But, you see, God had been preparing me for these kinds of blessings for years. And I am bold about what God blesses me with. I don't want to hide anything the Lord gives me and does for me. That's why I didn't build my house behind a big gate that you'd need a special card to get through to see the house. I built it out in the open so everybody who passes by can see it and get blessed.

I could have gone down to a country club and built a house someplace where nobody could find me. But how's that going to bless anybody—with me back in a hole of seclusion somewhere?

Don't Hide Your Blessings!

Many preachers who get blessed think they have to hide the fact that they're blessed. They think, *Man, I can't let those people know I'm blessed.*

But that's crazy! I'm not going to hide the fact that I'm blessed, because it's the Lord who's blessing me. *People* didn't bless me; *God* did. So I'm not going to hide it when God blesses me.

I'm putting God on display in my life. Some preachers say, "You'd better hide," but, no, you don't have to hide. If God is blessing you, come on out in the open and say, "Hey! Look what the Lord has done!"

People are afraid of persecution and flak for experiencing the blessings of God. But if they are hiding what the Lord has done, they are still going to get some flak even if they build their house in the *jungle!* Somebody's going to go back there and find them and get upset about their blessings. So they may as well go ahead and let people know what the Lord has done and how He has blessed them.

You know, I like to go out in my yard and turn the sprinkler on and wave to my neighbors. I don't want to live by myself out in the jungle somewhere. I like to put on my shorts and go for a walk in my neighborhood and wave to my neighbors as I pass by.

The Lord wants to show Himself strong, not just in your life, but also in the lives of others. So you need to be bold about what the Lord has done for you.

You need to make up your mind and say, "I'm going to make it. I'm going to prosper like God wants me to prosper. And I'm not going to hide my blessing." Then nobody will be able to stop you—not even the devil himself—because you'll have your mind made up.

After you have made up your mind, it might take a while for God to get you where you're going, but He'll get you there. He's setting it up for you. Those folks who are just sitting back with a wait-and-see attitude will be left behind in the dust. But you'll be making progress—financial progress—as you walk with God and obey Him. God is going to bless those who will be faithful to Him.

You know, we ought to be good advertisements for the Kingdom of God. But that old poverty spirit came on the Church, and people thought you had to be broke to be humble and serve God. They thought you had to be broke to be spiritual. But that's not spiritual— that's *stupid!*

Even after all the Lord has provided for us and all the scriptures He has given us that teach us about finances and what He wants for His children, some people are still talking about how humble and spiritual they are because they're broke.

Those people haven't read the Bible! The Bible says, **The Lord is my shepherd; I shall not want** (Psalm 23:1). The Bible also says in Psalm 23, **Thou preparest a table before me in the presence of mine enemies...** (v. 5). Well, I always thought that table was in heaven, but to my utter amazement, the revelation came to me that Psalm 23:5 is talking about a table right here on earth, because I will not have any enemies in heaven! God is talking about preparing a table for me right here on earth, in the presence of the devil, demons and worldly folks!

Come and Dine at God's Table of Blessing!

Get away from that "pork-and-beans" table, Body of Christ! Come on over to the table where the real butter is—the real thing! We don't have to be eating substitute butter. On God's table there is real butter!

I was preaching one time, and I heard the Spirit of God say, "Come on over to the table and dine with Me!"

Sometimes in the natural when a person gets to God's table, he may not know how to act because there's so much on the table. He's afraid he might knock something over. But the Lord says, "Let it fall over; I have plenty more."

Body of Christ, we've been eating at the wrong table. We've been eating at the enemy's table, and he's been holding the blessing back from us! But in Christ, there's no more bondage. There's no more bondage for you in your finances.

Whatever we need or desire, we can receive from Him at the table. That's true for all of us. In fact, your little heart is not big enough to think of something that God has not provided for you. Your heart is not big enough to think of something that God cannot get for you. You can think and dream as big as you want, but you won't be able to think and dream big enough.

I tell you, when you get in the will of God, you'll start thinking big! You'll sit in your favorite chair and see yourself with the blessings. And the Father will see to it that you get them because you're His son or daughter, and you're following His orders. There will be plenty of oil in your vessels just like there was for the widow we read about in Second Kings 4.

Second Kings 4:6 says, **And it came to pass, when the vessels were full, that she said unto her son, Bring me yet a vessel. And he said unto her, There is not a vessel more.** AND THE OIL STAYED.

That means that when they ran out of vessels, the oil stopped flowing. But it stayed. That also means that your oil will *stay!* In other words, your oil of provision will not leave you! It will stay!

Some people want the blessings of God that I'm talking about, but they don't want to yield anything to God. For example, they'll say, "Well, I'm not giving my tithe, because I don't know what that church will do with my money."

But, really, your business is to give your tithe and expect God to bless you. If something is wrong in that church, God will handle it. But even if there were something wrong in that church, it can't rob you of your blessing, because you believed and obeyed God when you tithed.

Don't misunderstand me. I'm not telling you to close your eyes to wrongdoing. If you see something in a church that you know is false and wrong, you need to find yourself another church. But your suspicion is not good enough. Suspicion is not basis enough because suspicion comes from the devil.

Most of the time, when God is telling you to release something, He's doing it because He wants to give you something better. But you have to give Him something to work with. A lot of times, the reason we don't get the better thing is that we're so enthralled and enthused with the thing we have, and we don't want to release it. Remember that so that the next time something like that comes up, you'll know what to do.

Let's look in First Kings at another example of yielding what you have to God so He can multiply it.

> **Arise, get thee to Zarephath, which belongeth to Zidon, and dwell there: behold, I have commanded a widow woman there to sustain thee. So he [Elijah] arose and went to Zarephath. And when he came to the gate of the city, behold, the widow woman was there gathering of sticks: and he called to her, and said, Fetch me, I pray thee, a little water in a vessel, that I may drink.**
>
> **1 Kings 17:9,10**

Look closely at verse 10. The prophet called to the woman and said, **Fetch me, I pray thee, a little water in a vessel, that I may drink.** Now, the average person would have said, "Preacher, get it yourself!"

God wants to bring honor back into the Body of Christ. He doesn't want you to bow down to the men and women of God or honor them as individual people. But there's a call on their lives that He wants you to respect.

In fact, if you're going to receive the full benefit of God's blessings, you have to have a certain respect for the call or office a minister stands in. Let me say it like this: The people who have respect for the call are going to receive more from God!

There's been an irreverence toward ministers in the Body of Christ. I remember a minister years ago who used to be my wife's pastor. People in that denomination didn't even know as much then as we know now about the Bible, but there was a certain dignity about that pastor, and people had respect for him. They didn't want to "mess up" while he was around. They'd say things like, "Man, here comes the 'Rev.' Straighten up!"

But in more recent times, it seems that people's attitudes have changed. Some people will say to the minister, "Hey, Boy!"

But that's irreverent. I'm not talking about playing around and laughing and talking with ministers. There's nothing wrong with doing that at times. But I'm talking about being irreverent and disrespectful of them.

Some members of my church know me well and will joke around with me. But in a ministry situation, they will switch gears in a split second. They'll change from saying "There's my buddy," to saying "There's my pastor."

When people have respect for the things of God and for God's ministers, they will receive God's blessing. It may sound like I'm trying to get people to act a certain way toward me because I'm a minister, but I'm not seeking my own gain. I'm at peace with God. He has given me an assignment to help bring reverence back into the Body of Christ.

In fact, it is a sacrifice to have to say some of the things I say. I could live my life as a blessed man without saying anything, and things would probably continue to be as they are in many people's lives. But I know what's in store for the person who shows respect for God and the things of God. So I say what God wants me to say, and I put my reputation on the line. I want people to have the blessings. That's why I teach the way I do.

Obedience to God May Involve Sacrifice

When Elijah said to this widow, **Fetch me, I pray thee, a little water in a vessel, that I may drink** (1 Kings 17:10), she never asked a question. She said, in effect, "All right, I'll get you the water."

Notice the widow went to fetch the water when the prophet asked for it. But today, if the minister wants people to give $10 for the church or to help support a missionary, that's a "horse of a different color" to them! They don't want to see the connection because they have to dig a little deeper to give their money than to simply go get water for the man of God. But I'm talking about the same thing: Yield what you have to God, and He will multiply it.

It's like having a revival meeting at church. People will start out coming to the revival every night, and they'll come for about four days. But when they have to sacrifice something in order to keep coming, it's a different story.

In other words, it was all right to go "fetch the water," but not to go the extra mile and actually give money to the church. That's too big a sacrifice, just like it's too big a sacrifice to keep attending those revival meetings after four or five days. Then they miss the very night they would have received the revelation the Lord was trying to get over to them.

Sometimes God will give you one thing to do, and that's the first test of obedience. In order to get you to the prosperity He wants for you, He sometimes gives you a series of tests. You can see that in First Kings 17.

We know that widow went to get the water for Elijah. The request for water didn't shake her. But verse 11 says, **And AS SHE WAS GOING TO FETCH IT, he called to her, and said,** BRING ME, **I pray thee,** A MORSEL OF BREAD IN THINE HAND.

You see, the Lord was speaking through the prophet because the Lord had told Elijah to go to Zarephath, and the widow would sustain him (v. 9). The Lord was doing a twofold thing. He was supplying the prophet's need, and He was using the prophet as an agent to bless the widow too. God always works from both ends. God will not let you give without setting you up to receive too. He will not let you sow without setting up your harvest for you! But He has to get you to sow first. He has to get you to plant first. He has to get you to *give.*

Your Giving Is God's "Ticket" To Prosper You!

Your giving is God's ticket to operate on the earth! Your giving gives God permission to speak to someone's heart to bring to your life exactly what you need. God can't come and operate on the earth on His own. Someone, through his or her actions, has to give God permission to come and operate on the earth.

Also, when you give God permission to bless you, the devil and demons, your worldly neighbors and even the person who doesn't like you can't stop your blessing, because God is going to see to it that you have it—you opened the door to Him! And when God comes through a door, His blessing comes with Him!

When you get set up on God's plan, no weapon formed against you can prosper (Isaiah 54:17). No weapon can stop you, and no lock can hold the blessing back that belongs to you. When God comes in, He brings the keys with Him. He says, "Let My child have the blessing. His faith is in action!"

So from verse 10 to verse 11, the prophet went from the water to the bread. He'd already asked for the water, but then he said, "Bring me a morsel of bread." And she said, **As the Lord thy God liveth, I have not a cake, but an handful of meal in a barrel, and a little oil in a cruse: and, behold, I am gathering two sticks, that I may go in and dress it for me and my son, that we may eat it, and die** (v. 12).

But then notice what the prophet said to her: "You don't have to die. You don't have to be in debt. You don't have to fail and go under."

God is saying that same thing to you today! You don't have to barely get by in life. You don't have to argue with that paycheck—the check says, "I need to go here," and you say, "No, you've got to go here to pay this." Then one bill stands up on the table and says, "Please pay me," and another one stands up and says, "No, pay *me!*"

God won't let you barely get by in life if you will yield what you have to Him and let Him multiply it. But you have to do what you know to do with the Word you've heard. Then you will be blessed in your doing.

Failing to do what you know to do with the Word is like sitting in a gold mine with no gold. When you are in disobedience, the world has your money, and they're "good-timing" with it, drinking and smoking and doing other ungodly things. Yes, they're out there buying cigarettes with your money!

But God has placed money here on this earth for us. Yet because many are not standing in their rightful place and doing what God has said to do, the enemy is running with their money. He's running with most of it because we haven't done what's right according to God's Word.

Learn To Put First Things First

Elijah said to the widow, **Fear not; go and do as thou hast said: but make me thereof a little cake FIRST, and bring it unto me, and after make for thee and for thy son** (v. 13).

He told her what to do *first.* God is telling *us* to take care of His things first. We have to trust God in the area of finances and put Him first.

Just trust Him! He will sustain you, just as He sustained the widow. Don't wait. Do what the widow did—she yielded what she had to God, and He multiplied it! She only had a handful of meal and a little oil. She told the prophet, **I am gathering two sticks, that I may go in and dress it for me and my son, that we may eat it, and die** (1 Kings 17:12).

Look again at verse 13: **Elijah said unto her, Fear not; go and do as thou hast said: but make me thereof a little cake FIRST, and bring it unto me, and after MAKE FOR THEE AND THY SON.**

Notice the audacity of the man of God in verse 13: "Bring me a little cake *first,* and *after* that, make some for you and your son." Notice those two words "first" and "after." A person who was not rightly informed in spiritual things would be fussing by now! He would say, "What do you mean, *after* I make a cake for you? I told you, all I have is a little meal and oil, enough for me and my son. I told you what I have. What do you mean *after!* There isn't going to be any *after!*"

But, no. In order for you to receive from God, you have to walk by faith. You have to obey His Word. Without faith, it is impossible to please God (Hebrews 11:6).

This widow walked by faith. Elijah said, "After you do what the Lord told me to tell you to do, then make food for you and your son." Now notice the next verse: **For thus saith the Lord God of Israel, The barrel of meal shall not waste, neither shall the cruse of oil fail, until the day that the Lord sendeth rain upon the earth** (v. 14).

We can see from this verse what the problem was. They had a drought. They didn't have any water. But despite her circumstances, this widow "went and did." She obeyed the words of the prophet, and God gave her a miracle.

"Go and Do!"

You see, there are blessings you just can't receive unless you obey God. There are certain blessings pastors and ministers can't bring to the people unless the people obey God. It doesn't matter how much those preachers pray for them or preach to them or try to teach them, those people aren't going to get to that place of blessing without some action on their part. They have to "go and do."

What are the results of "going and doing"? The Word of the Lord will come true for you! Notice what happened to that widow when she "went and did." It says, **And she went and did according to the saying of Elijah: and she, and he, and her house, did eat many days** (1 Kings 17:15).

She and her house ate for *many* days, not just for one day. It didn't tell us how many days they ate. It could have been for months because God said her meal barrel wouldn't fail until He sent rain upon the earth.

This woman gave that little bit of oil and that little bit of meal to God, and that little bit she yielded to God fed her and her family for many days!

When you are hooked up with God, your provision can't run out!

Let me show you something else that happened. We have seen that God took care of a widow and her family. He took care of a personal matter. Then, we also saw in Second Kings that God took care of the widow who was about to lose her sons to the creditors. That was a personal matter.

God will take care of your personal matters. But did you know that He will take care of your business matters too? God will take care of your business if you turn it over to Him.

Yield whatever you have to God. He can't help you if you won't cooperate with Him. So give God a chance to multiply blessings to you by yielding what you have to Him!

M any of you have heard and believed the message of prosperity—that prosperity is the will of God for you. But you might not be walking in the fullness of it yet. So the Lord wants you to know how to survive financially until prosperity arrives.

One of the things we're going to talk about is how to deal with creditors and the bills and debts you may have incurred over the months and years before you heard this message. I'm going to share with you some information about getting out of debt supernaturally, while at the same time applying some natural, practical principles to your situation.

If you've been believing God and confessing that money cometh, and you've been tithing and obeying the Word concerning your finances, then your prosperity is on the way! It's yours now, but it's on the way!

You may have already put yourself in position to receive divine prosperity. But we're going to discuss in this chapter how to *maintain* your position until prosperity arrives in its fullness in your life.

After you position yourself for the prosperity of God, there's a certain progression you must go through. If people don't realize that and don't know the steps God takes people through, they might feel they're fighting a losing battle, and they might give up before they arrive where they're going with the Lord.

You're not fighting any losing battle when you're confessing and believing in line with God's Word. One of our main texts said, **Let them shout for joy, and be glad, that favour my righteous cause: yea, let them say continually, Let the Lord be magnified, which hath pleasure in the prosperity of his servant** (Psalm 35:27). That verse didn't say, "Let them be sad." No, it said, "Let them shout for joy and be *glad!*"

Why is the Lord telling you to be glad?

Everybody knows about what I call the "bill table." That's the table where many people go every payday, trying to figure out how they're going to pay all their bills. Every creditor represented on that table hollers at them, "Send me mine now!"

Well, it's a joyous and glad time when you can get up from that bill table with all your bills paid and plenty of money left over! It's *not* a joyous time when you can't pay your bills.

Heaven Has Come to Your Rescue!

Part of that verse in Psalm 35 says, **Let the Lord be magnified, which hath pleasure in the prosperity of his servant.** One of the ways the Lord can be magnified in your life is by your permitting Him to do what He desires to do in your life in full measure. So be sure and put yourself in position for Him to do it. He wants to do it for you, but, you see, you have to initiate it here on earth so that heaven can come to your rescue.

God wants His children to be financially stable. And He wants them to be financially *able*—able to support their families and also able to support the Gospel of the Lord Jesus Christ. God wants us to evangelize the world so that all men might have the opportunity to be saved. But if we don't have the finances to support the Gospel, we can't do it.

It's up to you what happens in your life. "Money cometh" belongs to you, but you have to determine that if you're in debt, you're coming *out* of debt! You have to determine that you're coming into that good land of prosperity that the Lord has provided for you!

It will help you to say out loud continually, "Money cometh! Money cometh to the Body of Christ! That means money cometh to *me!*"

Look to God, Not to Man

I said this before, but it bears repeating. "Money cometh" to you as you stand on the Word of God for you concerning financial prosperity. And it cometh *without your trying to figure out where it will come from!* Just let it come because God said it would!

The Lord said to me, "Don't try to figure out *how* the money is going to come."

Some people will have a certain need, and they'll start thinking, *Let's see, I could ask Uncle Ben....* But Uncle Ben's not going to give you a quarter! Don't depend on "Uncle Ben" or "Aunt Sue." Depend on the *Lord!* If Uncle Ben hasn't given you anything yet, he's probably not going to! So just forget about it and look to the Lord.

Then some other people are just waiting for somebody in their family to die so they can become prosperous. But then, many times, after someone dies, someone else comes along who isn't supposed to be in the will—and he starts a big argument that ties the money up in the legal system for so many years that they're too old to spend it by the time they get it!

You need to realize that the money you need is going to come to you by your looking to the Lord and His Word and by your believing and confessing, "Money cometh!" You have to be obedient to do something with the knowledge you receive to get "Money cometh" working for you.

Obey Your Master!

You see, the wicked have our money because they're willing to obey their master. But our Master is stronger than their master! And if we obey our Master, the Lord Jesus Christ, He will bring our money back to us!

We're talking about how to survive until prosperity arrives. That's where most people are. They've got the revelation of "Money cometh." Now they must remain convinced that God doesn't want them broke. They must remain convinced that it doesn't matter who they are, what their background is or what their natural heritage is.

Your inheritance in Christ—your "Money cometh"—is not based on the natural; it is based upon the supernatural. You have to get that firmly settled in your mind. You are born of God's Spirit. You're in God's family now, and God has certain things in store for you because you are His child.

So we're not dealing with a natural blessing or a natural inheritance. We're dealing with supernatural prosperity that can come to any child of God who plugs into the divine will of God. This prosperity can come to any child of God who puts himself in position for God to pour out a supernatural manifestation of His prosperity in his life.

I believe that's why you're reading this book. *You want to put yourself in that position!*

Your Prosperity Comes by Faith

Now if you're going to survive until prosperity arrives, the first thing you're going to have to do is to *take hold of prosperity by faith.* In other words, that's where you must have prosperity first—in your heart by faith! Most of the time, God will not do anything for you without your having faith for it.

Understand What Prosperity Is For

So the first thing you need to do to survive until prosperity arrives is to take hold of your prosperity by faith. The second thing you need to do is to *develop and maintain a clear understanding of what prosperity is really for.* We already talked about that briefly, but, you see, God wants to get you ready for prosperity. He has to prepare you.

There are people who think that prosperity is just for houses, cars, clothes and plenty of money in their pockets so they can say how blessed they are. But that's not the real reason for prosperity.

The primary reason God wants you to have prosperity is to fulfill His covenant. He wants to get His Gospel out. Therefore, you cannot take God's prosperity and hoard it up for yourself. That's why we read previously that, first of all, God will humble you (Deuteronomy 8:2).

The worst thing that can happen is having these two fellows— pride and prosperity—running together. Talk about an accident waiting to happen! God has to get pride out of you before He can give you *plenty.*

Some people will say, "Well, that doesn't apply to me; I can skip that step." But if they've never had money before, they don't really know what they'd do if they had plenty of money. They can say right now, "Oh, I love You, Lord," but money can change some people. In fact, some people are desperate, and that's the only reason they stay with the Lord. And until they change their thinking, God is going to let them stay in desperation.

Balance

When I first taught this lesson, "How To Survive Until Prosperity Arrives," I received from the Lord a word in connection with understanding what prosperity is really for. As I was developing an understanding of what prosperity is for, He had me write down a word next to it and underline it. The word is *balance.*

People need to be balanced in this prosperity message. On one side, some are believing that you have to be broke to be humble and holy; and, on the other side, some just want prosperity to hoard for themselves. They don't care about the work of God.

Both of those sides are wrong, but if people develop a clear understanding of what prosperity is really for, that understanding will keep them balanced concerning the prosperity message.

Refuse All Temptation To Complain

The third thing you need to do to survive until prosperity arrives is to *refuse to grumble or complain about your situation another day!*

If you're in a hard place financially, don't tell anybody your condition. Dress up and smile brightly and act joyful, like you've got a million dollars!

Some people think that if they cry or confess a bad report, someone will give them money. If you do that, yes, someone may give you twenty dollars out of sympathy, but you'll never get out of debt, because that person who feels sorry for you isn't going to give you enough to get you out of debt. He'll just feel sorry for you and give you a little bit. Even if he gave you $100, if you were $10,000 in debt, you'd still be a while getting out of debt!

So refuse to grumble or complain about your situation another day.

Have you ever grumbled and complained to the Lord? Have you ever said, "If I just had more money...." You're not going to get blessed by nagging the Lord. The Lord doesn't appreciate nagging— and He doesn't appreciate bragging either! You see, you can make a good report sometimes and sound like you're bragging. So make sure you're reporting about what good things the Lord has done for you. The Lord has told me, "Go tell your friends what good things the Lord has done for you." That's a scriptural report (Mark 5:19). That's a testimony that glorifies God.

The Bible says in Revelation, **They overcame him by the blood of the Lamb, and by the word of their testimony** (Revelation 12:11). There's something about testifying of the good things that God has done for you. It glorifies God, and it inspires others. But don't brag about anything *you* have done. Remember it's *the Lord* who gives you the power to get wealth (Deuteronomy 8:18).

Rejoice in the Victory Right Now!

The fourth thing you need to do to survive until prosperity arrives is to *begin to rejoice now that God is bringing you out!*

Begin to rejoice that the Lord is Jehovah Jireh and El Shaddai, the God who is more than enough and the God who is bringing you out of debt, distress and discontentment! Get all your bills, put them on the floor and then dance over them! Put them out in the center of the floor and say, "Here we go, bills" and begin to rejoice!

I tell you, I've done things similar to that. If my spirit tells me to do something, I do it. I don't care how silly it seems. Some people don't want to do that. They don't want to demonstrate their faith outwardly, because they think it makes them look silly. But I'm telling you what, doing what my spirit told me to do has brought me out! I'm free!

Whatever God told me to do with my bills, I'd do it. If He told me to take all my bills and wave them to the left, I'd wave them to the left! If He told me to wave them to the right, I'd wave those bills to the right!

So whatever kind of instruction God gives you, obey Him. Sometimes He's trying you to see if you really trust Him. You can't go on another person's experience. God will tell you what He wants *you* to do. And if He doesn't tell you to do anything special, you know it's always right to stand on His Word and believe and confess it.

Don't Be Moved by Adverse Circumstances

The fifth thing you need to do to survive until prosperity arrives is to *refuse to panic when the circumstances don't look good.*

At the time a certain situation doesn't look good—and it's usually when you've gotten some revelation on prosperity—that's just the devil trying to pull you off the trail of prosperity by putting road-blocks and obstacles in your way. So don't panic when the situation doesn't look good. The devil is not going to let you march out of poverty for "free." He's going to fight you and try to bluff you. He's going to try to "rough you up" to keep you from going on with the revelation you have.

Pay No Attention to Critics

The sixth thing you need to do to survive until prosperity arrives is to *ignore others who are hecklers.* As you begin to prosper, some people will speak against you and persecute you because you're prospering and they're not. Don't pay them any mind! Just keep going. Just keep looking straight ahead. Wave at them and keep on going. Don't stop long enough to be offended. Just say, "Thank You, Lord. Prosperity is mine."

Learn the Secret of Contentment

Let's look at Philippians chapter 4 for the seventh thing you need to do to survive until prosperity arrives.

But I rejoiced in the Lord greatly, that now at the last your care of me hath flourished again; wherein ye were also careful, but ye lacked opportunity. Not that I speak in respect of want: for I have learned, in whatsoever state I am, therewith to be content. I know both how to be abased, and I know how to abound: every where and in all things I am instructed both to be full and to be hungry, both to abound and to suffer need. I can do all things through Christ which strengtheneth me. Notwithstanding ye have well done, that ye did communicate with my affliction. Now ye Philippians know also, that in the beginning of the gospel, when I departed from Macedonia, no church communicated with me as concerning giving and receiving, but ye only. For even in Thessalonica ye sent once and again unto my necessity. Not because I desire a gift: but I desire fruit that may abound to your account. But I have all, and abound: I am full, having received of Epaphroditus the things which were sent from you, an odour of a sweet smell, a sacrifice acceptable, wellpleasing to God. But my God shall supply all your need according to his riches in glory by Christ Jesus.

Philippians 4:10-19

The seventh thing you need to do to survive until prosperity arrives is to *remain content and refuse to compare yourself with others.*

The apostle Paul was writing this passage to the Philippian Church, but I believe the Holy Spirit had Paul write this down for us today so we could understand how to flow in prosperity and receive from God.

Notice what Paul says in verse 11: **Not that I speak in respect of want: for I have learned, in whatsoever state I am, therewith to be content.** Wherever you are now financially, have contentment along with your commitment to trust God. Don't envy someone else because he has more than you.

Remember that you are unique! Take your eyes off the other fellow and what he has and what he does. Concentrate on what God wants *you* to do.

My wife and I have walked this revelation of prosperity out progressively, and we continue to walk it out. We started at the bottom, and God has exalted us and our ministry.

Years ago when I quit my job to be in the ministry full time, I didn't tell anybody about it. I have two brothers and a sister-in-law who are members of my church. I never even told them I was leaving my job until I had already quit. But I also never went to their houses to ask for rice, butter, bread or a dollar or two. I stayed contented and committed to God. I was determined to trust God and let Him show Himself strong on my behalf. And He did!

I know if I would have asked my family for something, they would have given it to me because they love me dearly. But I knew I had to walk this out myself. Now I'm able to tell you about it and be a blessing to you!

I know for sure this Word works. And I know that this message of prosperity is true. But you have to get on God's system and stay committed in order to walk in the fullness of the blessing. Not everyone is willing to do that.

Anyone can go through something if he's floating on flower beds of ease all the time. But unless a person takes a strong stand on the Word, even when the circumstances look rough, he won't ever really know that the Word works! He'll just be guessing about it.

But I'm not guessing about it. I've been through it, and God has brought me out!

It seems as if God suspended my mind when I didn't have anything and I was just trusting Him. I got the revelation of this, and I wasn't troubled. I acted like I was rich all the time even when I was broke. I never changed strides. I just believed the Word of God, and I believed I was coming out!

I mean, if someone would say, "Let's have a picnic," my wife and I would say, "Well, how much money do we need to put in?" If it was twenty-five dollars, we pitched in and didn't complain. It may have been our last twenty-five dollars, but we put it like this: "Let the picnic go on!" We were going to laugh and eat, and people might have thought we had a million dollars in our pocket. But we were as broke as two frogs on a log on a rug, catching a ride!

People talk about living by faith, but most people don't know anything about living by faith. For example, if you've got all your confidence in that job you've got, you're not living by faith. Sure, you should work hard at your job, but your confidence should be in God.

Practice Patience and Perseverance

The eighth thing you need to do to survive until prosperity arrives is to *practice patience and perseverance in your faith.* I'm talking about how to survive until prosperity arrives. When you're on the "runway" from poverty to prosperity, your situation doesn't change overnight.

In the natural, it takes a little while for a big 747 airplane to get off the runway and become airborne. Sometimes those planes taxi so slowly, it seems as if you could go get your car and drive to your destination faster!

But, you see, on the runway, you have to be patient. The pilot of that plane is in the front, and he's constantly pulling this lever and that lever and operating those controls to get the plane to lift up and get off the ground. You have to be patient and let him fly the plane.

In much the same way, you have to know how to handle the runway from poverty to prosperity. You have to learn to be patient and consistent in faith. And here's one way to do that: **Not that I speak in respect of want: for I have learned, in whatsoever state I am, therewith to BE CONTENT** (Philippians 4:11).

If you've got the revelation of abundance and prosperity, but you're not there yet, just be joyous where you are, knowing that your situation is temporary. And it *is* only a temporary situation, so learn to be content.

As I said, my wife and I never complained when I quit my job to be in the ministry full time. I never griped because we didn't have enough. I never reconsidered the decision I made.

When I would pass the place where I had worked, I shifted into the passing gear in my car because I knew the Lord had sent me away from that place. And I never looked back. I never thought about it or said, "Boy, if I had my job, we could have this or that." The Lord told me to leave, so I left. I was gone forever from that job.

The Privilege and the Price

I'm trying to show you that there is a process to walking in divine prosperity. You already have the *privilege* of walking in prosperity by being a son or daughter of God. But most people will not pay the *price* to be prosperous.

Yes, there's a price you have to pay. Someone will say, "What do you mean, there's a price I have to pay! I have to pay for prosperity?" Yes, there's a price in your life. There's a price of commitment that you have to pay. God has to know that He can trust you with His goods. You're not going to be able to *tip* Him and *pay* the world and still expect to be prosperous.

I want you to understand that there's a position you have to get yourself into in order to be prosperous. And then you have to know that prosperity is progressive.

Let me show you what I'm talking about by using a natural illustration.

My son Leroy Jr. is twenty-one years old. My son Clayton is eight. A couple of years ago, I bought Leroy Jr. a shotgun. I could trust him with it. I could give him that shotgun, loaded, with the safety turned off and tell him, "The safety is not on." Leroy Jr. would take that gun and either punch the safety in place or not touch the trigger.

But I couldn't give that gun to my younger son, Clayton. He's only eight. Clayton would pull everything he sees on that gun because he doesn't recognize yet how to handle it!

Well, in the same way, unless you get yourself in a position where the Father God knows you're going to handle prosperity correctly, He's not going to permit you to have it.

Now, notice Philippians 4:12: **I know both how to be abased, and I know how to abound: every where and in all things I am instructed both to be full and to be hungry, both to abound and to suffer need.**

Paul said, "I'm not going to complain about it."

"Why, Paul?" we could ask.

"Well, I can do all things through Christ who strengthens me," Paul said in verse 13.

That boy was talking about finances! Then he went on to say, **Notwithstanding ye have well done, that ye did communicate with my affliction** (Philippians 4:14).

Giving and Receiving

In verse 15, Paul said, **Now ye Philippians know also, that in the beginning of the gospel, when I departed from Macedonia, no church communicated with me as concerning GIVING AND RECEIVING, but ye only.**

Notice this verse very closely: **No church communicated with me as concerning giving and receiving, but ye only.**

Why did Paul say "giving *and* receiving"? Because there is no receiving without giving. There is no receiving in the believer's life without his giving first.

If you want to prosper, you're going to have to learn how to give, especially to God's program. When I say "giving," I'm talking about beyond the tithe. Offerings are beyond the tithe. If you're not tithing, then you have to work on the tithe first. You're not even in position for God to bless you if you're not tithing. There will never be any prosperity for you from God without your being a tither. Yes, a person could have some money and not be a tither, but I can show you plenty of people with money who are not really prospering.

People with money who don't tithe and honor God with their money are not prosperous, because they don't have themselves fully covered or protected by God. They're still out in the open. They have money, but they're not fully covered by God; they don't have full spiritual insurance.

So everyone who has money is not necessarily prosperous. Real prosperity is being covered by God. It's having money, but it's also being in the position that's out of Satan's reach.

God will watch that money for you if you're in His program. But if God is not watching your money, the world could take it from you in one day.

Let's go a little further with Philippians 4:15: **Now ye Philippians know also, that in the beginning of the gospel, when I departed from Macedonia, no church communicated with me as concerning GIVING AND RECEIVING, but ye only.**

Underline that phrase "giving and receiving." I have already discussed this briefly, but you need to understand that God's system operates opposite the world's system. God said, "To receive, you have to give." Well, to the world, that doesn't seem logical. The world thinks, "Look, if I'm trying to receive, it doesn't look like I should *give* anything. If I *give*, I've got *less.*"

To the world, giving doesn't look like the smart way to receive something. The world says, "If I want to receive something, something ought to be coming *in*, not going *out.*" But in God's system, you give and God will multiply it back to you. God will *never* let you outgive Him. There's no way He will ever let you outgive Him.

It's not only important to give, but it's important to give *consistently.* Look at Philippians 4:16, **For even in Thessalonica ye sent ONCE AND AGAIN unto my necessity.** You see, the Philippian church didn't just give one time. It says they gave "once and again" to Paul's necessity. They didn't just send Paul a one-time offering and that was it.

We must be consistent givers in order to be blessed by God.

You know, the world just says, "Gimme." Have you ever heard the phrase, "My name is Jimmy. I'll take all you'll gimme"? Do you know some "Jimmy's"? But the believers should say, "Lord, make me a blessing. Thank You for seed to sow and for showing me where to sow it."

The next verse in Philippians 4 says, **Not because I desire a gift: but I desire fruit that may abound to your account** (v. 17).

Years ago, God gave me a revelation about this verse. If people really understood this verse, it would change their lives!

Paul said, "Not that I desire a gift." A lot of people just think preachers preach on prosperity for this reason. But most preachers are not preaching prosperity for this reason. They preach it because they want fruit to abound to people's account.

God is saying that as you make a deposit into what the Lord has called you to do, He is putting it on your account. In fact, He is *multiplying* it to your account!

And you can withdraw from that account. You can go to God and say, "Look, I'm a supporter. I give consistently to this work, and I need You to do something about my situation. I need such and such amount."

But you can't make any withdrawal if you haven't made a deposit. Just try doing that at one of your local banks! Go to the bank and say, "Hi. I need $18,000." The teller at that bank would ask you your name, punch a few keys on the computer and say, "Your name is not in the computer. You don't have an account here."

Then you might say, "Look, I know this bank has money. I just saw somebody else leave here, counting some money. I want some money too! You're supposed to have money, and I need money!"

That teller might say, "Well, let me check one more time." But do you know what she's doing? She's pushing a little button to call security. She's going to say, "Get this fool out of here!"

Well, security is being called on a lot of Christians! They'll say, "Lord, I love You. I'm demanding my rights in Christ. I'm demanding such and such amount of money." But the whole time they're saying that, a demon is pushing that little button, saying, "They don't have an account!"

There's no such thing in the natural *or* the spiritual realm as a withdrawal without a deposit. But if you're a tither and a giver, you can go to God in faith and say, "This is how much I need. Thank You. Praise God. Amen." And it's a "done deal." But you can't argue your case if you haven't done what you're supposed to do. You can't make a *withdrawal* if you didn't make a *deposit*.

If I weren't attending a church, or a storehouse, that I respected, where I could be fed spiritually and tithe and give offerings, I'd be running, trying to find a place to go so I could do what the Lord wanted me to do concerning giving and receiving. And, as Paul said, I would do it, not because the preacher desires a gift, but because this Gospel needs to be preached, the work of the ministry needs to go on and I want fruit to abound to my account!

So the gifts you give to your church are not just for the church's benefit. They are for your benefit, that fruit may abound to your account.

Now I want to talk about your favorite verse, Philippians 4:19: **But my God shall supply all your need according to his riches in glory by Christ Jesus!**

Some people are wondering why that verse hasn't been working in their lives. Well, it can't work without the rest of those verses we just talked about. The Bible doesn't play "skip." In other words, you can't skip over those other verses and just get excited about verse 19.

Look at what Paul is saying. In verse 18 he said, **I have all, and abound....** Do you know what he is saying? He is saying, "I'm not depending on you, but on God; I'm content." Then look at the rest of that verse: **I have all, and abound: I am full, having received of Epaphroditus the things which were sent from you,** AN ODOUR OF A SWEET SMELL, **a sacrifice acceptable, wellpleasing to God.**

Look at what Paul called that offering: "an odour of a sweet smell." In other words, money can smell sweet to the Lord. The Bible called that money—the offering given—**an odour of a sweet smell, a sacrifice acceptable, wellpleasing to God.**

The Lord talks about money a lot in Philippians 4. Paul said, in effect, "Concerning giving and receiving, I want to put something in your account" (vv. 15,17). *Then* he said, **But my God shall supply all your need according to his riches in glory by Christ Jesus.**

Now, if you understand giving and receiving and if you've deposited something into your account, then, as Paul said, "My God shall supply all your needs according to His riches in glory by Christ Jesus."

When you give God a sweet-smelling offering, a sacrificial offering, God can then channel money to you. He can supply all your needs according to His riches in glory by Christ Jesus. But Philippians 4:19 is not for everybody. That verse is not even for every Christian. No, that verse is for every Christian *who is in the will of God, doing what*

God wants him to do—supporting the Gospel, tithing, giving offerings, listening to the Spirit of God and giving where God tells him to give.

When you're positioning yourself to receive from God, you need to maintain your giving attitude and stay steady, doing what you know to do. Then there are practical steps to take too. For example, if you're deep in debt, you need to stop buying things you don't need on credit. You need to focus on paying your bills off in full, one by one.

I tell you, if you let Him, God will deal with debts, distress, discontentment *and* your creditors by giving you supernatural financing!

Creditors are hard on those who cannot pay their bills. But there's a spiritual answer to debt. Through your giving and faithfulness to God, He will cause money to come to you to pay your debts. But remember, when God blesses you, you must use what you have wisely.

Give Away Much and Get More

We need to get a wider vision of what money is for. The reason money comes to the believer is so he can give seed to the sower, not so he can eat up all his seed. In other words, as you give away much, you'll get more. God will take care of you. He can command a blackbird to drop one hundred dollar bills at your doorstep if He wants to!

Do you remember the widow we discussed who only had a little handful of meal? God used a widow to bless Elijah, and He blessed the woman abundantly because she sowed what little seed she had. She gave, and God gave back to her. Why did He use a widow instead of a rich man? Because He could get that woman's attention.

Can God get your attention? If He can, then you are in the proper position to receive the good life He has provided for you to have. You can rejoice right now that money cometh to *you!* You've claimed it, and it's on its way.

Pray this prayer out loud:

Money cometh unto me because my Father said it. Therefore, there will be no lack for preaching the Gospel, nor in my personal affairs. I am not covetous of the Lord's blessing, but I am a covenant partner with the plan, purpose and will of God. God is my Source. God is my Supplier. Therefore, I always have more than enough.

Money is not my master. Jesus is my Master. I master and manage my money according to the will of God. Money cometh! Money cometh! Money cometh! I'll never be broke another day in my life! I'm coming out of debt! I'm going to live financially free and have my needs and desires met, and I'm going to help send the Gospel throughout the world.

My Father wants me to be wealthy. I agree with my Father! From this day forward, I set my heart to be financially stable in all my ways. I'll listen to the Word of God. I'll give, and I know I'll receive. I'll plant, and I'll expect a harvest. I'll sow, and I know I'll reap. Hallelujah! Prosperity is mine. Money cometh!

8

I heard an older minister say that in order to find out what something is, we need to find out what it is *not*. This book is about
money and prosperity, but we have to understand poverty, too, so we
can get completely out of that condition and head on over into prosperity—*God's kind* of prosperity!

We'll begin this chapter by looking at some different types of poverty.

Poverty Because of Ignorance

Not all poverty is the same. There are different kinds of poverty.
One kind of poverty is *poverty because of ignorance*. In other words,
people in this kind of poverty just don't know that they're not
supposed to be poor! They haven't heard the Word, **Beloved, I wish
above all things that thou mayest prosper and be in health, even as
thy soul prospereth** (3 John 2). They haven't heard that God becomes
the supplier of all their needs when they cooperate with Him through
giving and receiving.

Then, there are some people who are candidates for prosperity, all
right. They tithe and give, but they're still in poverty because of ignorance—because of religious and traditional thinking that's taught
them that the more they have, the more ungodly they are.

Poverty Because of Ignored Truth

Another kind of poverty is *poverty because of ignored truth*. Jesus
said, **Ye shall know the truth, and the truth shall make you free**
(John 8:32). Some people hear the truth, but they ignore it. They go
on and do things the same way they've been doing them. They may
even take notes on the truth they hear. They might get happy in a
particular meeting and say, "I'm giving everything to the Lord!" But
then, after about two days, they'll say, "Oh, Lord, I need that money; I
can't give that."

But when you see the truth, you've got to stick with it like glue and refuse to change your course. Stick with the truth, because the truth is what will bring you through!

Poverty Because of a Good Income

Another kind of poverty is *poverty because of a good income.* People who have this kind of poverty think they don't need God. They have a well paying job. They have their two cars and a little boat on the side. But they have to work twice as hard to maintain that lifestyle because if they ever slacked up, they'd have to let the boat go. And they don't want the people next door to know they had to let their boat go! So they go out and work and work and work just to keep what they have.

Many people have well paying jobs, but they're still broke. God has provided them with good jobs so they could be good tithers and good givers and so they could be blessed. But they spend everything on themselves, so they're broke. They don't give anything to God, or they don't give to Him as they should give, so they don't have anything coming in but their little paychecks.

I've been there. I was making good money at the job I had before the Lord told me to quit to go full time into the ministry. But I'd get that money on Thursday, and by Saturday after all the bills were paid, we didn't have anything left. I'd just have to take some money out of my check to go get an ice cream or a bite of something to eat. I said, "I worked hard for this! No creditor's getting this little bit. *I'm* taking it." Really, I was stealing, because we had so many bills, that money really belonged to the creditors; it didn't belong to me. That money I was taking needed to go toward some bill.

Yes, we had a good income, but we were still broke because we were robbing God and not giving Him the pleasure of doing what He wanted to do for us. But, thank God, all of that has changed.

Poverty Because of Receiving Worldly Interest

Another kind of poverty is *poverty because of receiving worldly inter-est.* Now you know it's not wrong to put money in the bank. But it *is* wrong to put *God's* money, the tithe, in the bank! That's the kind of poverty I'm talking about here—poverty because of receiving worldly interest with God's money! People are putting God's money in the bank, and they're receiving a little interest for rainy days with that money. They're going to need it, too, because if they're not honoring God with their money, the devil will see to it that they have plenty of rainy days.

Poverty Because of Prosperity!

Now turn to Mark 10, and I'll show you another kind of poverty— *poverty because of prosperity!*

> And when he [Jesus] was gone forth into the way, there came one running, and kneeled to him, and asked him, Good Master, what shall I do that I may inherit eternal life? And Jesus said unto him, Why callest thou me good? there is none good but one, that is, God. Thou knowest the commandments, Do not commit adultery, Do not kill, Do not steal, Do not bear false witness, Defraud not, Honour thy father and mother. And he answered and said unto him, Master, all these have I observed from my youth. Then Jesus beholding him loved him, and said unto him, One thing thou lackest: go thy way, SELL WHATSOEVER THOU HAST, and give to the poor, and thou shalt have treasure in heaven: and come, take up the cross, and follow me. And he was sad at that saying, and went away grieved: FOR HE HAD GREAT POSSESSIONS.
>
> Mark 10:17-22

Verse 17 says, **And when he was gone forth into the way, there came one running, and kneeled to him, and asked him, Good Master, what shall I do that I may inherit eternal life?**

Notice it said, **There came one *running*.** You see, running doesn't mean anything to the Lord. People in the Church sometimes will get happy and run. But some of them are so tight when it comes to giving, they're probably running on credit!

Then in verse 17 it also says, [He] KNEELED to him [Jesus].... Did you know that kneeling doesn't move the Lord either? People can kneel before God and still be disobedient and tight with their money. Then it says, [He] **asked him, Good Master, what shall I do that I may inherit eternal life?**

He called Jesus "Good Master." You know, we've got all kinds of names we call the Lord. But not everyone who calls Jesus "Lord" or "Good Master" is letting Him be the Master of his or her money!

Jesus said to this rich young man, **Why callest thou me good? there is none good but one, that is, God** (Mark 10:18).

Now notice this fellow's life. It seems like he "had it all together." He knew how to run to Jesus, and he knew how to kneel. He even called Him "Good Master." He had respect for the Lord. And look at what kind of good lifestyle this fellow portrayed!

Jesus said to him, **Thou knowest the commandments, Do not commit adultery, Do not kill, Do not steal, Do not bear false witness, Defraud not, Honour thy father and mother** (Mark 10:19).

Notice how the man answered: **Master, all these have I observed from my youth** (v. 20)! This boy wasn't an adulterer. He didn't steal. He honored his father and his mother. He kept the commandments.

Then Jesus said, "Yes, but there's one thing you lack. Go, sell your possessions, and give to the poor" (v. 21).

Verse 22 says, **And he was sad at that saying, and went away grieved: for he had great possessions.**

This man had great possessions. You see, some people have money, yet they're living in poverty. Why? Because if you have money, and you're deciding what you're going to do with that money without consulting God, you're in poverty. Your "bottom" could fall out at any minute.

But, for a man or woman who's lined up with God's Word, there's no way for the bottom to fall out, because if that bottom goes out, God will put another bottom in before you even know that the first bottom went out!

It is dangerous to be blessed and not know it or fail to acknowledge God and show Him you appreciate His blessing you.

If you really want to honor God, when He is blessing you with finances, He should be able to tell you what to do with those finances.

Honor God With Your Tithing and Giving

God has already told us in His Word what to do with the tithe: **Bring ye all the tithes into the storehouse, that there may be meat in mine house, and prove me now herewith, saith the Lord of hosts, if I will not open you the windows of heaven, and pour you out a blessing, that there shall not be room enough to receive it** (Malachi 3:10).

You know, you can't split your tithe and send it wherever you want. For example, someone might say, "I like this TV minister. I'm going to send him 2 percent. Then I'll send 2 percent here, 2 percent there...."

But, no, the Bible says, **Bring ye ALL THE TITHES** [the tenth] **INTO THE STOREHOUSE, that there may be meat in mine house, and prove me now herewith, saith the Lord of hosts, if I will not open you the windows of heaven, and pour you out a blessing, that there shall not be room enough to receive it.**

"Tithe" means a *tenth.* You have to put 10 percent where the food and the blessing are coming out of the "spout"! In other words, your tithe doesn't go to some charity somewhere. All your giving to charity should be beyond your 10 percent. Your tithe should go to your local church where you are spiritually fed.

A pastor once told me that 17 percent of his congregation brought in 85 percent of the income of his church. My goodness! That's just a small percentage of the people who were carrying nearly the whole load!

God is going to support His churches and ministries whether the people who are getting blessed by those ministries act right and get hooked up or not. But those people who are not tithing and giving and obeying the Bible are not going to reap the blessings of the Bible. Others whom God sends will reap the benefit of supporting God's work and furthering His Gospel.

But why should the local people let someone else get their benefit?

I'm talking about letting God put you in a secure place in your finances. He does it through your obedience to Him.

Giving is a very important subject with God. Notice in Mark 10:20 after Jesus told the rich young ruler the commands to keep in order to have eternal life, the man said, **Master, all these have I observed from my youth.**

Then it says, **Jesus beholding him loved him, and said unto him, One thing thou lackest: go thy way, sell whatsoever thou hast, and give to the poor, and thou shalt have treasure in heaven: and come, take up the cross, and follow me** (v. 21).

In other words, Jesus was saying, in effect, "Yes, you've kept the commands, but this other thing—money—is just as important."

You see, giving properly is just as important as not committing adultery or some other sin. Mark 10:20 shows us the level of importance Jesus placed on giving. The rich young man said, "I did not commit adultery. I did not steal. I did not bear false witness. I did not defraud. I honored my father and mother." And Jesus said, "Yes, but what I'm about to tell you is just as important: Go, sell your possessions and give to the poor."

Jesus was saying, "I've got to untie you from your money. You told Me about your religion and how much you love Me. But here's the test: Sell what you have and give to the poor, and you shall have treasure in heaven" (Mark 10:21).

That rich young ruler said he didn't steal or lie, but, really, he *did* steal—and he lied when he said he didn't! How do I know that? Because the man was defrauding God and robbing Him of the right to do what He wanted to do with his money.

Are You Rich, Sad and Grieved or Full of Joy Unspeakable?

Now notice what happened after Jesus said all that. The next verse says, **And he** [the rich young ruler] **was sad at that saying, and went away grieved: for he had great possessions** (v. 22). He was rich, sad and grieved.

That's not true prosperity. We read about true prosperity in Psalm 35: **Let them shout for JOY, and BE GLAD, that favour my righteous cause: yea, let them say continually, Let the Lord be magnified, which hath pleasure in the prosperity of his servant** (v. 27). Joy and gladness will follow true prosperity!

I've read about several people who had millions, and even billions, of dollars. Some of them died in miserable conditions. Some died like paupers. Some died alone. Why? They were so worried about and consumed with their money that they locked themselves up and hid themselves away. Satan destroyed their minds and bodies.

You can read about many movie stars who are making big money. They don't have normal lives. Some of them can't even go down to the local ice cream store for a scoop of ice cream! They're scared somebody's going to see them. So they're locked up in luxury palaces, but their prosperity is not really doing them much good. Their prosperity is controlling them.

I tell you, there's nothing like a good walk in the yard! There's nothing like being free! You see, money is not all it takes to be prosperous. You can be consumed with money, and money can lock you up.

That's why God can't give money to some Christians. That money would lock them up. It would make them proud and boastful. Then they would send their tithes wherever they wanted to send them, regardless of what the Lord wanted. Or they might not send them at all.

Let's look again at that passage in Mark, chapter 10. Verse 22 says, **And he** [the rich young ruler] **was sad at that saying, and went away grieved: for he had great possessions.** Actually, that young man didn't have great possessions; great possessions had *him!* You see, money is made for you to use. Money is not made to use you.

On a certain occasion Jesus said to the disciples, **How hardly shall they that have riches enter into the kingdom of God!** (Mark 10:23).

Now some people look at that and say, "See, that's why I don't want to be rich. Jesus said it was hard for a rich man to go to heaven."

Have you ever heard anybody say that? Those same people will say, "There aren't many rich folks going to make it to heaven."

But they might be surprised to know that there will be a whole lot of poor folks in hell too. And the poor folks will have "caught hell" twice! They will have caught "hell" on the earth, living without God and His blessings, and then, if they don't accept Jesus as their Savior, they will literally go to a real hell. They will have never known the good life at all.

But the Master says in the Book that He desires for us to have days of heaven on the earth (Deuteronomy 11:21)! He wants us to be blessed on the earth. Then He wants us to go to heaven when we leave earth and never catch "hell" at all.

God wants you to be rich! No matter who you are or who your family is or where you were born, God has made provision for you to be rich in life.

There is a certain doctor in my congregation. Folks look at him and think, *Well, he's a doctor; he's* supposed *to prosper.* And there are business owners in my church, and people think, *Well, they're* supposed *to prosper!*

But just because you're not a doctor or lawyer or business owner doesn't mean you can't prosper. The Lord didn't say, "All doctors who give, it shall be given unto them." No, He said, **Give, and it shall be given unto YOU; good measure, pressed down, and shaken together, and running over, shall men give into YOUR bosom. For with the same measure that YE mete withal it shall be measured to YOU again** (Luke 6:38).

Let's read some more of Mark, chapter 10, to see how Jesus views earthly riches:

> **And Jesus looked round about, and saith unto his disciples, How hardly shall they that have riches enter into the kingdom of God! And the disciples were astonished at his words. But Jesus answereth again, and saith unto them, Children, how hard is it for THEM THAT TRUST IN RICHES to enter into the kingdom of God!**
>
> **Mark 10:23,24**

And the disciples were astonished at his words (v. 24). Why do you think they were so astonished at Jesus' words? Because they were rich! People read Mark 10:23 and talk about how broke the disciples were. But those disciples were businessmen! They were not broke! That's why they were astonished at Jesus' words.

Then in verse 24, Jesus added some clarification: **Jesus answereth again, and saith unto them, Children, how hard is it for them that TRUST IN RICHES to enter into the kingdom of God!**

Don't Trust in Money, but in the Living God

As I said, Jesus wasn't talking about the disciples when He talked about how hard it was for a rich man to enter the Kingdom of heaven. When the disciples became astonished at His words, I could imagine Jesus saying something like, "Well, let Me explain, boys. I'm not talking about you. I'm saying, 'Children, how hard is it for them *that trust in riches* to enter into the Kingdom of God!'"

Then He went on to say, **It is easier for a camel to go through the eye of a needle, than for a rich man to enter into the kingdom of God** (Mark 10:25).

Boy, some preachers can really mess up that verse! They read that verse and go to talking about a needle and a piece of thread! They don't understand what Jesus is saying.

I saw the "eye of the needle" when I was in Jerusalem once. It is an opening into a fortress or city that a camel had to bow down on his knees to get through. A man couldn't even be on the camel's back. When the camel bowed down to get through that eye, there was just enough room for the camel. The reason that opening was so small was so an enemy couldn't get into the city.

The reason I know some preachers really mess up that verse is because I used to mess it up myself! I thought Jesus was talking about the eye of a small needle that you sew with.

Preachers who don't understand that verse will tell you that you can't go to heaven with riches. But if they really believe that, why do they keep taking up offerings in their churches! Why don't they just let the churches go broke! It just doesn't add up!

Remember, it said the disciples were astonished at Jesus' words (v. 24). Verse 26 says, **And they were astonished out of measure, saying among themselves, Who then can be saved?**

Well, why would they say, "Who then can be saved" if they themselves were not rich? They had to have had some money, or they would have said something such as, "Well, all of us poor boys will go to heaven then."

The disciples had money. And, in essence, they said, "What one of us can be saved then?" The Lord had to help them. He said, **With men, it is impossible, but not with God: for with God, all things are possible** (v. 27).

Then Peter said, **Lo, we have left all, and have followed thee** (v. 28). Peter had money, but he wasn't trusting in his money—he was trusting in God. Peter was serving the Lord.

Blessings—With Persecutions

Now here's an important point I want to make. Jesus answered Peter and said, **There is no man that hath left house, or brethren, or sisters, or father, or mother, or wife, or children, or lands, for my sake, and the gospel's, but he shall receive an hundredfold now in this time, houses, and brethren, and sisters, and mothers, and children, and lands, with persecutions; and in the world to come eternal life** (vv. 29,30).

First, let me say this about those verses: Jesus won't cause you to leave your husband or wife and commit adultery. He wouldn't divide a marriage. He's talking about surrendering your life to Him **for my sake, and the gospel's.** Then He said, **But he shall receive an hundredfold now IN THIS TIME, houses, and brethren, and sisters, and mothers, and children, and lands, with persecutions; and in the world to come eternal life.**

I like the Lord. The phrase "in this time" is talking about receiving all those blessings in *this* time—on the earth. Then the Lord goes on to say *and* **in the world to come eternal life!**

Notice that the Lord said we could receive a hundredfold in this time: houses, brethren, sisters, mothers, children and lands. But then He said something else was coming along with it: *persecutions.*

I know what I'm talking about when it comes to receiving persecution for walking in the blessings of God. For example, God specifically told me to build the house I live in now. And it wasn't a "regular" house that He told me to build. So I built the house. If I *hadn't* built the house, I would have been in sin, because He had told me what to do. And I would have been in disobedience if I had been afraid to do what He told me to do.

But some persecution came with my building that house. And persecution will come with your receiving God's blessings too. If you can't take persecution, then stay in your shack and eat green onions and wild rice, because if you rise up in life, persecution is going to come.

You see, in my case, I have realized that there's always going to be somebody who doesn't want the preacher to have much of anything or to do well in life. People like that will say about a preacher, "I bet he's stealing the people's money."

But why don't people like that ever point to the bank president and say, "I bet *he's* stealing"? Or why don't they point to the president of a big corporation and say, "I bet *he's* stealing"?

They put that mark on the preachers. But I don't receive those kinds of accusations. I'm not going to be in the same category with those other preachers who aren't doing right. I am of the crowd that has integrity, intelligence and a spirit of excellence in all things! We serve a holy God.

I'm telling you about persecutions so you'll know about them ahead of time. When you start rising up in life and getting blessed, the persecutions are going to follow.

So since you know about it ahead of time, don't let it bother you that persecutions are coming. Just go on and enjoy your prosperity, because the persecution is *supposed* to come with it—the Bible says so. The persecution is going to come from unbelieving church members, and it's going to come from the world.

You see, the world is going to get mad because you're not out there with them drinking and smoking, clowning around and committing adultery. They're mad because you're at home, happy and free, and you're living better than they are. They're mad, so they have to persecute you.

But that doesn't mean you have to be afraid of prosperity. God is on your side, and He is greater than the persecution the world gives. So if you are born again and you have the right ambitions and desires, go ahead and speak your rights in Christ, claiming your blessings and walking in divine prosperity. Don't pay any attention to the persecutions.

Poverty Because of Unbalanced Teaching About Prosperity

We've talked about several kinds of poverty in this chapter. The last one we talked about was *poverty because of prosperity.* Another kind of poverty believers experience is *poverty because of unbalanced teaching about financial prosperity.*

Prosperity is not always a popular teaching. Years ago when men and women of God got hold of the revelation of divine healing, healing was not always a popular subject to teach on. You could talk about healing, and the traditional people would just sort of blink their eyes like a frog in a fog, sitting on a log! Many of them would just sit there and look at the preacher and say, "Leave me alone. Don't bother my sickness. I'm going to keep my sickness. I know I've got to be sick with *something* in life. So don't talk to me about healing."

It's the same way with prosperity teaching. People say, "Preach the Bible to me," but when you start talking to them about prosperity, it seems like you run up against a hard wall! But we preachers who know the truth have to try to get people into their "promised land." Christians are already out of "Egypt," so to speak, but now they need to enter into *all* the blessings God has for them.

As I said before, some believers think "broke is better!" They think you're unholy, unrighteous and ungodly if you have money.

That's unbalanced believing. Then, others think that money is just to finance their selfish lifestyles. Those people don't care what happens to the church or to the work of God. That's unbalanced believing too.

We have to be balanced in this teaching. If we're not, we'll have people go off and say we're teaching something that we're not. They'll say, "Those people are just after money." And the devil will make a lot of noise about that because he doesn't want us to have money. So he'll come up with some false ideas and accusations and say that money is all we're aiming for.

Two Kinds of Prosperity

We talked about poverty and about the fact that it's God's will that you walk in prosperity. But there are actually two kinds of prosperity: a *worldly* kind and a *godly* kind. There is a worldly kind of prosperity, which creates covetousness in a person. A covetous person will scheme to get money any way he can get it.

But there's also God's kind of prosperity. God has given His children the power to get wealth (Deuteronomy 8:18). Being wealthy means being well provided for. God gave us power to be well provided for!

There's a balance in this prosperity message. And if you're going to be balanced, you have to understand the covenant, covetousness and the curse.

A fear of becoming covetous is the thing that has held many Christians in bondage. They've believed that when Christians come to a certain level of financial blessing, they are out of the will of God. But they have that backwards. Religion and men have taught us that being wealthy is wrong. But God said in His covenant that He gives us the power to get wealth (Deuteronomy 8:18)!

Preachers will preach poverty and tell people, "Don't believe God for too much. You don't need much, because money will cause you to sin."

Well, I know of a lot of broke folks who don't have any money, and they're sinning plenty! They're sinning and sneaking around, doing things that are wrong. Well, if people who have money sin *because* they have money, then why do some who *don't* have money sin?

A person doesn't have to have money to sin. *He could sin on credit!*

Let's read a verse that has been used to try to prove that we are supposed to live in poverty.

> **No man can serve two masters: for either he will hate the one, and love the other; or else he will hold to the one, and despise the other. Ye cannot serve God and mammon.**
>
> Matthew 6:24

God and money are what this scripture is talking about. Some people believe that if you have money, you are serving money instead of God. But that's not necessarily true.

Money Has No Power in Itself

Money in itself has no power. I mean that money is neither evil nor good. Money is what a person *makes* it.

You see, I drive a nice car, but when I drive down the street, I'm not uppity. I wave to almost everybody I see. That car doesn't make me; I make the car. In other words, that car is not who I am. I know who I am. And I'm going to stay down-to-earth. I'm not going to be high-minded.

A person can have plenty of money and still live right. He can pay his tithes, help get the Gospel out and help the needy.

Don't Be Afraid of Money

We talked about First Timothy 6:10, **For the love of money is the root of all evil...,** in a previous chapter. We saw that it is really people with corrupt minds who love money. People who do not have the truth of God's Word in their hearts love money.

But those people who love God and His Word do not have corrupt minds, and they don't love money. In fact, many of them are afraid of money. They are afraid of having it.

The Spirit of God has revealed to me some things from First Timothy 6 that will help believers stop being afraid of money. It will keep them from being afraid to walk in God's kind of prosperity.

> **If any man teach otherwise, and consent not to whole-some words, even the words of our Lord Jesus Christ, and to the doctrine which is according to godliness; He is proud, knowing nothing, but doting about questions and strifes of words, whereof cometh envy, strife, railings, evil surmisings, Perverse disputings of men of corrupt minds, and destitute of the truth, supposing that gain is godliness: from such withdraw thyself. But godliness with content-ment is great gain. For we brought nothing into this world, and it is certain we can carry nothing out. And having food and raiment let us be therewith content. But they that will be rich fall into temptation and a snare, and into many foolish and hurtful lusts, which drown men in destruction and perdition. For the love of money is the root of all evil: which while some coveted after, they have erred from the faith, and pierced themselves through with many sorrows.**
>
> **1 Timothy 6:3-10**

First Timothy 6:3 says, **If any man teach otherwise, and consent not to wholesome words, even the words of our Lord Jesus Christ....**

"If any man consents not to wholesome words." What kind of words? Wholesome and right words. This verse is talking about someone who will not consent to wholesome words, even the words of our Lord Jesus Christ.

Well, is that verse talking about *you?* My goodness—no! That verse isn't talking about you if you are one of God's children and you're keeping your heart right. No, we are *with* the Lord; we are not against Him. That verse is not talking about us.

The last part of verse 3 says, **And to the doctrine which is according to godliness.** Well, we believe in the doctrine of godliness. We believe in living right as Christians.

This passage in First Timothy 6 is talking about people with corrupt minds—people who are against the doctrine of Christ—not people who have the mind of Christ!

People with corrupt minds can't handle riches, because they won't do the right thing with money. But when I talk about godly prosperity, I'm not talking about those "devils" who do that! I'm talking about men and women with integrity. (That's where some preachers have messed up. They didn't have integrity. They were out doing what the sinners were doing.)

As I said, First Timothy 6:5 is describing someone who would become covetous with money. The next part of that verse says, **Supposing that gain is godliness....**

Well, we know better than that!

I know that money can't make me walk with God properly. I know I have to be led by the Spirit of God. I know money can't take the place of my prayer time, my worship, my praise, my fellowship and my intimacy with God. I know I can't come to the altar with $300 and put it on the altar and then tell God what to do.

I know better than that. Don't you?

Then Paul goes on to explain something: **But godliness with contentment is great gain** (v. 6).

Godliness and Contentment
Are Irrespective of Money

A person could be as godly and contented *without* money as he could be *with* it. But he could be *more* contented with some money in his pocket! I have been contented without money. I served God with all my heart without a bit of it. But then I found out in His Word that I didn't have to be without it!

I stayed contented, and I stayed godly, but I added something to that—financial prosperity. And I tell you, life is much better *with* prosperity than *without* it!

I figured since I'm going to be in this world, I might as well have a good life. So I added some money to my godliness and my contentment, and I tell you, the three go well together!

But, you see, someone will take First Timothy 6:6 and think the Spirit of God is saying, "Now you should only be godly and content. You have to be godly and content and *broke.*"

But that's like saying God wants you to be content under the curse and just waste Jesus' blood and the redemption He bought for us! That's like saying God wants you to stay at the bottom.

But that's not what He is saying at all. He is saying, in effect, "If you have a corrupt mind and are destitute of the truth, you need to learn the lesson of godliness and contentment."

I'm not going to let anything separate me from the love of God. There's not enough money or gold in the world to keep me from God, because I know money and gold are a temporary thing. But the things of God are eternal. And when you have the Spirit of God and the Word of God inside of you, you can properly handle every dollar that comes to you. You become the master of money instead of money becoming the master of *you!*

Most of the people who are just after money in life are the folks who don't have it. And, as I said, people who love money and who would become covetous with money will do anything to get it. They will scheme. They will break the law, and they will degrade themselves for money.

Paul went on to say in First Timothy 6:7, **For we brought nothing into this world, and it is certain we can carry nothing out.** You know, when you die, your family is not going to stuff your pockets with your money and bury you!

I'm not planning to take any money with me, but I *am* planning to leave something for my seed because the Bible told me to do so: **A good man leaveth an inheritance to his children's children...** (Proverbs 13:22).

In the passage in First Timothy, chapter 6, Paul is trying to bring correction to those people who don't understand the right way to handle money—covetous people. He's not talking to *covenant* people, because covenant people aren't stupid. Covenant people know they are not going to bring anything to the grave with them.

First Timothy 6:9 says, **But they that will be RICH fall into temptation and a snare, and into many foolish and hurtful lusts, which drown men in destruction and perdition.**

That couldn't be talking about the kind of "rich" or the kind of wealth Deuteronomy 8 talks about. It says, **But thou shalt remember the Lord thy God: for it is he that giveth thee power to get wealth, that he may establish his covenant which he sware unto thy fathers, as it is this day** (v. 18).

But they that will be rich... (1 Timothy 6:9). That means *they who want to be rich for the wrong purpose and with the wrong attitude about money.* Those people will fall into temptation because they will scheme and connive and do anything they can to get their hands on a dollar. Do you know some people like that?

Just having money does not mean that you don't love God. I disagree with the kind of thinking that says money is evil, because it doesn't line up with the Word and with what the will of the Father is for you. You can be holy with a pocketful of money! Money in itself is not evil. Money has no life. The only life money has is the life we give to it, so to speak, by our attitudes about money.

You see, if First Timothy 6:9 were talking about God's kind of prosperity in Deuteronomy 8:18, then if we became rich, the Lord would be a partner in our falling into temptation and a snare. Why? Because Deuteronomy 8:18 says, **For it is HE that giveth thee power to get wealth, that he may establish his covenant which he sware unto thy fathers, as it is this day.**

But, no, First Timothy 6:9 and Deuteronomy 8:18 are talking about two different types of prosperity! One is a worldly type. The other kind of prosperity is a godly type. It's a covenant type of prosperity. A person has to come into agreement with God and His covenant to get this kind of prosperity. A person who receives this kind of prosperity has to want to see the Gospel preached. He has to want to see the world evangelized and the Kingdom of God go forward.

There's God's kind of prosperity, and there's a worldly type of prosperity. When the Bible talks about men going after riches, it's not talking about God's kind of prosperity. That's the worldly kind. And God is telling us not to go this route.

Covenant, Covetousness and the Curse

Poverty is a curse of the law. God's kind of prosperity is a blessing that comes as a result of keeping God's law. To know the difference between the curse and the blessing, you need to know the difference between covetousness and the covenant.

The *covenant* is the power God gives to individuals to receive financial freedom so that they may be blessed and that they may *be* a blessing!

God told Abraham, "I'll bless you and I'll make you a blessing" (Genesis 12:2). And when you're walking under the covenant, you'll be blessed, and you'll *be* a blessing.

Covetousness is going after money and wealth to hoard it for yourself. You are living under a curse if you are in covetousness when it comes to the blessings of God.

The *curse* is nothing but Satan having his hand on you to keep you down. Being under the curse is being under Satan's bondage and under the condition of fallen mankind instead of under the blood of Jesus.

Now many Christians live like that—as if they're under the curse—because they don't have the revelation of how to get out from under that bondage, pressure, distress and discontentment.

Health and Wealth: Part of the Covenant Package

God doesn't mind your being *wealthy* in the same way He doesn't mind your being *healthy*. But we preachers have to teach the Word and teach people how to rightly divide the Word of truth in order to get them to walk in God's kind of prosperity.

It's not always easy to get people to believe that they don't have to be poor or sick. As a matter of fact, we preachers have really had to plow some fields to get people to believe they don't have to be sick!

I remember when I first started preaching on healing. I found out that healing belonged to us, and I started preaching it. But people would just look at me and say, "But, Reverend, you always taught me in the past to *keep* my sickness. Now what are you talking about! Here you come, just a 'whippersnapper,' saying now that people are supposed to be healed and well. But I've had my sickness for fifteen years. I've been serving the Lord with my sickness. What do you mean, talking to me about healing!"

I remember when I first started preaching healing to the church I pastor now. Some of my members looked at me like a bullfrog that had just come out of a windstorm! Some of them protested, "You're not going to take my sickness!" "You're not going to take my high blood pressure!" "You're not going to take my arthritis!"

It's funny now, but it wasn't then. Back then, it seemed as if we were healing-free in the part of Louisiana I'm from—the deep, deep South.

Do you know what I mean by "healing-free"? I mean that, to a large degree, people didn't know a thing about divine healing.

Now I'm talking about prosperity. I'm preaching that you don't have to be in debt. You don't have to be in distress. You don't have to be in discontentment. You can be free and have plenty of money in your pocket and be a blessing to others. God *wants* you to be rich! He wants you to be wealthy!

After what I went through when I first started preaching healing, when I first received the revelation on prosperity and started preaching it, I thought, *Here I go, sounding like a pioneer again.* People would look at me and say, "Yes, Pastor, that's good teaching. But a person has to be broke *sometime.* He can't *always* have money!"

Those are some of the thoughts the devil brings to people's minds when they hear the good news that money cometh! It almost sounds too good to be true, but it is the truth: God wants us to be prosperous and have plenty of money.

God wants you to have money, but He doesn't want you to connive for money. You don't have to lust for it. I don't waste a wink of sleep thinking about money. Money cometh! Money comes and rings my doorbell and says, "Here I am!" I just go to bed, go to sleep, get up and praise the Lord because money cometh!

You Need Money!

We need to get our thinking straight once and for all about money and about God's kind of prosperity. First Timothy 6:10 says,

For the love of money is the root of all evil: which while some coveted after, they have erred from the faith, and pierced themselves through with many sorrows.

Some people love money, but I love God. God is my first love. And no money in the world can make me leave Him. But that doesn't mean I'm going to separate myself from money, because God wants me to have money. He wants me to support this Gospel, and money is our means of exchange in this world.

You need money. Ministers have to travel, but they can't get on a plane and fly somewhere without a ticket. When the airline agent asks for a minister's ticket, that minister can't say, "Hallelujah, John 3:16 says, 'For God so loved the world that He gave His only begotten Son.' Where's my seat? Hallelujah!" The airline agent is going to say, "Sir, I need your ticket!"

You see, you need money! And God has provided a covenant whereby you can have it!

In Genesis 25, we read about Jacob and his older brother, Esau. Once when Esau was really hungry, Jacob said to Esau, "All right. I'll give you some stew. But give me your birthright first. Then I'll give it to you" (v. 31). You see, the son who had the birthright got all the inheritance. Jacob was a rascal because he was tricking his brother out of the birthright.

Then Jacob and his mama played a trick on Daddy. Daddy's eyes were dim, and Jacob's mother Rebekah put goat hair on Jacob's arms to make him feel more like Esau. Then Jacob went into his daddy Isaac's tent and got his daddy to bless *him* instead of blessing Esau. Daddy thought Jacob was Esau, so he blessed Jacob with all of Esau's blessing (Genesis 27:6-29).

Jacob schemed to get that blessing. Then Jacob finally met God and they wrestled. Jacob said, "I'm not going to turn You loose till You bless me" (Genesis 32:26).

Then Jacob met his match as schemers go when he met his Uncle Laban. (See Genesis 29.) Uncle Laban was an even better schemer than Jacob! There they were—two schemers! (A schemer will always meet up with another schemer.)

But we're not schemers, and we're not covetous. We're in *covenant.* God wants to get the negative side across to people because, although He wants us to have money, He wants us to have it *properly.* The Body of Christ at large has been broke. Some of them don't even have a quarter, and that's sad. Others are getting along pretty well, but "getting along pretty well" is not the covenant.

Jesus Himself said, **The thief cometh not, but for to steal, and to kill, and to destroy: I am come that they might have life, and that they might have it more abundantly** (John 10:10). That includes material blessings too. Jesus came that we might have life, and have it more abundantly. "More abundantly" means *more than enough,* not just "getting along pretty well."

We are walking in God's covenant of "more abundantly." We are not walking in covetousness. Deuteronomy 8:18 says, **Thou shalt remember the Lord thy God: for it is he that giveth thee power to get wealth, that he may establish his covenant which he sware unto thy fathers, as it is this day.**

You see, you need the wealth this verse talks about to get the covenant established in your life.

Error and Extremes

Many people have let First Timothy 6:10, **The love of money is the root of all evil,** rob them of divine prosperity because they didn't rightly divide the Word of truth. They thought that *money* was evil. On the other hand, others who didn't have balanced teaching on prosperity started confessing for money, got caught up with the money and forgot God. They didn't understand God's kind of prosperity.

I have actually seen ministers in our generation who got hooked on money and the message of prosperity, and they got out of balance. They went into covetousness and error and **pierced themselves through with many sorrows** (1 Timothy 6:10).

I've seen that happen. Money was all those ministers would talk about. Every time a prophecy came forth, it was about money. They prophesied money *out of* others' pockets and *into* theirs!

Those ministers may have started out all right with this prosperity message, but they became false prophets. They were consumed with money and started merchandising the anointing by taking up four and five offerings in one service.

One particular minister who died several years ago erred because of money. I've been told that the Holy Ghost moved in spectacular ways in his services. But then this man would stop right in the middle of the move of God and receive an offering! Well, people were excited because the Spirit of God was moving, so some would give everything they had in their pockets.

What that minister did is called merchandising the anointing. But the anointing is not for sale! That minister died young. The power and anointing of God were on his life, but he became covetous and consumed with money, and he erred from the faith. But the money didn't do it. *He* did it. You see, it's not the money's fault if someone errs from the faith!

Sometimes people who are broke get into covetousness and err from the faith just like some rich people do. For example, they may be broke, and somebody will offer them a business deal that is not quite right; it's shady. But they've been broke for so long, they want money, and they want it now! So they err from the faith.

But if somebody wants you to get involved in something shady, just keep moving. Avoid all that if you want to be really blessed by the Lord.

Don't Put Your Trust and
Confidence in Uncertain Riches

We know by now that God wants us to have money, but He wants us to have it *properly* and *honestly!*

> **But thou, O man of God, flee these things; and follow after righteousness, godliness, faith, love, patience, meekness. Fight the good fight of faith, lay hold on eternal life, whereunto thou art also called, and hast professed a good profession before many witnesses. I give thee charge in the sight**

of God, who quickeneth all things, and before Christ Jesus, who before Pontius Pilate witnessed a good confession; That thou keep this commandment without spot, unrebukeable, until the appearing of our Lord Jesus Christ.

1 Timothy 6:11-14

These verses are talking about the requirements to have godly prosperity operating in your life. We looked at *covetousness* and the worldly kind of prosperity. Now we're going to look some more at the *covenant* part of prosperity, or *God's kind* of prosperity.

As we already discussed in detail, there are certain marks that you must bear—certain characteristics that must mark your life—if you're going to walk in the covenant of prosperity.

Verse 17 says, CHARGE THEM THAT ARE RICH in this world, THAT THEY BE NOT HIGHMINDED, nor trust in uncertain riches, but in the living God, who giveth us richly all things to enjoy.

You see, Paul didn't say you couldn't be rich. He just said, "Don't be high-minded or trust in money, in uncertain riches."

What are we to trust in? The rest of that verse says, **But in the living God, who giveth us richly all things to enjoy.**

Paul also said in Romans 12:3, when he was talking about faith, **For I say, through the grace given unto me, to every man that is among you,** NOT TO THINK OF HIMSELF MORE HIGHLY THAN HE OUGHT TO THINK; **but to think soberly, according as God hath dealt to every man the measure of faith.**

Paul was saying, "If you think correctly and walk by faith, you won't think more highly of yourself than you ought to think." Why? Because everything we get from God, we get by faith.

Faith will cause you to get healed. Faith will cause you to come into prosperity. It's all by faith. All of the blessings God has provided come by faith. They don't come by our own works apart from God.

So Paul admonished us not to think more highly of ourselves than we ought.

Can you handle money and not think of yourself more highly than you ought to think?

You know, the blessings that I have this day—the blessings the Lord has placed in my life—I couldn't have handled ten years ago. That's why I said there's a test every one of us has to pass before God brings us into His kind of prosperity.

God will bring people through a series of tests before they arrive at walking in divine prosperity. And if you don't pass the test, you take the grade over!

Some people have stayed in the third grade for fifteen years! God's been trying to get them ready for what He has for them.

I'm telling you, when you rise up in life and have material gain, you'd better be hooked up to the Man. If you're not, when that material wealth starts saying to you, "Look who you are. Boy, you're something!" you won't know what to say. But you have to tell that wealth, "Shut up! I am who God says I am. And wealth, you are going to give glory to *Him*, not to *me!*"

Unless you come through a series of tests, you're not going to be able to handle money properly. But the Lord will get you ready. Some people say, "What are you talking about, saying I'm not ready! Don't make that confession! Don't say I'm not ready!"

But if you are not where you want to be financially, find out where the problem is. Maybe you haven't been using your faith as you should have been. Maybe it's because you're not ready spiritually to handle money.

If that's the case, you can get ready. Start believing God now that money cometh! If you will, He will take you step by step through His plan and will see to it that you become ready. He will prepare you and bring you into a good land of prosperity and plenty.

The Lord may test you with certain things. For example, He may try you with $15 until you do with it what He wants done with it. If you can't handle $15, you can't handle $15,000!

Here's the deciding factor: Suppose you have $15. You tell the Lord, "Lord, I don't have much, but I have You as my Provider. So I'm going to go ahead and listen to You and do what You tell me to do with this $15."

When you have that attitude, God will move you up the ladder. Then He will give you more.

Some people say, "I'm ready! I can handle it. I can handle plenty of money, Lord, so give it to me!"

But if those same people received $20,000 tomorrow, would they bring $2,000 to the church and tithe? Many of them wouldn't. They would begin shuffling that money around and start thinking, *Man, two thousand dollars! I'm not going to give that much money to the church!*

Or suppose someone just inherited $40,000. But when it came time for him to go to the church to tithe $4,000, he got behind closed doors and decided to give only $400.

You see, a person's heart is not right if he would do something like that. And many times, a person like that will bring his $400 to church and not even want to put *it* in the offering basket. Instead, he'll want to march straight into the pastor's office and brag to the pastor about his gift. He'll want the pastor to show him great appreciation—for giving God what is rightfully His!

People like that are not ready for the covenant of prosperity. They need to judge themselves.

It's good to picture yourself with a lot of money. But all that money isn't going to do you any good if you're not going to do what's right with it. In other words, if you receive $50,000, $5,000 belongs to God. When I receive money, I write the Lord's check first. I can hardly wait to give it. I want that money out of my house! It's the Lord's money! That should be your attitude too.

Remember, First Timothy 6:17 says, **Charge them that are rich in this world, that they be not highminded, NOR TRUST IN UNCERTAIN RICHES, but in the living God, who giveth us richly all things to enjoy.**

You see, money is uncertain. The value of money goes up and down. Your trust should not be in money, but in the Lord. The Bible says, **Trust in the Lord with all thine heart; and lean not unto thine own understanding. In all thy ways acknowledge him, and he shall direct thy paths** (Proverbs 3:5,6).

Acknowledge the Lord, and He'll direct your path. You can acknowledge the Lord with or without money. But did you know that if you acknowledge Him with money, He can do more for you? He can direct you to use that money for His glory, and He'll show you ways to use your money to multiply it for your own personal needs too.

Some people will only acknowledge the Lord and pray and trust Him when they're broke and they need something from Him. But I can trust in the Lord just as well with money as I can without money. I don't need to be broke to pray. I've got to pray if I'm going to pastor a church! You can't pastor a church with just money!

The Lord wants you to have money; He just doesn't want you to trust in money—in uncertain riches. So what does a person trust in if he doesn't trust in uncertain riches? The answer is in the rest of that verse: **But [trust] in the living God, who giveth us richly all things to enjoy** (1 Timothy 6:17)!

You see, when you come into financial prosperity, you've got to continue to trust in the living God and not put your trust in money. When you trust in the living God, you're still going to serve Him. You're still going to work in the ministry of helps in the church.

Some people think, *I've got $250,000, and you want me to work in the church? You don't know who I am! I'll buy you, you poor thing!* That's the way some people talk when they get a little money. I've actually seen guys with $40 or $50 in their pockets who thought they owned the world!

We need to trust in the living God, as First Timothy 6:17 says, because God is the One who gives us all things richly to enjoy.

What does that word "richly" mean? Well, for one, it means *plentifully.* Why does He give "all things" plentifully to us? To *enjoy!*

Someone said, "Well, those two words 'richly' and 'enjoy' couldn't go together." Some people think you've got to be poor to enjoy anything and not feel guilty about it. They think people are sinning if they're rich and enjoy anything in life!

They think you're in sin if you sit at your nice dining room table and eat a nice meal and don't have to buy your groceries on credit!

Some corner stores still sell groceries on credit. You can go in there, and there's an account in your name. I remember a man in my town years ago who had money, but he still bought groceries on credit. One day I was behind this man, and I watched him sign that paper for his groceries. When he left, I said to the store owner, "Doesn't that man know that money is made to spend? He should quit signing those papers and just pay for the stuff!"

But, you see, sometimes when a person gets in one groove and has his way of doing things, he just stays in that groove. He doesn't have to, but he does.

Some people have to buy their groceries on credit. But wouldn't it be wonderful if they could go through the supermarket and just put whatever they wanted in the grocery basket?

I've seen some people in the grocery store calculating what they're buying. And sometimes they have to put some stuff back because they don't have enough money to buy everything they put in the basket.

But I made up my mind years ago to walk in prosperity, and now when I roll my basket up to the cash register, my basket's going through the line! I'm not going to put anything back! I found a way through the Word of God to have plenty of money in my pocket so that when I go to the grocery store, I can put what I want in that basket!

I'm just being honest. As I said, some preachers think they have to hide their prosperity. But I don't hide my prosperity. *People* didn't bless me; the *Lord* is the One who brought me to where I am.

The same thing can happen to you, too, when you don't trust in uncertain riches, but in the living God who gives us all things richly to enjoy!

Christians Should Enjoy Life!

Christians ought to be able to enjoy life. They ought to enjoy the holidays and vacation time. I particularly like Thanksgiving week. I don't usually work that week. I like to be around the house and smell what's in the oven and on the stove in the kitchen!

Of course, Christians should enjoy the fact that they're saved and going to heaven and missing hell, but I believe God wants us to enjoy life here, too, because the Bible says He gives us all things richly to enjoy.

Sinners need to be enticed and come over to God's way when they see you blessed and enjoying life and praising God.

They should want to know what kind of God you're serving. Then you can tell them, "Jesus made me what I am."

But it's different when you've been a Christian for twenty-five years, and you don't have anything in the earth to show for it. Yet you're talking about your El Shaddai and Jehovah Jireh, the God you serve. Sinners will hear you talking like that and see you not prospering and say, "Those Christians are crazy. El *Diablo* is better than their El Shaddai. My needs are met. I'm doing better than they are."

Really, salvation is the most important thing, and it is more important that a person accept Jesus and go to heaven than it is for him to have financial prosperity. But, really, what a sinner has on the earth shouldn't "hold water" compared to what a believer has on earth! Over a period of time, you, as a Christian, should bring a sinner to open shame.

I give dope pushers a headache because I'm so prosperous. I've got them so confused. I drive my car through certain parts of town, and when I pass by, the dope pushers bow. They think I'm "king of the dope" or something. They think, *Hey, he's so prosperous, he's got to be selling dope.*

But, no, I've got inside information! It's called the Bible! I found out about my covenant with God and held fast to my confession. I live holy and purely, and God has raised me up.

The Lord wants to show Himself strong on your behalf and raise you up in the financial arena, and He will do it if you let Him.

Let me share with you a word I received from the Lord during a meeting I preached:

> *Those who'll let Me do it for them, I'll do it swiftly, says the Lord. They'll be out* [of debt] *before they know it. Yield to My*

Spirit. Yield to My Word. Yield to My will. Yield to My way, and you'll see just what I say.

God wants us to walk in His covenant blessings. The devil wants to keep us under the curse, but we are under the covenant. We've got that old devil by the neck. Christ has redeemed us from the curse of the law, and money cometh!

We're going to build big, beautiful buildings, and sinners will run in and get saved and baptized. We're going to plant pretty flowers on the grounds and let them see the glory of God on earth. We're going to preach the Gospel of the Lord Jesus Christ in all the world, because money cometh!

Be Rich in Good Works

We saw that one characteristic of a person who is walking in God's covenant of prosperity is that he doesn't put his trust in uncertain riches. What is another mark, or characteristic, of someone who is walking in this covenant? Someone who walks in this kind of prosperity is *rich in good works.*

> **Charge them that are rich in this world, that they be not highminded, nor trust in uncertain riches, but in the living God, who giveth us richly all things to enjoy; That they do GOOD, that they be RICH IN GOOD WORKS, ready to distribute, willing to communicate.**
>
> **1 Timothy 6:17,18**

Look at that phrase, **That they do good....** This is what you have to do when you come into the land of prosperity. You have to do good, that you may be rich in good works.

What does the rest of that verse say? It says, **Ready to distribute....** That means "ready to give."

When God prospers you, it's really God's money that you have. And you have to be ready to give it up at any time when He gives the word.

So you can't just go around blessing whom you want to bless. You might be blessing a person who doesn't have any socks on and whose coat is ragged and about to fall off. You might be really proud because you blessed somebody whose coat was falling off, but that might not be the person the Lord wanted you to bless!

In this chapter, we've seen two marks, or characteristics, of the person who is walking in God's prosperity: He doesn't *trust in uncertain riches,* and he is *rich in good works.*

In other words, we could say that the person who walks in God's kind of prosperity puts God and His Word first.

> **Therefore take no thought, saying, What shall we eat? or, What shall we drink? or, Wherewithal shall we be clothed? (For after all these things do the Gentiles seek:) for your heavenly Father knoweth that ye have need of all these things. But seek ye first the kingdom of God, and his righteousness; and all these things shall be added unto you.**
>
> **Matthew 6:31-33**

Now this scripture doesn't mean that you don't tell the Father your needs. Matthew 6:8 says that the Father knows what you need even before you ask Him for it. But He still wants you to ask.

Let me share with you a word from the Lord that I received during a meeting I once preached.

> *Open your heart so you can see clearly the things that I have provided for you. Yield not to the voice of the evil one, but yield to My Spirit, because it is I who desire to bring you out. Yea, yield to My Spirit this very day. Yield to My way. Yield to My will. Yield to My Word, and those yokes and bondages that you've carried will be gone forever. It is My desire that you walk freely in the yoke with Me, for My yoke is easy, and My burden is light.*
>
> *Do not give so men will see. Give in secret, and I will reward you openly. Yield to the Spirit of truth. Yield to My direction, and as you're led by the Spirit, you'll begin to live like you never thought you could live. For it is My desire for you to give and live, not keep and go deeper—deeper into the darkness and snares of this world.*
>
> *But give and live, says the Spirit of the Lord. Move up into your inheritance, for I have provided for you to have such an abundance that it will flow over, and others around you will be blessed—just as those around Abraham were blessed, says the Lord of hosts.*

There are those who have a burning desire to be tithers, yet they start out tithing, and any little "checkmate" will stop them, and they panic and go back to doing things the way they were done before.

But, no, turn your back on worldly prosperity and turn your way toward godly prosperity. Just begin to do what I tell you to do, and you'll see results.

If you'll do what I say, you'll see that day. Come closer to Me. Dive into what I say and see how sweet and how good it is. It will pay off if you follow My instruction.

The Lord wants you to move in His flow of prosperity, not in the world's flow. God's way is always better.

God will help you move into His flow and enter His good land of prosperity. As you learn to key in on His prosperity and walk in His ways, you will be blessed!

Part 1

**And if ye be Christ's, then are ye Abraham's seed,
and HEIRS according to the promise.**
—GALATIANS 3:29

In this chapter, I'm going to point out a few things from the Word of God to help you understand the importance of your heritage—your inheritance in Christ. God wants you to understand the heritage that was left for you and the legacy He wants you to leave behind concerning the things of God.

There are three phrases Paul is emphasizing in our text, Galatians 3:29, **And if ye be Christ's, then are ye Abraham's seed, and heirs according to the promise:** (1) "If ye be Christ's"; (2) "then are ye Abraham's seed"; and (3) "heirs according to the promise"!

What does Paul mean by **If ye be Christ's...?** Paul is saying, "If you are a Christian—if you are born again—then certain things belong to you."

Let's take Galatians 3:29 a step further. It says, "If you are Christ's, then you are Abraham's seed."

Now God is doing two things in that verse. First, He is assuring you of something if you are Christ's. Second, He's giving you the example of a man, Abraham, who received the blessings and benefits of walking with God. Abraham was called the Father of the faithful.

The third thing Galatians 3:29 says is, "You're heirs"!

Now the word "heir" implies that there is an *inheritance.* If you are someone's heir, there is an inheritance waiting for you.

God wants us to honor what He has left for us. He has had people throughout history and throughout the Bible walk ahead of us in that vein of the inheritance so we would know how to receive what is ours and live in the blessings God has provided for us.

We do have an inheritance because we're the children of God—because we're in Christ. There's a certain inheritance that belongs to us—the physical manifestation of prosperity. I'm not talking about a *spiritual* inheritance. Certainly, we have a spiritual inheritance, but *financial prosperity* is an inheritance of God's heirs too.

God wants His children to be financially stable, with our needs met and a surplus of blessings besides! These things belong to the seed of Abraham. That means they belong to us because we are in Christ!

Honor Your Inheritance by Walking in the Fullness of It

By honoring your inheritance of prosperity, God can get the Gospel out because you're taking your rightful place. But if you aren't taking your rightful place, you haven't become a full partner with the Lord in the area of prosperity.

You know, you can read about something in the Bible and see some information on a certain subject, and you can even make a request about the information that you have seen. You can realize that some benefit belongs to you. But until that information gets from just the *mental* realm to the *spiritual* realm and becomes a revelation in your spirit man, you will not walk in the fullness of that benefit.

You see, you can realize mentally that prosperity belongs to you, but until you get a revelation—not from man but from the Holy Ghost—that God wants you to prosper, you will not arrive at a place of financial prosperity in your life.

The Holy Ghost will have to expose your spirit to that truth, and that will not come overnight. And it will not come without your having the tenacity to press in to find out about it.

Many lost souls will miss the Kingdom of God because some in the Body of Christ lived below their rights and privileges. I am convinced that some will not enter the Kingdom because the Body of Christ missed the part of the Gospel that would have brought them into the prosperity that God provided through His promise to Father Abraham and through the Lord Jesus Christ.

Why? One reason is that it's through this inheritance of financial prosperity that the Gospel of the Lord Jesus Christ is preached in every place in the world the Lord wants to send it. But when the Church has a poverty mentality, the Gospel can't go forth as God wants it to go forth.

You see, because we are in Christ, everything that the Father owns on earth is ours. And when we tap into that revelation, lack leaves us, and we have what Jesus was sent for. We have salvation and eternal life, and we have health and wealth in this life here on earth!

When we don't realize what God has done for us in the area of finances and prosperity, we are denying to a certain degree the right of Jesus to bless us. We are denying the Holy Spirit the privilege to show us the pathway that the Father wants us to travel while we're here on earth.

For your needs not to be met—for you not to walk in the abundance that God has provided for you—is to deny Christ the right to enjoy one of the things He died for: your prosperity.

Prosperity Is a Godly Doctrine

Remember Jesus said, **I am come that they might have life, and that they might have it more abundantly** (John 10:10). How does Jesus want you to have life? *Less* abundantly? No! *More* abundantly!

Then John wrote, **Beloved, I wish above all things that thou mayest prosper and be in health, even as thy soul prospereth** (3 John 2). This is God's will for you, but it has to be a revelation to you. It has to be a revelation in your spirit that you are in Christ; therefore, you are Abraham's seed; *therefore,* you're an heir of the promises of God!

You as a Christian are an heir to prosperity! But a poverty syndrome and a "barely-getting-by" mentality have crept into the Church. For this reason, when someone stands up and preaches a message of prosperity, it seems he's preaching some strange doctrine!

But the prosperity of God that belongs to us in Christ is not a worldly or strange doctrine.

We talked about paying tithes as one of the requirements for walking in your inheritance of prosperity. You see, there is a reason the Father wants you to tithe. It's not just so there will be meat in His house (Malachi 3:10). It's so He can open the windows of heaven and pour you out a blessing that there shall not be room enough to receive it!

You need to get the revelation of why the Father wants you to tithe. You need to get the revelation of why the Father talks about giving and receiving, or sowing and reaping. He only wants you to enjoy your heirship and what He has provided for you!

See the Truth and Believe It!

We talked about some other requirements, or qualifications, for walking in your inheritance of divine prosperity. For example, you have to be a tither and a giver if you want to be financially blessed. Also, we saw that there are certain characteristics, such as humility, that should mark your life as a financially blessed child of God.

Now we're going to look at some more things that have to be in place for you to understand and receive the prosperity of God as your heritage.

First, the Spirit of God will have to teach you, so you'll have to be open to Him and hungry for the Word. He will lead you into the revelation of divine prosperity as you seek Him.

Second, in most cases, nothing is received from God without a person's having faith for it. So you have to understand that not only are you Abraham's seed, but that Abraham is the father of the faithful or of those who walk by *faith*. Why? Because Abraham walked by faith, and he was blessed by God as a result.

So two things have to be in place for you to receive prosperity: (1) the revelation in your spirit that God wants you to prosper and that He has provided prosperity for you; and (2) faith to receive the prosperity that belongs to you.

To receive an inheritance in the natural, first you have to know that you're an heir. Well, we are heirs of God and joint-heirs with Christ!

> **The Spirit itself beareth witness with our spirit, that we are the children of God: And if children, then heirs; heirs of God, and joint-heirs with Christ; if so be that we suffer with him, that we may be also glorified together.**
>
> **Romans 8:16,17**

Pay close attention to verse 17: **If children, then heirs; heirs of God, and joint-heirs with Christ....** *We are heirs!* We have a heritage left to us by Abraham, and it has been carried down through a biblical lineage. Throughout the Bible, we see men and women of God who walked by faith and who were prosperous.

We who are in the Body of Christ are not Old Testament servants. We are *sons.* (See John 1:12; Galatians 4:6; 1 John 3:1,2.) Since God had pleasure in the prosperity of His *servants*—those people under the old covenant who were not born again—then how much more does He have pleasure in the prosperity of His *sons!*

Those people in the old covenant were just *serving* the Lord. I serve the Lord, but I am more than just a servant. I'm an heir! You're an heir, too, if you are born again (Galatians 4:7). I like the way Paul put it in Romans 8:17: **And if children, then HEIRS; HEIRS of God, and JOINT-HEIRS with Christ; if so be that we suffer with him, that we may be also glorified together.** Paul tells us three times in that verse that we are heirs!

God is trying to tell you through many witnesses in His Word that He wants you to be in a position where you can be blessed and be a blessing. These scriptures contradict the lifestyle of so many in the Body of Christ who are barely getting by financially. Spiritually, they are enjoying some of God's blessings. They get those spiritual "goose bumps" from time to time. But when it comes to other parts of the benefits, such as prosperity, they are not enjoying those blessings.

Let's look at another passage in Romans 8.

> **He that spared not his own Son, but delivered him up for us all, how shall he not with him also freely give us all things?**
>
> **Romans 8:32**

God spared not His own Son, but delivered Him up for us all. Since God gave us the benefits or the provisions of His Son, how shall He not with Him—along with the Son—freely give us all things besides?

When God says "all things" in this verse, He is talking about our inheritance. He is talking about what He has provided for His children and what He wants them to have. God has already given us His Son. Since He gave us Jesus, what wouldn't He give us?

We need to honor our heritage in Christ and appreciate what He has done for us. In this chapter, I'm discussing how to get in position to walk in God's kind of prosperity, and one way to do that is by showing honor to your heritage in Christ. You can't get in proper position to walk in prosperity if you are not honoring that part of your inheritance that God has freely given you in Christ.

Now Abraham honored God and the promises of God. He feared the Lord by walking in all of God's ways and by trusting and obeying Him. And we know that Abraham was a blessed man.

Let's look at another Old Testament man who feared the Lord. The Bible says Job **feared God, and eschewed evil** (Job 1:1).

Usually when we talk about Job, we talk about the fact that he missed it in some areas. We talk about the negative aspect and the fact that Job lost everything he had.

But, actually, God gave Job back twice as much after Job prayed for his friends (Job 42:10).

Let's look at the life of this prosperous old covenant man.

> **There was a man in the land of Uz, whose name was Job; and that man was perfect and upright, and one that feared God, and eschewed evil.**
>
> **Job 1:1**

God said, **That man was perfect and upright, and one that feared God, and eschewed evil.** Now why would God give us such a description of this man?

The Lord really bragged on Job. Don't feel sorry for Job just because the first thing you think about is Job's sores and everything he lost. As I said, when you read the end of the book, you discover that Job was healed and had twice as much as he'd had before.

Whatever Job had at the beginning of the book in terms of blessings, you can double at the end of the book! Then the Bible says Job lived to a good old age, so he *enjoyed* all that God did for him too!

In verse 1, God began by detailing the life of Job. Let's continue reading what God had to say about this man:

> **And there were born unto him seven sons and three daughters. His substance also was seven thousand sheep, and three thousand camels, and five hundred yoke of oxen, and five hundred she asses, and a very great household; so that this man was the greatest of all the men of the east.**
>
> Job 1:2,3

Now, when some people read verse 1, **There was a man in the land of Uz, whose name was Job; and that man was perfect and upright, and one that feared God, and eschewed evil,** they will say, "Oh, Job was a holy man," and everybody gets happy. But when they read the following verses and see how rich Job was and how much *substance* Job had, they almost become afraid. They think, *I thought Job was holy, but look at everything he had! He couldn't have been walking with God, because he had too much!*

Look at the last part of verse 3: **So that this man was the greatest of all the men of the east. God said that about Job!**

Everybody wants to be upright like Job, but many people are afraid to have money, because they think you have to be broke to be holy. But that wasn't the case with Job.

Holiness Does Not Preclude Prosperity

I want you understand that this man Job was living in prosperity because he was keeping his covenant with God.

You see, if God wanted us to be holy and *broke,* it seems He would have just stopped at verse 1. God should have just written that Job was holy and then stopped right there. If the fact that Job was upright and eschewed evil was the only characteristic that pleased the Lord, why would the Lord write about or detail anything else about Job's life?

Or maybe verse 1 should have read, "There was a man in the land of Uz, whose name was Job; and that man was perfect and upright, and one that feared God and eschewed evil—and was *broke* because people who eschew evil and walk uprightly are supposed to be broke!" That's what much of the Church as a whole believes!

Now, concerning Job, why did the Lord tell us, **And there were born unto him seven sons and three daughters** (v. 2)?

We know Job was upright and holy. We know God was pleased with Job and loved him and gave him a nice family with children. But how was Job going to take care of that family?

Listen, friend, in this world, you need *substance.* You need *money!* You can be as holy and spiritual as you want to be, but you still need some substance in this world. You need some material, temporal blessings in order to survive in this physical world. You might as well face up to that fact.

You can pray and praise the Lord as much as you want, but when you finish praying, you still have to pay your bills. Prayer and praise are good, but you have to have money to take care of yourself and your family. You can't just say, "Hallelujah!" and have your bills come up paid!

I told you about how holy Job was; I told you he had a nice little family. Now look at verse 3 again: **His SUBSTANCE also was seven thousand sheep, and three thousand camels, and five hundred yoke of oxen, and five hundred she asses, and a very great household; so that this man was the greatest of all the men of the east.**

Job had 7,000 sheep and 3,000 camels. That's 10,000! Then he had 500 yoke of oxen and 500 "she asses" or donkeys. And the rest of that verse says, **So that this man was the greatest of all the men of the east.**

Read the rest of Job chapter 1. Job didn't hold to his confession at times, but I want you to see how blessed he was. Not only did he walk with God and have a nice family, but God also blessed him financially.

You are an heir of God and a joint-heir with Christ, and there are certain blessings that belong to you as a result. But you have to tap into God's prosperity by faith in order for it to happen for you. You can't waver or be hesitant about your inheritance and then expect to walk in the fullness of prosperity.

Some people are always saying there's more to life than money. That's true, but you can't convince me that they enjoy life to the fullest being broke and living without the financial blessings of God. Without the financial blessings of God, they can't enjoy life in the measure God wants them to, and they can't give to the Gospel like God wants them to.

But if they want to be broke, that's their decision. God won't violate their wills and force them to walk in His prosperity.

But I'm going to walk in it! I'm not going to be broke! I'm going from one level of faith to another—from glory to glory, from faith to faith and from strength to strength. I'm going all the way in receiving from God and walking in my inheritance in Christ because I see the truth of God's Word that says I can have it.

Who will go with me? Will you take what belongs to you and walk in your inheritance, honoring God and the heritage of prosperity that you have because of Him?

The God Who Is More Than Enough!

The Spirit of God says, "Money cometh!" He says that so we can get hold of the truth and let the truth bring us out of debt, distress and discontentment.

Now, as I said, when you're confessing "Money cometh," don't worry about where the finances are coming from. Don't worry about your own resources, because God is your Source, and He is the God who is more than enough. God said, **For every beast of the forest is mine, and the cattle upon a thousand hills** (Psalm 50:10). God said, **The silver is mine, and the gold is mine, saith the Lord of hosts** (Haggai 2:8). God is the Source of your prosperity, and He has plenty!

All the things that God owns—the earth and the fullness thereof—belong to us too because we're heirs. All we have to do is give God permission to bless us by believing and obeying Him. And He *will* bless us!

Our Lost Prosperity Has Been Found in Christ!

Adam lost his prosperity in the Garden of Eden. God put Adam in the garden, blessed the garden and told him to have dominion. God told Adam he could eat from all of the trees except for the tree of the knowledge of good and evil (Genesis 2:17). Adam had prosperity in the garden!

But, you see, what Adam lost through disobedience—through eating of the tree of the knowledge of good and evil—Jesus came to bring back to us. Jesus came to put us in that garden, so to speak, where we'll have sufficiency in everything.

When Adam sinned and missed it, he really had to work the land. He worked by the sweat of his brow (Genesis 3:17-19). The ground wouldn't yield a harvest to him as it had before. Everything went against him.

But Jesus bought back our ability to fellowship with the Father and to have *sufficiency in all things!*

Financial prosperity is a heritage of the sons and daughters of God, but just reading about it will not cause it to come. Simply realizing it, in general, will not give you the breakthrough you need. Just repeating prosperity verses will not cause you to enjoy your inheritance. Making a request for it will not necessarily bring it to pass if you're not requesting it in faith.

No, to obtain and maintain prosperity, you must have revelation knowledge of your inheritance. You must believe and know for a fact that a great heritage has been left for you.

Old Testament men of God, like Abraham and Job, are our forerunners, so to speak, who walked in the blessings of God and left us some idea of what our inheritance is. So from the Old Testament through the New Testament, we cannot deny our heritage in Christ, which includes divine prosperity.

Don't Let Prosperity Pass You By!

Sometimes I say that people who don't walk in the blessings God has provided for them are either *lazy* or *crazy!* People who are lazy just sit back and let prosperity pass them by. They hear about prosperity, but they never do anything about it! They're not excited enough; they don't want it badly enough. The preacher will preach about redemption and our heritage in Christ, and they will just sit there, nodding their heads, as dead, dry and unbelieving as they can be.

Most of the time, they will be thinking, *Well, this church service will be over after awhile.* They don't understand what the Spirit of God is trying to teach them. If the preacher shouts and preaches a fiery sermon, they might get a *little* excited. But they're unbelieving too!

Why? Because excitement alone doesn't pay the bills. No, you have to *apply* yourself to understand what God has done for you and what He wants you to have in life. It's easy to hop and jump in church, but without proper teaching of the Word of God, you're just hopping and jumping "broke," because it's revelation knowledge from the Word that is *acted upon* that will produce results for you.

Sometimes when a preacher delivers the Word, people will just sit there, saying, "Oh, yes, amen, Preacher! That's good! Job was rich, but I'm not too concerned with what Job had. Just give me my little spiritual feeding and let me go home, back to my bills."

What I'm saying is this: You are not going to be able to receive from God until you get the revelation of His Word and get excited in faith about His blessings!

There was a time when I didn't have this revelation concerning prosperity. But I was hungry for it. I would stand in long lines to get in meetings where I knew I would be taught the Word. I have stood out in the cold until my feet have turned numb, because I wanted the revelation of prosperity. There's some suffering involved in that, but you have to be hungry for the things of God, and you have to be willing to pay the price to walk in the blessings of God.

God has brought me and my family a long way. We haven't always walked in divine prosperity, but God has brought us out of poverty, and I give Him all the glory for it. Since the time we came into prosperity, people have gossiped about us. But they don't know us. They don't know what God has brought us through. We learned we were heirs of God and joint-heirs of Jesus Christ, and we will never be the same again!

It's one thing to know about your inheritance. It's another thing altogether to act on what you know and receive the full manifestation of that inheritance. Jesus talked about working the principles of God to receive divine prosperity when He said, **Give, and it shall be given unto you; good measure, pressed down, and shaken together, and running over, shall men give into your bosom. For with the same measure that ye mete withal it shall be measured to you again** (Luke 6:38).

Some of the *results* of acting on our inheritance are written in Ephesians 3:20: **Now unto him that is able to do exceeding abundantly above all that we ask or think, according to the power that worketh in us.**

These two verses are descriptions of abundance! If God didn't mean for you to have it, why would He have described it in so much detail? It's like the passage we read in Job. Why would God waste His time to tell you how much substance Job had if He didn't want you to have some material and financial blessings too?

God Is a Good Father to His Children

God didn't tell us only Job's *spiritual* qualities. Through Job's story, He is saying to us, "I am the God of abundance. And you are the *heirs* of abundance! Do not let this world system hold you from My *Word* system. Work the Word and come out of your situation, and give Me the glory for being a good Father."

Let's look at the natural and compare God the Father's goodness to a natural father's goodness toward his own son. To illustrate this point, let's suppose that every time you saw my son Leroy Jr. he had on a suit that was torn in the seat, shoes with big holes in them and a necktie that looked like it dated back to 1714! What would you think about me? You'd think, *That preacher ought to be ashamed. That preacher is able to get that boy a better suit and tie and better shoes than that! What's the matter with him, anyway!*

Of course, I'm able to do better than that for my son, and I do provide well for him.

Well, what about God? What if you were going around barefoot and wearing rags, saying, "I'm a child of the King"? You know the devil would be laughing at you. He would say, "Surely God is able to take better care of His child than that!"

Can you see the comparison? If I had a closet full of nice suits, neckties and shoes, and my son showed up at church with a tattered suit, an old necktie and a dirty, yellowed shirt, what would you think?

Now, my son happens to have a closet full of nice clothes. And I'm announcing to you, Body of Christ, that your "closet" is full of the good things of God. Your Father wants you to go into that closet and get yourself dressed up right and represent Him properly in life. He wants you to dig in and look in the mirror of the Word before you go out to represent Him. His Name is Jehovah Jireh. He is your Provider, glory to God, so *act* like it!

Meditate on that truth. Christ has redeemed us from the curse of the law—from the curse of poverty, **that the blessing of Abraham might come on the Gentiles through Jesus Christ; that we might receive the promise of the Spirit THROUGH FAITH** (Galatians 3:14).

Christ Has Done the Work— The Rest Is Up to You!

You see, God has made the promise, and Christ has done the work. Now *you* need to use your faith. Some people don't want to use their faith when they see some blessing God has promised them in the Word. They just want the blessing to fall on them like ripe cherries off a tree. They feel it takes too much sacrifice to study, meditate on, believe and act on the Word. It's too hard on their flesh to believe in something they can't see. So they don't receive the promise.

Another reason some don't enter into their inheritance as they should is found in Galatians 4:

> **Now I say, That the heir, as long as he is a child, differeth nothing from a servant, though he be lord of all; But is under tutors and governors until the time appointed of the father. Even so we, when we were children, were in bondage**

under the elements of the world: But when the fulness of
the time was come, God sent forth his Son, made of a
woman, made under the law.

Galatians 4:1-4

We already stated that an heir is one who is set up to receive an
inheritance. And we, as heirs of God, have received a godly inheritance. A legacy has been left to us—a lifestyle of walking in the prosperity of God.

But if you are an heir of God and you don't understand your
inheritance, Satan will see to it that you don't possess it. So you will
have to build yourself up in knowledge and in faith in order to claim
what is rightfully yours.

Galatians 4:1 says, **Now I say, That the heir, as long as he is a
child, differeth nothing from a servant, though he be lord of all.**

In the natural, when an heir is a child, he has not reached the age
to receive his inheritance. And, naturally speaking, some inheritances
are actually given back because nobody claims them!

Well, spiritually speaking, many inheritances belonging to God's
children are going back because nobody's claiming them!

You see, in the natural, a child can't receive his inheritance
because he wouldn't know what to do with it. Spiritually, you need to
grow and know what is rightfully yours so you can claim it. Then
once God sees that you have the revelation of your inheritance and
that you have faith for it, you can step up in prayer or in your confession and say, "It's mine; I have it now." You don't have to see it with
your eyes; however, with the eyes of your faith, you see it.

Over the years, my wife and I have claimed certain things by faith,
and once we did, we started acting like we had the things we claimed.
We started walking, talking and acting like they were so. And those
things came into existence. We received because we saw the revelation—we saw what was rightfully ours—and we acted on it in faith.

There should be a difference between a sinner and a saint. Do
you think the only difference between a sinner and a saint is that
one is going to hell and the other is going to heaven? No, there

should be a distinction *here on earth* between the child of God and the child of the devil.

But if the child of God doesn't come into the revelation of who he really is, he'll be sitting around like the sinners who don't know that God has provided anything for them! Yet God has provided for man everything he needs to be on top of every situation, including every financial situation.

The Place of Confession and Obedience

Look at that verse again: **Now I say, That the heir, as long as he is a child, differeth nothing from a servant, THOUGH HE BE LORD OF ALL** (Galatians 4:1). I believe you should be lording it over your economic situation and over everything that concerns your finances! And to do that, you have to get yourself in position by believing it and acting upon the Word in faith—by your confession and your obedience.

For example, to properly act on what you believe about divine prosperity, you need to pay your tithes.

> **Bring ye all the tithes into the storehouse, that there may be meat in mine house, and prove me now herewith, saith the Lord of hosts, if I will not open you the windows of heaven, and pour you out a blessing, that there shall not be room enough to receive it. And I will rebuke the devourer for your sakes, and he shall not destroy the fruits of your ground; neither shall your vine cast her fruit before the time in the field, saith the Lord of hosts. And all nations shall call you blessed: for ye shall be a delightsome land, saith the Lord of hosts.**
>
> **Malachi 3:10-12**

Verse 12 says that "all nations shall call you blessed, for you shall be a delightsome land!" Why are all nations going to call you blessed? Because they will see that you are a delightsome land! They won't need a spiritual revelation that you are a delightsome land; all they'll need are their eyes!

Church, you are heirs of God and joint-heirs with Jesus Christ. You have a heritage of prosperity that you must walk in.

Will you do it? Will you seek the Lord through His Word and take your rightful place, honoring the Lord and your heritage of prosperity that He has provided? If you will make the decision to be a receiving heir, the revelation of your glorious heritage and your "Money cometh" will become a living reality in your life; and not just you, but many will be blessed!

Part 2

Christians have a heritage in Christ that many have not tapped into. Many have not honored their heritage of prosperity because they've failed to receive what God has provided for them.

Do you want what God says is yours? If I can prove your heritage to you from the Scripture, will you take hold of it? Will you go after it if you see it in the Word?

Are you a son or daughter of God? Do you think God is broke? Some people act as if they think He is broke. But not only is God not broke; He has given His children—His sons and daughters—a heritage of prosperity that can cause their struggling days to be over. Their days of lack can end.

Throughout the Old Testament, we can see that those people who really served the Lord and knew the rights of the covenant had more than enough. As I said previously, there is a lineage of prosperity throughout the Old Testament—from Abraham, Isaac and Jacob to Christ—that we can partake of. Those men in the Old Testament showed us the heritage—and left us the legacy so we could see how God blesses His servants *and* His children!

> **The Spirit itself beareth witness with our spirit, that we are the CHILDREN of God: And if children, then heirs; heirs of God, and joint-heirs with Christ; if so be that we suffer with him, that we may be also glorified together.**
>
> **Romans 8:16,17**

We saw how God blessed His *servants* in the Old Testament. But what do these verses in Romans say? We are the *children* of God!

Claim Your Benefits Today!

There are certain benefits that belong to me and you, as heirs and children of God. The thing that makes our heirship unique is that the Person who left us the inheritance died, rose again and has presented the inheritance to us. We are not *going to* receive the inheritance. We can go ahead and collect our inheritance *now!*

Jesus has left us a great inheritance. He died, and now He is sitting at the right hand of God, making sure that if we claim our belongings, we will get them! Our situation is unique in that the Person who left us the inheritance arose from the dead and made the astonishing statement, **I am he that liveth, and was dead; and, behold, I am alive for evermore, Amen; and have the keys of hell and of death** (Revelation 1:18)!

He's alive! But the inheritance has been bequeathed, so you can go ahead and claim your inheritance! And Jesus will see to it that you get it!

So, you see, it means something to be an heir of God. God told us we are heirs, but He didn't want us just to "hang loose" as heirs as if it didn't mean anything to be an heir. He went on to clarify what it means to be an heir. We are heirs of *God!* That means that what He has is ours!

Then after the Word said we are heirs of God, it went a step further and said, **And joint-heirs with Christ...** (Romans 8:17).

In other words, whatever belongs to Christ belongs to you!

Now, prosperity has been a problem in the Church—because we haven't had it. We've been taught how to be broke. Some of the same churches that teach poverty will take up nine offerings to try to get by. *But how are people going to have anything to give if preachers haven't taught them how to have something to give?*

God's Divine System for His Heirs

How are preachers going to teach God's people how to have something to give? By teaching them the Word and by teaching them how to get on God's system of tithing and giving offerings. Many people in the Church today are falling short of that prosperity goal one dime at a time. They are letting a dime rob them. But God has a divine system. And divine prosperity doesn't come any other way than by getting in on God's system.

God wants you to have abundance. He wants you to have more than enough. But it's not just going to fall on you. You have to go after it. You have to be serious about obeying Him in tithing and giving offerings. And you have to tell Satan to take his hands off your finances in the Name of Jesus. You have to be determined and say boldly, "I'm coming out of debt! I'll never be broke another day in my life!"

Christians have heard, "God wants you to be rich." Then they've heard, "No, He wants you poor." They need to decide what to believe, and they need to decide it according to the Word.

What It Means To Be Rich

What does "rich" mean? "Rich" doesn't mean you have $5,000,000 in the bank. But it does mean that all your bills are paid and you are out of debt. It means driving the kind of car you want. It means having the kind of house you want. It might not be tomorrow when you'll have it, but you will have it if you stick with the Word.

God is not holding houses or cars back from you. It doesn't make any difference to God what kind of house you live in. As a matter of fact, He'd rather you live in a big house. He would rather you drive a big car or the kind of car you want. He would rather you have money in your pocket.

Some people say, "It's not spiritual to talk about houses and cars." But those same people will do everything they can, spiritual or not, to have a better house or a better car and to do nicely in life! Why else would they be working so hard on the job? Why are they taking all of that overtime?

Actually, I don't know of too many people who don't want to improve themselves. So why not improve *correctly*? Why not improve *God's* way?

If people don't want to improve themselves and have some of the good things in life, something is seriously wrong. They need prayer!

Not wanting any of the good things in life is really a selfish attitude, because "rich" means that you have more than enough to take care of your family, to take care of the church and to help your neighbor if he needs help. You can help him with finances, and you can help him understand God's system so he can get it for himself. But if you are not prosperous, you can't bless your family, the church or your neighbor.

Let's look at another scripture that reveals what it means to be rich.

> **The thief cometh not, but for to steal, and to kill, and to destroy: I am come that they might have life, and that they might have it more abundantly.**
>
> **John 10:10**

In this verse, Jesus revealed the thief as the devil. And the thief, the devil, has been stealing from you if your bills are not paid. I mean, you're an heir, and your bills are not paid? Your Father owns all the silver and the gold and all the cattle on a thousand hills, and your bills are not paid? He says to ask and it shall be given unto you, and your bills are not paid?

> ASK, and IT SHALL BE GIVEN YOU; seek, and ye shall find; **knock, and it shall be opened unto you.**
>
> **Matthew 7:7**

Well, do you know how to ask? We need to learn how to appropriate the things God has provided for us, because there's a thief out there who wants to keep us broke. But we don't have to worry about the thief who comes to steal, kill and destroy, because Jesus said, I AM COME THAT THEY MIGHT HAVE LIFE, AND THAT THEY MIGHT HAVE IT MORE ABUNDANTLY (John 10:10).

Let me ask you a question: Is it "life more abundantly" when you can't pay your bills? Is that the life that Jesus was talking about? No! Is it abundant life when you can't go out to a restaurant and eat what you want? No! You know, the sinners are out there eating filet mignon, and the Christians are eating hamburgers!

Do You Want Your Inheritance?

You know, there's no in-between when it comes to God's kind of prosperity. You are either *for* your prosperity—the inheritance that's been given to you in Christ—or you are *against* it. Do you want your inheritance?

I tell you, God has raised me up to teach this message of prosperity. He has blessed me with exceeding abundantly above all I could ask or think so I could teach this. I've been broke and I've been rich, so I know what I'm talking about.

My wife and I were broke when we took the pastorate of our church. We had thirty-five members at the time. We'd take up an offering and barely get forty dollars! It was a miracle if seventy-five dollars was in the offering!

We weren't able to buy clothes. My wife sewed her own clothes. But we kept preaching the Word and staying faithful to the truth, and it paid off for us in so many ways. Now I wish I could pour my heart into your heart to let you know what the Father has in store for you if you will pay the price to obey Him fully and faithfully!

We looked at John 10:10 to prove that God wants us to have abundance. Many Christians don't live that verse. But God's Word is true. He said, **Yea, let God be true, but every man a liar...** (Romans 3:4).

God wants us to have abundance!

Give, and it shall be given unto you; GOOD MEASURE, PRESSED DOWN, and SHAKEN TOGETHER, and RUNNING OVER, shall men give into your bosom. For with the same measure that ye mete withal it shall be measured to you again.

Luke 6:38

What does that verse sound like to you—*lack* or *plenty*? It's talking about plenty! "Good measure, pressed down, shaken together and running over" sounds like plenty to me!

The psalmist David knew what it meant to have plenty too!

The Lord is my shepherd; I shall not want.

Thou preparest a table before me in the presence of mine enemies: thou anointest my head with oil; MY CUP RUNNETH OVER.

Psalm 23:1,5

God wants *your* cup running over too!

Put all these verses about abundance together with Malachi 3:10: **Bring ye all the tithes into the storehouse, that there may be meat in mine house, and prove me now herewith, saith the Lord of hosts, if I will not open you the windows of heaven, and pour you out a blessing, that there shall not be room enough to receive it.**

That there shall not be room enough to receive it! You see, tithing ignites your prosperity! And, beyond the tithe, *giving* further ignites your prosperity, as we read in Luke 6:38.

God has done this for me, and He's doing it for me every day. And God is no respecter of persons (Acts 10:34). What He's done for me, He'll do for you too. So rise up and take your inheritance, child of God! Get up in the morning and tell the Lord, "I want my inheritance; show me the direction to go." And He will!

Now let's look at two more "abundance" scriptures. The Bible says in the mouth of two or three witnesses, let everything be established (2 Corinthians 13:1). I've already given several "witnesses" for you to ponder and meditate on!

Therefore let no man glory in men. For all things are yours.

1 Corinthians 3:21

He that spared not his own Son, but delivered him up for us all, how shall he not with him ALSO freely give us all things?

Romans 8:32

Notice that word "also" in Romans 8:32. God gave us His own Son, the very best gift He could give. So, since He gave us His best, we can be sure that He will freely give us all other things!

First Corinthians 3:21 says, **All things are yours.** When you start thinking poverty and lack, stop yourself and remember this verse and say, "All things are mine!"

The Lord is trying to teach us something. All things are ours. All we have to do is claim them.

You *can* come out of debt and walk into the prosperity of God. You can do all things through Christ who strengthens you (Philippians 4:13)!

Now I'm going to give you yet another scripture so you can know for sure that the Father wants you to claim your inheritance of prosperity!

> **For the Lord God is a sun and shield: the Lord will give grace and glory: no good thing will he withhold from them that walk uprightly.**
>
> **Psalm 84:11**

Some people stop reading that verse halfway through. They'll say, "Thank You, Lord, for Your grace and glory." But that's not all this verse says. It says, NO GOOD THING WILL HE WITHHOLD FROM THEM THAT WALK UPRIGHTLY!

God Will Give His Children Good Things

God will withhold no good thing from those who walk uprightly. What are some of the good things that this verse is talking about? Well, material and financial blessings are good things, aren't they? For example, if you saw a nice house in a nice neighborhood that you liked or had blueprints to a nice house, is that a good thing? Well, the Lord said He would not withhold any good thing from those who walked uprightly!

Remember, I said that it's not wrong for you to live in the house you want, drive the kind of car you want or eat at the restaurants you like. Those are good things, and God will give them to you if you'll walk uprightly before Him.

Why do you think Job was blessed? Because he walked uprightly! All you have to do to walk in the blessings of God is to claim them by faith and then *continue* in faith, walking uprightly according to the Word.

Know Your Rights and Stand Your Ground!

As important as walking uprightly is to receive your rights as a child of God, just walking uprightly alone won't bring you into prosperity. Just claiming the promise alone won't do it either. No, you have to walk uprightly *and* claim the promise if you want to walk in the fullness of your rights in Christ.

You see, Satan will try to hold the blessings back. He will let you walk uprightly and be broke! As a matter of fact, he wants to keep you broke *because* you walk uprightly.

There are a lot of people who are as upright as they can be, but they haven't been taught properly how to have the things in life that God wants them to have.

But when you know what belongs to you, and you are walking uprightly, you need to come in like a tornado and say to Satan, "Hey, Satan! I know you're trying to hold prosperity back from me, but I've come to get my goods in Jesus' Name!"

You have to learn to confess and tap into your rights in Christ!

Let's look at the account of the "prodigal son" who claimed his rights or his inheritance, but he wasn't walking uprightly at first.

> **And he said, A certain man had two sons: And the younger of them said to his father, Father, give me the portion of goods that falleth to me. And he divided unto them his living. And not many days after the younger son gathered all together, and took his journey into a far country, and there wasted his substance with riotous living. And when he had spent all, there arose a mighty famine in that land; and he began to be in want. And he went and joined himself to a citizen of that country; and he sent him into his fields to feed swine. And he would fain have filled his belly with the husks that the swine did eat: and no man gave unto him. And when he came to himself, he said, How many hired servants of my father's have bread enough and to spare, and I perish with hunger! I will arise and go to my father, and will say unto him, Father, I have sinned**

against heaven, and before thee, And am no more worthy to
be called thy son: make me as one of thy hired servants.
And he arose, and came to his father. But when he was yet a
great way off, his father saw him, and had compassion, and
ran, and fell on his neck, and kissed him.

Luke 15:11-20

All of us can identify in some way with the younger son. In other
words, all of us have sinned and have missed it in some way. We have
all done something wrong in our lives at one time or another.

This younger son said to his father, **Father, give me the portion of
goods that falleth to me. And he divided unto them his living** (Luke
15:12). Then it says, **Not many days after the younger son gathered
all together, and took his journey into a far country, and there
wasted his substance with riotous living** (v. 13).

Verses 14 and 15 say, **And when he had spent all, there arose a
mighty famine in that land; and he began to be in want. And he
went and joined himself to a citizen of that country; and he sent
him into his fields to feed swine.**

Some Christians are perishing because they don't want to go by
the Father's rules. That's why that boy left—he didn't want to go by his
father's rules. He didn't want to take any orders or be in submission to
any authority.

Submit to the Authority of the Father and Be Blessed!

You see, some Christians are feeding swine, so to speak. But they
won't pay their tithes, so they have to get money any way they can.

Now, notice verse 16: **And no man gave unto him.**

Let's go on to verse 17: **And when he came to himself, he said,
How many hired servants of my father's have bread enough and to
spare, and I perish with hunger!**

That boy repented!

You who have heard the truth about tithing and giving offerings but are still not doing it, you're just like the prodigal son. You say to the Father, "Help me. I want what's mine." Then, when the Father blesses you, you head for the good times.

You are like a prodigal son if you're not in the will of God financially. You've gone away from home, so to speak. You've asked the Father for your share, and He's constantly giving you your share. Every time you get your check, you're getting some of your share, but you've cut yourself off from the Lord's ability to *increase* you, because you take that check and go out to the pigpen!

There are a lot of Christians out there enjoying their riotous living, throwing God's money away on cigarettes and booze, but they won't tithe. They need to repent for their riotous living and for robbing God! They've been robbing Him of the good pleasure of blessing them in the way He wants to bless them.

This boy in Luke 15 had enough sense to repent. And, you know, if you'll repent, the Father will welcome you back into the house. If you haven't been tithing, just say, "Father, I've been stealing Your money. But I see the truth, and I'm sorry for my sin."

You see, you have to humble yourself like the prodigal son did when he "came to himself" while feeding those swine. You have to be humble like a child. Jesus said, **Verily I say unto you, Whosoever shall not receive the kingdom of God as a little child, he shall not enter therein** (Mark 10:15).

Receive God's Instruction in Humility

But you can't be as a little child if you're not teachable. If you're saying, "Well, I'm my own person," you won't be able to receive what the Lord is saying to you through His Word.

You see, your spirit has to receive this revelation of divine prosperity. You're not going to receive it if you're not teachable and if you don't admit you need help in this area.

Let's look at Luke 15:17: **And WHEN HE CAME TO HIMSELF, he said, How many hired servants of my father's have bread enough and to spare, and I perish with hunger!**

Verse 20 says, **And he arose, and came to his father. But when he was yet a great way off, his father saw him, and had compassion, and ran, and fell on his neck, and kissed him.**

Notice the son was trying to get his confession out: "Father, I have sinned against heaven, and in your sight, and am no more worthy to be called your son." But the father was busy saying to his servants, **Bring forth the best robe, and put it on him, and put a ring on his hand and shoes on his feet** (v. 22)!

This is how the Father thinks about us! He wants us to have the best. Verse 23 says, **And bring hither the fatted calf, and kill it; and let us eat, and be merry.**

Now let's keep reading in this passage and learn something about the *elder* son in connection with prosperity:

> **Now his elder son was in the field: and as he came and drew nigh to the house, he heard musick and dancing. And he called one of the servants, and asked what these things meant. And he said unto him, Thy brother is come; and thy father hath killed the fatted calf, because he hath received him safe and sound. And he was angry, and would not go in: therefore came his father out, and intreated him. And he answering said to his father, Lo, these many years do I serve thee, neither transgressed I at any time thy commandment: and yet thou never gavest me a kid, that I might make merry with my friends: But as soon as this thy son was come, which hath devoured thy living with harlots, thou hast killed for him the fatted calf. And he said unto him, Son, thou art ever with me, and all that I have is thine. It was meet that we should make merry, and be glad: for this thy brother was dead, and is alive again; and was lost, and is found.**
>
> **Luke 15:25-32**

You know, people are always talking about the boy who left home. But the boy who stayed home was as unwise as his runaway brother.

Verses 29 and 30 say, **And he answering said to his father, Lo, these many years do I serve thee, neither transgressed I at any time thy commandment: and yet thou never gavest me a kid, that I might make merry with my friends: But as soon as this thy son was come, which hath devoured thy living with harlots, thou hast killed for him the fatted calf.**

Now look at verse 31 and see what the father said to the elder son: **And he said unto him, Son, thou art ever with me, and all that I have is thine.**

You see, that elder son is just like you if you are not tapping into what God has for you. You are sitting in the Father's house, in the Kingdom of God. Everything belongs to you, and you're walking uprightly, but you're grumbling and complaining about how everything's against you.

But God is saying to His sons and daughters, "You're in My Kingdom. You are always with Me. All things are yours. All that I have belongs to you. You're in the family, and you're an heir. You're a joint-heir with Jesus. No good thing will I withhold from you as you walk uprightly, so put a claim on what is yours. Lay hold of it."

We need to heed the words of our gracious, loving heavenly Father. We need to claim and receive from Him our inheritance in Christ. As we do, we will be honoring the heritage of prosperity that our Father has provided for us.

In this book, we've been talking about scriptures on money and financial prosperity. If you stay broke after reading this book, shame on you—*that is,* if you stay broke *over a period of time.* You see, if you haven't been walking in it, divine prosperity is not going to happen overnight in your life. You didn't get into debt overnight, but if you keep applying the principles of prosperity, you will come out of whatever situation you may be in, and you'll get into a better situation! Things will start changing for you.

We've already talked about some of the qualifying factors to walking in divine prosperity. One of these factors can be found in a phrase in Psalm 35:27: **Let them shout for joy, and be glad, THAT FAVOUR MY RIGHTEOUS CAUSE: yea, let them say continually, Let the Lord be magnified, which hath pleasure in the prosperity of his servant.**

You see, you have to favor God's righteous cause to walk in God's prosperity. One minister said, "Don't *dress* better than you *give,* and don't *shout* better than you *live."* In other words, don't dress like you have prosperity while you're just tipping God.

Psalm 35:27 is talking about tithing and giving offerings, because God's righteous cause is the propagation of His Gospel to all the earth. If you tithe and by faith start doing things that are right, then you qualify for divine prosperity. You can shout for joy, because you are favoring God's righteous cause!

Love God, Not Money

I can tell you that in every scripture God gives us about being prosperous, He has a qualifier in it. And that qualifying factor keeps you from destroying yourself, because it sees to it that you put first things first. That qualifier puts you in a position where you love God more than you love anything else. And by loving God, when you are elevated financially and in those high places in the blessings of God, you are still stable.

223

Can you see that? It is just like our wise Father to put us in a position not to hurt ourselves. He puts us in a position where we love Him, and by loving Him, we will not destroy ourselves when the blessings begin to come. We will not separate ourselves from Him. Therefore, we can shout for joy and be glad.

Do You Qualify?

Many times, when a minister preaches or teaches about prosperity, people will get excited. They might say, "Hip-hip-hooray!" But not all of them *stay* excited after the Lord poses this question to them: "Do you qualify?"

One way the enemy has tried to disqualify us is by telling us that poverty is godly and that prosperity is *un*godly. I've gone over this before, but I'm going to go back over it again because that statement is a lie. Poverty is not godly. Poverty is of the devil! The Bible says in Galatians 3:13, Christ has redeemed us. If poverty were godly, why would we need to be redeemed from it?

So poverty is not godly; it's of the devil. But we have been redeemed.

Once you know how to qualify for prosperity, it won't be anybody else's fault if you don't prosper. If I tell you how to do it, and if you don't prosper, it's not going to be my fault, your church's fault, your pastor's fault, God's fault or the devil's fault! *It's going to be your own fault!*

Now you know that the curse of the law is threefold. It includes *the second death* (or *spiritual death*), *sickness* and *poverty*.

But through the blood of the Lord Jesus Christ, we have been bought with a price. First Corinthians 6:20 says, **For ye are bought with a price: therefore glorify God in your body, and in your spirit, which are God's.**

You are bought and paid for, and your prosperity is paid for. Now, I ask you the question, "Do you qualify to prosper?" You might say, "Well, yes, I qualify—I'm a child of God!"

But the fact that you are a child of God doesn't qualify you completely to walk in what has been provided. By way of illustration, you may be on a sports team. You may have made the team, but that doesn't necessarily mean you're *playing* in the game.

Well, spiritually, if you are a child of God, you're on the "team," all right. You're in the Body of Christ, so you're on the team. But are you playing in the game? You could play if you practice hard enough. Practice what? Practice God's Word! In other words, practice doing what the Lord told you to do.

Don't Sit on the Sidelines— Get in the Game!

You see, not everybody on a team plays in the game. Some boys and girls hold down the bench! Now, thank God, you are on the team if you are a Christian. And you might get some sprinkling of a blessing while you're on the bench. But if you really want to make some points and bring up the score for the Body of Christ, you need to qualify to get in the game!

Galatians 3:13 lets you know you're on the team, but verse 14 adds a qualifier to show you how to play in the game:

> **Christ hath redeemed us from the curse of the law, being made a curse for us: for it is written, Cursed is every one that hangeth on a tree: That the blessing of Abraham MIGHT come on the Gentiles through Jesus Christ; that we MIGHT receive the promise of the Spirit THROUGH FAITH.**
> **Galatians 3:13,14**

Look at that phrase in verse 14, **through faith.** Somebody might say, "Oh, goodness. I thought the blessing was an automatic thing. I thought that, just because I got saved, was baptized in water and shook the preacher's hand, all the Bible promised me was just going to be mine to enjoy."

No, you still have to qualify. And one of the ways you qualify is by faith. In other words, you have to believe in the blessings of God and learn to walk by faith to obtain them for yourself.

Changing the "Might Nots" to the "Mights"!

It seems that there is many a "might not" in the Body of Christ. In other words, there are people who "might not" ever see the goodness of God on this side of heaven. Certainly, they'll see it in heaven, but in heaven they won't have needs like they have down here. They need to see God's blessings and His goodness in their lives financially on *this* side of heaven! There might be people who will slap themselves when they get to heaven and find out how many of the blessings of God they missed on the earth. They'll say to themselves, *You crazy thing, you! You missed all the blessings of God down on the earth. You could have enjoyed yourself on earth and had a good time on your way to heaven. But you missed it!*

The thief cometh not, but for to steal, and to kill, and to destroy: I am come that they might have life, and that they might have it more abundantly.

John 10:10

Notice Jesus didn't say, "I am come, and you *are definitely going to* have life more abundantly." No, He said, "I am come that you *might* have life more abundantly."

The "might" is where *you* come into the picture. In other words, *you* have more to do with your prosperity than *God* does!

That the blessing of Abraham MIGHT come on the Gentiles through Jesus Christ; that we MIGHT receive the promise of the Spirit through faith.

Galatians 3:14

There's that word "might" twice in one verse! What does that mean? It means there's a possibility that you will walk in the promised blessing. But it does not say that it's necessarily going to happen. Galatians 3:14 means you *might* make it, and you *might not* make it! You might be broke the rest of your life if you don't learn to qualify for divine prosperity!

That's why I want to discuss qualifying for prosperity: I want you to change those "mights" into *realities* in your life. I don't want you to be a "might not" Christian.

Now that's three times we've seen that word "might"—in John 10:10 and Galatians 3:14. And we know that means we *might* and we *might not* walk in God's kind of prosperity and the abundant life.

What we want to do is get rid of the "might nots" in our own lives.

I don't know about you, but I don't want that "Well, I *might* prosper" business in my life. I don't even want there to be a question about it, because where there's a "might," a "might not" will always be right behind me! I want to get as far away from "might not" as I can.

There is a way to be sure you qualify for divine prosperity. You don't have to live in the land of "might nots"!

Stand Your Ground Against the Devil!

Many people have thought, *Well, I'm a Christian, so God is just going to pour the blessing out on me. I'm going to pray all day, and God is just going to give it to me.*

No, He's not. You have to bypass Satan to get the blessing, because Satan is not just going to stand there and let you get God's blessings like they were ripe cherries falling off a tree. No, the devil will oppose you to see if you really believe what you say you believe. So God set those qualifications in place for you to bypass Satan, who's trying to keep the blessing from you.

It's like being on a sports team. If you know the plays of the other team, you are really going to be a good player. Well, you have to know how to get by Satan. Satan is here to cut off your prosperity.

You see, faith is involved here. You have to have faith to stand on God's Word until you see the things you've been believing for. Satan can't stop you or cut you off from the blessing when you are walking by faith and in obedience to God's Word.

Many believers are on the bench when it comes to prosperity. They can jump up and shout and wave their hands and talk about what they're going to do. They can make a lot of noise and fuss, but when it's time to "put the horse to the wagon," so to speak, and actually *do* something, they're not able to play in the game.

Actually, qualifying for your prosperity and playing in the game is not hard. You just have to obey the Bible. It's very simple—if you obey, you eat the good of the land. But if you refuse and rebel, you're *not* going to eat the good of the land (Isaiah 1:19,20).

Choose God's Way, Not the World's Way

There are things to do to qualify for divine prosperity, such as obeying God and walking by faith. But there are also some things you're going to have to *turn down* or *refuse* in order to qualify for prosperity.

> **By faith Moses, when he was born, was hid three months of his parents, because they saw he was a proper child; and they were not afraid of the king's commandment. By faith Moses, when he was come to years, refused to be called the son of Pharaoh's daughter; Choosing rather to suffer affliction with the people of God, than to enjoy the pleasures of sin for a season.**
>
> Hebrews 11:23-25

Look at verse 24: **By faith Moses, when he was come to years, refused to be called the son of Pharaoh's daughter.** What was Moses refusing? He was refusing the throne of Egypt. He could have been in line for the throne and become the pharaoh of Egypt, but he refused it.

If you want godly prosperity, there are some things you, too, are going to have to refuse. Do you remember what Abraham once refused after a battle? The king wanted to give Abraham some of the victor's spoils. But Abraham refused. He said, "No, I don't want any man to say he made me rich" (Genesis 14:23). Abraham did not want that king to contaminate his prosperity.

Don't Be Fooled by Uncertain Riches

You see, you can't go after money. Not everyone who brings you money or who wants to give you something is from God. I tell the ministers who work with me, "Now, I don't mind you being blessed. I *want* you blessed, but don't let anybody 'buy you out' against me." I tell them, "Don't eat at just anybody's house." You see, some people want to feed you, but when they *feed* you, they want to *lead* you!

You have to have the wisdom of God. You don't have to hurt people's feelings; you can just say, "No, thank you."

There are certain things you have to refuse in order to walk in God's kind of prosperity. You can't just grab everything that comes your way.

Now, in refusing the throne of Egypt, Moses refused worldly riches too. Somebody might say, "Moses was crazy to pass up something like that! He could have been rich!" But, you know, there is no such thing as a real "get-rich-quick" scheme that gives you something for nothing.

Certain people will mail you letters that promise you a free gift if you make an appointment to go pick it up. My wife and I received one of those one time. We drove for miles, and when we finally arrived, they told us we had to further qualify for the "gift." They said we had to look at this, that and the other thing before we could claim our prize. It was a sales presentation. I just went back to my car. I said, "There is another way to become prosperous besides all of this foolishness!"

Why do people fall for certain money making schemes? Because they want prosperity! Most people want to prosper, and if a person sees something that looks like a good opportunity to make money, he will go after it.

Some of these people who offer "get-rich-quick" schemes will keep egging you on, feeding you information, little by little, until they have you right where they want you. It's like a man going fishing. He has to keep putting a little bait on that hook or the fish won't bite.

In the same way, some of these schemers will put out a little bait by showing you a really nice prize, but after you drive for miles and miles to see whatever they want to show you, you realize you could have taken the money you spent on the trip and bought *yourself* a TV or some nice "prize." And, many times, when you do business with certain places like that, they will sell your name to other companies, and before you know it, you'll have thirty-five other companies to deal with!

One time I received another letter saying I had been chosen to win a really nice prize. I remember at first I said, "This is it! We've hit the jackpot!" But come to find out, I ended up being the "jack"!

At first I thought, *They chose my name! I'm the chosen of the Lord!* But after it was all over with, I felt so foolish. We should have known better than that. There is no such thing as getting something for nothing.

Even God put some qualifications ahead of His prosperity. There are some things we need to do because if a person gets something for nothing, he's not going to appreciate it or handle it properly.

Refuse All Substitutes

So we could say that another qualification for entering into godly prosperity is refusing a substitute for the real thing. Hebrews 11:25 says, CHOOSING **rather to suffer affliction with the people of God, than to enjoy the pleasures of sin for a season.**

You see, a choice has to be made. Moses chose to suffer affliction with the people of God rather than to enjoy the pleasure of sin for a season. Pleasures came and presented themselves to Moses as substitutes for the real thing—the real call of God upon his life. And Moses made the choice to suffer with the people of God so he could fulfill *God's* purposes for his life rather than to accept the pleasures that Egypt and the throne had to offer.

Sin's pleasures only last for a season. That's why you have to make the right choice. Godly prosperity consists of choices. You have to choose to favor God's righteous cause and not to try to get your prosperity some other way—by being worldly.

Nobody, not even the preacher, can make people tithe if they don't want to. *God* won't even make them tithe. They have a choice. They can choose not to obey the Word. They can choose to forfeit the blessings that come with obedience. But *I* choose to obey God because I know that if I do, I'll eat the good of the land, and I'll be a blessing to others!

So it's a choice, not a feeling. For instance, you can't feel tithing. You just choose to *do* it!

What else does it say about Moses and the choices he made? Hebrews 11:26 says, ESTEEMING the reproach of Christ greater riches than the treasures in Egypt: for he had RESPECT unto the recompence of the reward.

That word "esteeming" means *honoring*. Actually, this verse is a comparison between Christ and Moses. Jesus esteemed the will of God as greater riches than the world. And Moses turned down the treasures of Egypt for Christ.

You, too, will have to make the decision that you'll turn down the treasures of this world for Christ and that you'll honor His righteous cause. And when you do, He will give you even better treasures!

Look at Hebrews 11:27: **By faith he [Moses] FORSOOK Egypt, not fearing the wrath of the king: for he endured, as seeing him who is invisible.**

Remember those four words in Hebrews 11:23-27: (1) *refuse;* (2) *choose;* (3) *honor;* and (4) *forsake.*

Godly Prosperity Is Related to Your Spiritual "Altitude"

We need not try to talk about qualifying for divine prosperity—for God's best for you financially—without going to the book of Third John.

The elder unto the well-beloved Gaius, whom I love in the truth. Beloved, I wish above all things that thou mayest prosper and be in health, even as thy soul prospereth.
3 John 1,2

Now, notice verse 1: **The elder unto the well-beloved Gaius, whom I love in the TRUTH.** Remember, Jesus said something else about truth in John's gospel.

Jesus saith unto him, I am the way, the TRUTH, and the life: no man cometh unto the Father, but by me.
John 14:6

And ye shall know the TRUTH, and the truth shall make
you free.

John 8:32

Do you see another qualification for prosperity in these verses?
John was talking about your soul prospering as a qualifier for experiencing godly financial prosperity. How does your soul prosper? By
your walking in the truth!

Now look at Third John 3 and 4: **For I rejoiced greatly, when the
brethren came and testified of the TRUTH that is in thee, even as
thou walkest in the TRUTH. I have no greater joy than to hear that
my children walk in TRUTH.**

The word "truth" is mentioned three times just in those two verses.

So to qualify for godly prosperity, you have to favor God's righteous cause (Psalm 35:27) by being willing and obedient. You have to
be a doer of the Word by tithing and giving offerings, and you have
to believe in the blessings of God. You have to obtain them through
faith by walking in the truth.

Refuse, Choose, Honor and Forsake

To walk in godly prosperity, you have to *refuse, choose, honor* and
forsake, just as Moses did.

Let's look more closely at those four words:

Refuse. You have to *refuse* the pleasure of sin for a season. In other
words, you have to refuse to get your prosperity the world's way.

Choose. You have to *choose* to do things God's way and to obey
and trust Him in every situation and circumstance.

Honor. You have to *honor* the Lord and His Word by obeying it.
For example, the Bible talks about honoring the Lord with the first-fruits of your increase (Proverbs 3:9).

Forsake. You have to *forsake* the world's system of prosperity and get
into God's system. To do that, you have to learn to pay tithes and give.

I told you that if you are in Christ, you're on the "team," all right,
but that doesn't mean that you are actually playing in the game. You

play the game, so to speak, by doing the things you know you're supposed to do according to the Word.

How would you like to be on a basketball team, for example, and never get the ball? Well, in the Body of Christ, I want the ball! If I'm going to be on the team, I want to get in the game. And I don't just want to get in the game—I want the ball! I wouldn't like to be on a team and just run around on the court, never get the ball and never actually play in the game.

In other words, I want to *do* something in the Body of Christ. And that takes money. And receiving money and divine prosperity takes doing what is right with my finances.

You know, there are some people who, in the natural, will get the ball and hold it from everybody else except their best friend. But, thank God, on *God's* team, we can *all* have the ball!

On God's team, everybody can have his own ball. I've got mine, and I'm shooting every day for higher scores in the Kingdom of God.

Do you have the ball? Are you doing something with the truth you've learned?

I tell you, God's truth is marching on. It will set you free! It'll set you free in the area of finances. It'll put you in a place of being prosperous.

Now I said that if you're willing and obedient, you'll eat the good of the land. Some people are not qualifying for godly prosperity and eating the good of the land, and yet they are good people. But there are guidelines—rules and laws—that have been set in motion for us to follow. And you have to follow those laws.

For instance, the law of sowing and reaping is a law that has to be followed to gain godly prosperity. In other words, you aren't being willing and obedient if you aren't being a giver. You can't claim "good measure, pressed down, shaken together and running over" without meeting the qualification of that verse.

You see, you can't claim the promise or the blessing without meeting the qualification. And I tell you, there is one word that qualifies you to partake of the blessing part of that verse—the "good measure, pressed down, shaken together and running over." What is that one word? *Give.*

Now let's look at some scriptures that support the qualification of walking by faith and walking in the truth of God's Word in everything you do.

> **Blessed is the man that walketh not in the counsel of the ungodly, nor standeth in the way of sinners, nor sitteth in the seat of the scornful. But his delight is in the law of the Lord; and in his law doth he meditate day and night. And he shall be like a tree planted by the rivers of water, that bringeth forth his fruit in his season; his leaf also shall not wither; and whatsoever he doeth shall prosper.**
>
> **Psalm 1:1-3**

These verses contain many qualifications. But there is a complementary verse that goes with them.

> **This book of the law shall not depart out of thy mouth; but thou shalt meditate therein day and night, that thou mayest observe to do according to all that is written therein: for THEN thou shalt make thy way prosperous, and then thou shalt have good success.**
>
> **Joshua 1:8**

Notice the word "then" in Joshua 1:8. It's not *"before* then." "Then" is just like "might" in Galatians 3:14, which says you *might* have the blessing, and you *might not* have it. It's up to *you.* If you obey the first part of Joshua 1:8, **This book of the law shall not depart out of thy mouth; but thou shalt meditate therein day and night, that thou mayest observe to do according to all that is written therein...**, then you will have the blessing of the second part of the verse: **For THEN thou shalt make thy way prosperous, and then thou shalt have good success.**

Now, Joshua 1:8 says you will make your way prosperous *after* you do certain things. The blessing will come *after* you "let not the Word depart out of your mouth." The blessing will come *after* you "meditate therein day and night." The blessing will come *after* you "observe to do according to all that is written therein."

Now, according to this verse, who's going to make your way prosperous? It says, **THOU shalt....** Who's "thou"? "Thou" is *you!* And what is the qualifying factor for you to be able to make your way prosperous? You have to be a doer of Psalm 1:1-3 and Joshua 1:8.

Remember, we read in Third John 2, **Beloved, I wish above all things that thou mayest prosper and be in health, EVEN AS THY SOUL PROSPERETH.** Well, these passages in Psalm 1:1-3 and Joshua 1:8 are talking about *soul* prosperity.

The psalmist said, **Blessed is the man that walketh not in the counsel of the ungodly...** (Psalm 1:1). Walking in the counsel of the ungodly will keep you broke. The next part of that verse reads, **Nor standeth in the way of sinners....** Standing in the way of sinners will keep you broke. The rest of that verse says, **Nor sitteth in the seat of the scornful.** Sitting in the seat of the scornful will keep you broke too.

Verse 2 says, **But his delight is in the law of the Lord; and in his law doth he meditate day and night.** Then what happens? **And he shall be like a tree planted by the rivers of water, that bringeth forth his fruit in his season; his leaf also shall not wither; and whatsoever he doeth shall prosper** (v. 3).

And he shall be like a tree.... What kind of tree? A planted tree. A planted tree by the rivers of water—a tree "that bringeth forth his fruit in his season."

What else? His leaf shall not wither! And the rest of that verse is almost too good to read! It says, **And WHATSOEVER HE DOETH SHALL PROSPER!**

Go for the Gold!

Listen, Christian, there is a place you can get to with God where it seems like everything you touch turns to gold! That may sound sacrilegious or even fictitious, but our God is a big God! He is able to do exceeding abundantly above all we can ask or think by His Spirit who works in us (Ephesians 3:20)!

I'm at that place by the grace of God. I'm at that place, and I'm going to stay there. I've gotten to the place where I sometimes just *think* about the blessings, and here they come! Somewhere down the line I may say what it is I want. But I don't have to say it over and over again. I don't have to be a "parrot" anymore, just parroting the same scriptures over and over again before I'm in faith enough to receive whatever it is I desire from God.

Someone once said, "Well, do you have any scriptures for that prayer?"

I answered, "Well, do you have any that are against it?"

Ephesians 3:20 says, **Now unto him that is able to do exceeding abundantly above all that we ask or think, according to the power** THAT WORKETH **in us.** Things start happening when that power is at work in you!

I tell you, angels get tired of sitting around with nothing to do because Christians are not talking right or acting right. When they hear somebody so much as *think* right, they probably say, "Well, he hasn't said anything yet, but let's go. We're ready; we're tired of sitting here on our wings."

Those angels are so ready to go, they say, "We just *dare* him to think it out loud!" I mean, they are just *looking* for somebody to give God's blessings to!

The Role of Angels in Prosperity

You need to know how to put your angels to work. Your angels will go out and get that money for you and bring it to you. They'll go out and influence somebody to give to you.

Somebody asked, "Do angels really work for us?" Look at Hebrews, chapter 1:

> **But to which of the angels said he at any time, Sit on my right hand, until I make thine enemies thy footstool? Are they** [talking about God's angels] **not all ministering spirits,** SENT FORTH TO MINISTER FOR THEM WHO SHALL BE HEIRS OF SALVATION?
>
> **Hebrews 1:13,14**

All through the Bible, we see angels ministering to people. Angels are real today, and they are still activated or sent forth on behalf of men. As a matter of fact, every individual has his own angel (Matthew 18:10).

Supernatural things are real. Some of my own church people have seen angels. One of them is my oldest son.

My son Leroy Jr. had bunkbeds in his room when he was younger. One day years ago, he was lying on the top bed with his hands behind his head, just looking up at the ceiling. Suddenly, he saw a big creature, an angel, with his wings spread out. The angel was hovering over my son's bed.

My son tried to call out to us. He told us later that his mouth was moving, but nothing would come out! He was in awe of this creature. I tell you, a holy reverence will come upon a person when he comes in contact with the supernatural things of God.

Another time when Leroy Jr. was even younger, we were vacationing in Orlando, Florida, at Disney World with my brother and sister-in-law. We watched a parade, and later, when we were all talking about what we'd seen that day, my son asked his mother, "What else did you see?" They talked back and forth a few minutes about various aspects of the parade. Then my son said, "I saw Jesus! He was standing right over there," and he pointed in the direction where he saw the Lord.

My wife asked him, "Well, what did He have on?"

Leroy Jr. described Jesus as wearing a white gown with sandals. My wife continued to question our son. He was only four or five years old at the time. We knew he wasn't just trying to show off or get attention, because he said, "Don't tell my uncle or aunt." You see, sometimes spiritual things will bring a fear and a reverence upon you, and you don't want to "blab" them to everybody.

I'm talking about the supernatural things of God because I want you to realize that angels and the things of the Spirit are real. I'm telling you about some supernatural incidents that will help you to understand that the things of the Spirit of God are real.

My daddy died in a train accident in 1969. He was coming back home from taking my sister to work, and he drove into the path of a train. It hit him on his "blind side."

I never knew of my daddy confessing the Lord Jesus Christ. I never knew of my daddy ever going to church, telling me about Jesus or reading the Bible. He was just a good man, and he took care of his family.

I used to go to church with my mama. I went through all the church programs, got sprinkled and said prayers, but I wasn't saved. I was raised as a lost church boy!

When I became a preacher, I wanted to "shoot straight" and not lie or exaggerate about the truth. Some people are always wanting to put everybody who dies in heaven by saying, "Well, who knows, maybe they made a last minute decision and made it at the last second."

But I didn't want to do that. I'd never heard my daddy confess Christ, so I just said, "My daddy went to hell. I won't see him anymore."

Well, one day, my family and I were sitting at the kitchen table, and my youngest son had a vision. You see, many times children are more in tune to God than we adults are. As adults, we make up our own minds about how we're going to do things and how we're going to believe. But the Bible says you have to become as a little child to receive the things of God and His Spirit (Mark 10:15; Luke 18:17).

Well, my youngest son had a vision. Afterward, he told me, "Daddy, I saw your daddy when he was killed in that train accident."

My son said that he was up in heaven in the vision and then came down, right through the roof of the car and saw my daddy lying there in that car. Then my son said he saw him in his coffin (he called it a box).

Now, my son never met my daddy. He'd never seen him and didn't know much about the train accident except little bits and pieces he'd heard here and there.

My son said, "I went back up into heaven and saw your daddy again. I was about to ask him, 'What are you doing here?' but the Lord told me, 'No.'"

That's what my son said! As I sat there listening to him, I got the interpretation of that quickly. I knew exactly what that meant. The Lord was telling him, "That's none of your business what he is doing here." But from that point on, I knew beyond a shadow of doubt that my daddy was in heaven. My son spoke to us at that table with divine authority and with the anointing. I knew I'd heard from God.

The Lord did that to set me straight about my daddy. I repented. I tell you, a lot of people are going to be in heaven who you think aren't going to be there. And some people you think are going to be there *aren't* going to be there!

I shared all that with you because I want you to know that the things of the Spirit are real. There are supernatural beings to help you in the realm of finances. The Bible says, **Are they not all MINISTERING SPIRITS...** (Hebrews 1:14).

What does that phrase, "ministering spirits," mean? That means angels are there to *minister!*

When my wife and I were first coming into the land of prosperity, we would send out angels, saying, "In Jesus' Name, go, ministering spirits, and cause the money to come." And we believed with all of our hearts that undoubtedly they went when we gave the command. And the money always came!

Put Your Angels To Work!

As I said, I believe angels get disgusted sometimes. I believe they go back to the Lord and say, "Lord, assign me to someone else. This person is as ignorant as he can be. He doesn't know that supreme help is available to him. I'm tired of following him around when he's so ignorant. Give me another assignment or let me go help *Reverend Thompson's* angel!"

I'm being humorous, but I said that to get my point across. Every one of us has an angel. And you can speak to your angel according to the Word and send him out in Jesus' Name.

Goodness, how we live below our means as children of God! The Bible says that God made man **a little lower than the angels, and hast crowned him with glory and honour** (Psalm 8:5). We are in a divine setup by God Almighty! Jehovah Jireh is our Provider. We have a divine commodity, a divine force, called faith that can cause things to come out of the spirit world and into the natural world to help us.

The Bible says, **Blessed be the God and Father of our Lord Jesus Christ, who hath blessed us with all spiritual blessings in heavenly**

places in Christ (Ephesians 1:3). God has blessed us with all *spiritual* blessings. But we have to realize that that which is physical was spiritual first, because it came from God!

You see, we have the ability to frame our own world by calling things that be not as though they were (Romans 4:17)! So we need to call prosperity into being and line ourselves up with the qualifications for prosperity. We should not sit in the seat of the scornful or stand in the way of sinners. We need to delight ourselves in the Lord and in *His* Word (Psalm 1:1,2)!

So we know that ministering spirits are angels that are sent forth to minister for us. It says, **For them who shall be heirs of salvation** (Hebrews 1:14).

Who are heirs of salvation? You are! Well, do you qualify? It's up to you—*you* decide.

As I said before, some people don't qualify because they haven't heard that God is the God of prosperity. They still think He's the God of poverty. Others don't qualify because they don't believe it when they hear that God is the God of prosperity and that He wants us to have abundance.

One time I heard a minister say that if you're barely getting along in life, you're serving the wrong god! He said you're serving the "barely-getting-along" god.

But God Almighty—El Shaddai—is not a "barely-getting-along" god! He is the God who is more than enough!

I know what that minister was talking about. I served that "barely-getting-along" god for years before I found out the truth that God wanted me to prosper. Back then, I only had one suit, and it was so old and had been ironed with so much spray starch, it was shining like lightning! I pressed that thing every which way but loose! All the lining was falling out.

I was serving the wrong god. I was serving the traditional, religious, poverty god. But we, as Christians, are heirs (Romans 8:17)!

We are heirs of God and joint-heirs with Jesus Christ. We are heirs of salvation, and Hebrews 1:14 said, **Are they not all ministering spirits, sent forth to minister for them who shall be heirs of salvation?**

Now to relate that to prosperity, ministering spirits will minister to you in the area of finances. But you have to believe that prosperity is for you before you can act on it by faith. If you believe that money cometh, then those ministering spirits can minister finances on your behalf.

Learn To Think Big in God!

Sometimes it's a person's wrong thinking and wrong beliefs that hold him back and disqualify him from receiving divine prosperity. Some people need to learn to think "rich" instead of thinking "poverty and lack" and doing without.

I never used to fly first class. God had to really work with me. I would pass those big seats in first class and go right back to the small seats on a plane. Like a trained dog, so to speak, I'd go back to row twenty-six, right over the wing!

The Spirit of God once said to me, "Why do you keep passing up those first class seats? When are you going to have faith for those seats?"

I said, "Lord, I don't want to spend money like that," and I'd go on back to row twenty-six.

One time something happened, and the airline bumped me to first class. I was with two other gentlemen, and there was only one seat left in the coach section. So they put two of us up in first class.

I sat in that big, nicely upholstered seat with plenty of elbow room and privacy to meditate and pray quietly. And it felt good!

Then, another time, something else happened, and I ended up in first class again. (I know it was the Lord who kept bumping me up to first class!) But then, after that, I made up my mind that God is a first class God, and from that day forward, I began to fly first class!

I made up my mind I wasn't going to pass up those big seats anymore! So I fly first class now, and I'm not bothered by it at all.

Some people will never change until someone shows them it can be done. For example, a fellow minister, one of my sons in the faith, used to drive for miles to attend some of our meetings. I talked him into believing God for a nice big car. I said, "Son, you're killing your-self driving all those miles in that car you have!"

Well, I preached a meeting for him at his church, and afterward, his church membership doubled. And in the process of time, the finances increased too. Then he, too, got blessed with more money and went out and bought himself a nice big car. He had long legs, so he really needed a larger car!

Then I talked him into flying first class. I told him, "With those long legs of yours, you need to sit in first class when you fly."

He took my advice. Now he can stretch out and lay his seat back and be comfortable when he flies.

You see, if someone can show you something can be done, it helps you have faith for it. Before someone showed you a particular thing could be done, you might not have even considered doing it. But once someone shows you that it can be done, it can help you change your thinking and increase your faith.

Some people say, "Well, we need to fly in the coach section to save money." But God has plenty of money! You don't need to be "tight" and try to hold on to every penny you have. That is what's wrong with some people. They're tight, their faith never grows and their circumstances never change; they end up eating where they don't want to eat, sleeping where they don't want to sleep and going in the financial direction that they don't want to go!

You need to change some of the ways you've been thinking in the area of finances! If you're thinking poverty, you're not in the will of God, because poverty is not God's will. *Prosperity* is God's will for you.

The devil has tried to keep Christians, and especially preachers, broke. A congregation will be like their preacher. In other words: Like teacher, like pupil. But I'm not broke anymore! I'll never be broke another day in my life! God is giving me the good measure, pressed down, shaken together and running over. He's giving me exceeding abundantly above all I can ask or think according to the power that worketh in me!

If you want to walk in godly prosperity, you don't need to be in a church that is just scraping by, where the pastor just talks about having God's blessings in the "sweet by-and-by."

The "sweet by-and-by" is going to take care of itself. You need to talk about the "now-and-now"!

Learn to think big. It will help your faith. I read a book titled *Gifted Hands* by Ben Carson,[1] a black author who grew up in a lower-class family. As he was growing up, his mother worked in other people's houses for a living. She would see all the nice things others had, and she would go home, sit her son down, and tell him about the things those people had in their houses. Then she'd tell him, "Son, you can have the same things. You can live like that too."

She was shaping that young boy's thinking. She was teaching him to think big and to dream big. She'd tell him, "You can be anything you want to be," and she pushed him to excel at school.

Her son rose up to be head of his class. Then he went on to college and medical school and became a leading surgeon in the country, making some of the most money in the world.

So, you see, you have to get your thinking straight. Thinking in line with God's Word is a part of qualifying for divine prosperity. If you grew up poor or you're not prospering now in life, you can't think according to the past or according to your circumstances. You have to think big according to God's Word. When you obey, believe and act on the Word, you will be well on your way to qualifying for abundant prosperity and entering into God's land of plenty for you!

---

[1] Benjamin S. Carson. *Gifted Hands.* New York: Zondervan, 1997.

Part 1

For ye know the grace of our Lord Jesus Christ, that, though he was rich, yet for your sakes he became poor, that ye through his poverty might be rich.
—2 CORINTHIANS 8:9

You know, anyone can go after money, but the Lord has made it possible for money to come after you!

You see, when those two words "Money cometh" came to me, God didn't say to me, *"You* go to money." No, He said, "Money *cometh!"* And, really, that's in line with Luke 6:38: **Give, and it shall be given unto you; good measure, pressed down, and shaken together, and running over, shall men give into your bosom. For with the same measure that ye mete withal it shall BE MEASURED TO you again.**

In this chapter, we're going to look further at the difference between the world's system of prosperity and God's system of prosperity. There is a difference. God wants the Body of Christ to be rich, but He doesn't want us to be going after money.

Also in this chapter, I'm going to help you so that you'll never have to worry or be concerned, saying, "Am I worthy to have money?" or "Is this too much money for me to have?" or "Should I even be thinking about and believing for money?" The devil will not be able to hoodwink you and convince you that because you have money, you're out of the will of God. We're going to deal with those areas in this chapter.

Let's look again at our text:

For ye know the grace of our Lord Jesus Christ, that, though he was rich, yet for your sakes he became poor, that ye through his poverty might be rich.

2 Corinthians 8:9

Look at this phrase, **that ye through his poverty might be rich.** How did our Lord Jesus Christ become poor for us? By being made a curse for us:

> **Christ hath redeemed us from the curse of the law, BEING MADE A CURSE for us: for it is written, Cursed is every one that hangeth on a tree:**
>
> **That the blessing of Abraham might come on the Gentiles through Jesus Christ; that we might receive the promise of the Spirit through faith.**
>
> Galatians 3:13,14

One of the reasons why people have thought that it is ungodly to be rich is that they have thought that Jesus Himself was poor when He was here on the earth.

But Jesus became poor when He died on the cross as our Savior, Redeemer and Substitute. *That's* when Jesus became poor—when He became a curse for us—not in His earthly ministry.

Jesus Was Not Poor in His Earthly Ministry

In Jesus' earthly ministry, He ruled the laws of nature. I mean, Jesus could have guests of more than 5,000 and take five loaves and two fishes and feed them all (Matthew 14:19,21)! That doesn't sound very poor to me!

And when it came to tax time, this "poor" Jesus told Peter, "You go catch a fish, and the first fish you catch, reach in its mouth, and our tax money will be there" (Matthew 17:27). That doesn't sound poor to me!

Also, if the Man was so poor, why did He have a treasurer? Poor people do not have treasurers. To have a *treasurer,* you have to have *treasures!* And there must have been quite a bit of money in that treasury, because Jesus had a large staff traveling with Him, and He had to feed them and take care of them. And then, when Judas, the treasurer, was stealing out of the bag (John 12:6), there was apparently enough in the bag that the others wouldn't even notice that he was taking some of the money out for himself.

We've been taught about "poor Jesus." But, Jesus wasn't poor. Those who teach that He was poor use this scripture: **The foxes have holes, and the birds of the air have nests; but the Son of man hath not where to lay his head** (Matthew 8:20).

But, you see, Jesus was a traveling evangelist, so He wasn't worried about having a home. One of Jesus' followers was the rich Joseph of Arimathea. Jesus could have stayed at Joseph's house from time to time if He'd wanted to.

Jesus knew the earth wasn't His permanent dwelling place. Actually, we'd better know that too. One of the things that robs us in this life is that we try to have and hold on to what we have as if we were going to be here for eternity, but we're not.

Jesus knew He was "just passing through." He knew He was going back to the Father's house. But He came down here to tell us how to live on the earth. And during His three years of ministry, He showed us every angle of how to be blessed and how to draw from the wealth of the Father.

Jesus always had what He needed in His earth walk. He wasn't poor. For example, when the Lord got ready for His donkey ride, He told two of His disciples to go and get the donkey. He told them, "When they ask you why you want it, just tell them the Master needs it." Then it says that the man who apparently owned the donkey told the disciples to go ahead and take the donkey to Jesus. (See Matthew 21:1-11.)

Then when the Master got ready to have what we call the Lord's Supper, He didn't need to worry or concern Himself with renting an auditorium or convention center. No, He sent His disciples to tell a certain man to prepare his upper room (Matthew 26:18)!

I mean, Jesus lived in complete authority over His financial situation. So when it says in Second Corinthians 8 that Jesus became poor, it isn't talking about Jesus' becoming poor when He was here on earth. The Bible says Jesus had the Spirit without measure (John 3:34). He knew how to flow with His Father! Jesus had no problems in the area of finances. Whatever He needed, He had.

Over and over again in Jesus' earth walk, we see Him controlling nature by the laws of prosperity. Jesus operated the laws of prosperity while He was here on earth to show us how to put those laws into operation in our own lives.

No, Second Corinthians 8:9 wasn't talking about Jesus' becoming poor in His ministry on earth. You need to identify just when Jesus became poor, so you can stop believing in Him as "poor little Jesus" and start believing that He was *made* poor so that you *would not have to be.*

In Jesus' death on the cross, a great exchange took place. When Jesus became poor on the cross, in His great act of redemption, there was a place-swapping!

Jesus Became Poor on the Cross— That We Might Become Rich!

Many people need to get beyond believing Jesus was poor just because He had nowhere to lay His head! That verse doesn't mean He didn't have the means to get lodging! It means that He was constantly traveling, and to be His disciple meant you had to travel too. His disciples had to keep on "rolling." They wouldn't be able to sleep in the same beds all the time.

(I've done my own share of traveling in the ministry. Man, I'd stay in one hotel room, and about the time I'd get comfortable, I'd have to go to another meeting and stay in another hotel room someplace else. I might be in one city, and just about the time I'd get to know which street to turn on to get somewhere, I'd have to go to another city and relearn all the streets!)

Jesus was not poor in His earthly ministry. I'm sharing with you some of the things the Lord taught me when I first started down the road to prosperity. But since we're talking about "Money cometh" and not going after money, I should say it like this: The Lord showed me these things when prosperity started down the road to *me.*

When You're in Faith, Prosperity Will Find You!

I made it possible for prosperity to start down the road to find me because I left a trail of faith behind me by operating in the laws of prosperity. Deuteronomy 28 says that the blessings of God will *overtake* you! You don't have to go after the blessings. You don't have to go after money. Money will come after you!

"Money cometh" does not mean going after money. It's not covetousness. It's not thinking, *Money, money, money. I've got to have more money.*

No, "Money cometh" means that when you begin to fulfill the Father's will and you see that it is the Father's will for you to be blessed, money will constantly be finding its way to you. But you have to operate in faith. That means giving or sowing in faith and reaping in faith too.

Really, when you are doing the Father's will, obeying Him and His Word and acting on it in faith, you don't have to be concerned about money. You just put Him first, and He will make sure you have the money that you need.

You see, godly prosperity is opposite worldly prosperity. Someone who is seeking worldly prosperity, always thinking about money, going after it, conniving to get it and scheming every way he can to get money.

As the revelation of godly prosperity dawns on the Body of Christ, you can be sure the devil will zoom in and begin to tell the Church, "Look here, you can't accept this prosperity message. You're getting worldly if you do, because accepting this message means you've just got money on your mind."

The devil and even some church people will accuse you, saying, "All you think about is money. You should be thinking about feeding the poor and needy."

But you can't feed the hungry without money! You'll be hungry yourself if you don't get ahold of this prosperity message!

So you can't look at the prosperity message with the understanding that Jesus was poor on the earth, because He wasn't. It was somewhere else that He became poor. And we have to see that in order to understand how we can receive prosperity.

Let's look at our text again:

> For ye know the grace of our Lord Jesus Christ, that, though he was rich, yet for your sakes he became poor, that ye through his poverty might be rich.
>
> 2 Corinthians 8:9

Look at that phrase **Though he was rich....** Some say, "Well, yes, when Jesus was up in heaven with the Father, He was rich." But we already established that Jesus was prosperous on the earth too. You see, if you have the means to get money as Jesus did, you can't be poor!

Prosperity is due you as a believer, because in Jesus' death, burial and resurrection, He took your place in poverty. He took your place in *poverty* so you could take His place in *prosperity*.

Jesus took our place in poverty, but He didn't stay there any longer than three days! Having taken on the sinful state of man, He couldn't stand being broke any longer! He came up on the third day! He said, in effect, "Enough of this!" and He arose, victorious over death, hell and the grave, and over your poverty. Poverty should not keep you down anymore since Jesus arose victorious over the devil and poverty!

Second Corinthians 8:9 says, **Though he was rich....** But that's not just talking about when Jesus was with the Father in heaven. Jesus came down and took on the form of man and existed here on earth for thirty-three years. But for those thirty-three years, He was prosperous. He was in control of nature and had authority over the laws of prosperity.

Let that truth dawn on you. If you've been bound by a poverty mentality, you can rise above it through the Word and move out in the area of prosperity where the Lord wants you to be.

Notice another phrase in Second Corinthians 8:9, **Yet for your sakes he became poor, that ye through his poverty MIGHT be rich.**

There's that word, "might," again. We already learned that the word "might" in this context means you *might* or *might not* be rich. It all depends on what you believe and whether your actions correspond to your faith.

You see, it's through faith that you turn your "mights" into realities. Jesus redeemed you from the curse of the law. He was made a curse for you. He took your poverty for you. He redeemed you from poverty. In His going to the cross, He swapped places with you, that, through His becoming poor, you *might* become rich!

Jesus Redeemed Us So That We Might Receive Blessings, Not Curses!

So what are you going to believe?

On the cross, Jesus became poor. He became a curse. For a moment in time, He stripped Himself of His power and His ability to operate in the laws of prosperity so that He could swap places with us. He was temporarily separated from God. Then, He took authority over the enemy, rose from the dead and went to glory to endorse us as recipients of what He did for us. He enabled us to walk in the same law of prosperity that He Himself walked in when He was on the earth.

Jesus became a curse for us, **that the BLESSINGS of Abraham might come on the Gentiles through Jesus Christ; that we might receive the promise of the Spirit through faith** (Galatians 3:14).

Notice, that says, "That the *blessing* might come on us." It doesn't say, "That the *curse* might come on us!" Being broke is a curse; it's not a blessing. You don't have to have the mind of a genius to figure that out. When you're broke, your car's out of gas, your refrigerator is empty, your baby's crying because he's hungry and your spouse is grouchy because of debt, distress and discontentment—that is a *curse!* It's *terrible* to be broke!

Let's look again at the blessing of Abraham. One aspect of Abraham's blessing was that he was *very* rich. Lot, Abraham's nephew, settled down for awhile with Abraham and became very blessed. His blessing was a result of his relationship with Abraham. Abraham blessed that boy so much that when they were in the same place with their sheep, their servants and workmen began arguing over whose sheep were going to eat where. Abraham said, "Look, you just go ahead and take the place you want, and I'll just go where you're not going because the two of us can no longer stay in the same place. We've got too much." (See Genesis 13:5-12.)

Four Little Words—One Simple Rule:
Always Keep God First!

Abraham was made rich by God because he obeyed God fully and always put God first. "Money cometh" today means a person is falling in line with God's laws of prosperity. Money will run that person down just like it did Abraham.

Money will look for you and find you when you are doing the right things according to God's Word! I'm going to show you how to do that.

There is a clear and simple principle to set up for yourself if you want to walk in "Money cometh" and not in "money covetousness." Following this principle will set you up to operate and function properly in God's laws of prosperity. It will always ensure that you are thinking about money properly and that you're handling your money properly.

What is the principle? It's made up of four little words: *Always keep God first.*

You see, when the devil or people come to accuse you that you're worldly because you're walking in prosperity, you can always tell which side of the ledger you're operating on by measuring yourself by those four words. If you're operating in godly prosperity, those four words will be the line of demarcation. They will decide for you whether you are operating in godly prosperity or not. They will decide whether you're operating in "Money cometh" or "money covetousness."

Every demon and every person who wants to argue over your prosperity can be put to silence by those four simple words. When you're operating in the principle of always keeping God first in your heart, in what you say, in your giving, in your praise, in your worship—in your entire lifestyle—then no devil, no tradition, no ecclesiastical authority nor anyone else can tell you that you're out of the will of God.

Now think about that for a minute. In every avenue of your life, do you have Him first? Do you have something else on your agenda that has a little more value in your life than pleasing God and doing His will and His Word?

You see, when you talk about loving God, you're talking about loving His will, His Word, His way, His covenant, His program, His desire and His heart! That means you are willing to fulfill Isaiah 1:19, **If ye be willing and obedient, ye shall eat the good of the land.**

So always keep God first. When you do, you are saying, "I am willing, and I am obedient in whatever God tells me to do."

You are either in line for godly prosperity or out of line for godly prosperity. Just ask yourself, *Am I putting God first?* (If you need help judging yourself, here's one guideline: If you kept God first, then this morning, the first person you talked to was Him.)

If you're going to keep God first, you're going to have to be conscious of His presence all the time. You must constantly have the consciousness of His presence, His goodness and His provision uppermost in your heart and mind. You're going to have to live aware that He's the One who's keeping you breathing. He's the One who's keeping your heart pumping.

Having constant communion and fellowship with the Father is keeping God first. Consecrating yourself to Him is keeping Him first. For example, asking Him what He wants you to do with your legs, feet, hands, mouth and pocketbook is being consecrated to Him!

> **But seek ye first the kingdom of God, and his righteousness; and all these things shall be added unto you.**
>
> **Matthew 6:33**

I like to say it this way: "Seek ye first the Kingdom of God, and His righteousness; and *all things are yours*"!

> **Therefore let no man glory in men. For ALL THINGS ARE YOURS.**
>
> **1 Corinthians 3:21**

Are you seeking first the Kingdom of God and His righteousness? If you are, then the Bible says all things are yours.

If you're *not* seeking first the Kingdom of God, you can repent and make an adjustment today. Too many people just say, "Oh, yeah, I'm seeking first the Kingdom" without even thinking about what they are saying. But it is damaging to your character to say you're living something you're not really living, especially if you are a preacher.

A Practical Example of "Seeking First the Kingdom"

Let me give you a good example from a preacher's point of view of how to seek first the Kingdom of God.

I used to attend funerals from time to time in a certain denomination, and from the pulpit, some of the preachers who were ministering at those funerals would publicly attack what I believed. You see, I'd gotten filled with the Holy Ghost and had become involved in Word of Faith circles. Instead of comforting the dead person's loved ones, these preachers would actually start fussing about the Holy Ghost. I mean, this dead person's relatives might all have been going to hell, but instead of ministering to them, the preacher would cut down my doctrine about the Holy Ghost and faith from the pulpit!

I told the Lord, "I don't like to go to these funerals. But Lord, I want to experience what it means to seek first Your Kingdom in this situation. You know I need to go to some of these funerals to be there for the friends and family members. I need to be there when they're suffering. So please show me how to handle this situation. I'm tired of handling it myself."

I asked the Lord, "If I get called on or get a chance to say anything from the pulpit, what shall I say? What would You have me say?"

I started praying that way because it dawned on my spirit, "Ask the Lord Jesus what *He* would say tonight." So I began to pray, "Jesus, You know what You would say if You were ministering. What would *You* say? I want to say what You would say."

I'm talking about seeking first the Kingdom of God. I would ask myself, *What would Jesus do? He would seek the Kingdom.* And I knew He knew how to seek the Kingdom, too, because in His earth walk, He always sought the Father and spoke what God would have Him speak.

Jesus' seeking the Father was a matter of the Kingdom seeking the Kingdom! Jesus was and is and always will be the King of the Kingdom.

So I knew that if I could find out what He would do, I would be seeking the Kingdom of God too.

Jesus left us a manual, so to speak, in the Word that tells us what He would do in certain situations. If you really want to operate in the laws of godly prosperity, then practice putting God first, always, in everything, in every situation. At every gathering you attend, make sure you "save a seat" for Jesus. Make sure the Lord is welcome at all your functions.

We're actually talking about the balance of prosperity—how to tell if you're walking in godly prosperity or if you're trying to get prosperity the world's way. In other words, "Is money coming after you, or are you going after money?"

God Owns Everything—We Own Nothing

Here's another way to stay balanced in godly prosperity: Thoroughly understand the fact that we don't own anything—God just lets us use the things He gives us. Keep that in mind, and that will keep you balanced! In other words, you don't own your house, your cars and so forth. God is letting you use those things. Having that attitude will keep you from getting caught up with money and material possessions.

Certainly, a person could get caught up in just following after things. But we need to realize that a person can prosper with the right attitude and not be sinning at all. In fact, it is the will of God that we prosper. We just have to remember to always keep Him first and think, *God owns everything; I own nothing.*

Thinking that way will help you detach yourself from things and always keep God first so God can give you more. This is where the blessing comes. We don't own anything. God just lets us use things. And He'll let you use some good things if you get in His will. I mean, He'll let you use His best!

So think, *God owns everything, and I own nothing. The things that I have, God is letting me use.*

Every now and then, I lift both hands in the air to the Lord and call out my wife's name, my children's names and everything I have. I name it all out loud and say, "Lord, do whatever You want to do with me and with all that I have—we're Yours."

I tell Him, "Every dollar and everything I have—my cars, my yard and the trees in my yard—belong to You. And I want to bring glory to You in my life."

And, you know, as often as I do that, the Lord says, "I'm going to trust you with more. You're the kind of fellow I'm looking for to really bless."

We're talking about balance, but lest you go to the other extreme and think God doesn't really want you to have anything, you need to settle in your mind once and for all the fact that God wants you blessed! He wants you rich. He wants you out of debt. That's why we've been talking about tithing and giving, sowing and reaping and putting God first in everything. Don't hoard what the Lord gives. Loose it, and more will come!

Here's another guideline to follow to keep yourself balanced in prosperity and tap into God's kind of prosperity (we've already referred to it briefly in the book of Deuteronomy): *humility.* The following are some scriptures that talk about being humble before the Lord:

> By HUMILITY and the fear of the Lord are riches, and honour, and life.
>
> **Proverbs 22:4**

> True humility and respect for the Lord lead a man to richest honor and long life.
>
> **Proverbs 22:4** TLB

> HUMBLE yourselves therefore under the mighty hand of God, that he may exalt you in due time.
>
> **1 Peter 5:6**

Blessed are the MEEK [or humble]: for they shall inherit the earth.

Matthew 5:5

What does it say about the meek? Does it say they shall inherit *heaven?* Yes, they'll inherit heaven, but it says they shall inherit the *earth!*

Humility and the Fear of the Lord

What is true humility and the fear of the Lord? *Always keeping God first and realizing that He owns everything; we own nothing.*

Respect for the Lord means reverence for Him. What does that mean? Well, it would be irreverent for you to be blessed by God and then not follow His guidelines for your business affairs. When you don't follow His guidelines and His Word, it's as if you were saying to Him, "I don't care what You say." And then telling Him how much you love Him is vain. He doesn't believe you. He *can't* believe you, because if you really loved Him, you'd be following His guidelines and keeping Him first. You see, your actions speak louder than your words.

Tithing and giving are not for God's benefit. *Tithing and giving are not even for the church where you are giving.* Certainly, the local church will benefit from your tithe. That's the way God set it up. But tithing and giving are for *you* because a freedom and an abundance of joy and peace come upon you when you get in the will of God, especially in the area of money.

When I first learned to turn loose of God's money, I became a giant in the faith realm. I didn't have much money then, but I became a giant in faith. I felt big for loosing that money, even before I had very much money! I felt rich by faith before I ever saw a dime, because I'd acted in faith on God's Word. I knew I was in the will of God.

Before I started obeying God concerning the tithe, when others would get up and testify about tithing, I would sit there, wishing they'd talk about something else. That's what you'll do if you're guilty. I was guilty. But then, when I started tithing and giving like I was supposed to, heaven came down to bless me, and I've been blessed ever since!

Some people are just waiting for a revelation that will make them loose their tithes to God. But they will not get the revelation until they get *into* the revelation. They need to go ahead and respect and revere the Lord and do what they know He wants them to do.

Do you desire to prosper? Do you desire to prosper and be in health even as your soul prospers (3 John 2)? Here's where it starts: in true humility and respect for the Lord. The Bible says that is what leads a man to riches, honor and long life.

Jesus as Lord + Consecration to Him = Blessings!

You know, receiving Jesus, not just as Savior, but as *Lord* is directly connected to your coming in line with God's laws of prosperity. If Jesus is really the *Lord* of your life, you'll be a doer of whatever is spoken to you in the Word. Can you see how that is connected to your prosperity?

You cannot walk in the laws of prosperity unless Jesus is the Lord of your life. Jesus being the Lord of your life means He directs the way you go in every aspect of your life. A lot of people have accepted Jesus as *Savior,* but they have not accepted Him as *Lord.*

So many Christians don't want Jesus to be their Lord. As I said, they accept Him as Savior, but He is not really Lord in the sense that He controls their lives.

People like that don't want a pastor or shepherd. And it doesn't matter how many revelations a person receives, he is still a sheep, and he still needs a shepherd! People who don't want to make Jesus their Lord don't want to obey church doctrine or sit under the ministry of anyone who will speak the truth in love or rebuke them in love, resisting their error. They want to praise God and then do what *they* want to do and give like *they* want to give and show up for church when *they* feel like it!

There have been some people like that in my church. I just fed them and loved them and tried to make sure they were going to heaven and were passing up the hospital and the bankruptcy court on the way. But I couldn't help them like I wanted to and like God wanted them to be helped, because they weren't submitting to Jesus as Lord. They didn't have Him as the absolute Lord of their lives.

> **And he said to them all, If any man will come after me, let him deny himself, and take up his cross daily, and follow me.**
>
> Luke 9:23

Jesus said, **If any man will come after me, let him deny himself....** That means letting Jesus be Lord of your life. The rest of that verse says, **Let him deny himself, and take up his cross daily, and follow me.** That means we are to follow Jesus and do what He says to do.

Is Jesus the Lord of your life? I mean, is Jesus in full control of everything in your life and everything that you have? Does the Bible govern your life, or have your flesh, relationships, unbelieving preachers or traditions kept you blinded to the truth and held you back from walking in the fullness of God?

You can settle that question in your heart once and for all. With every fiber of your being, you can make the declaration that from this day forward, everything you have is going to belong to God to be used for His purposes.

When you do that, Jesus becomes the Lord of your life. He can tell you, "Go right," "Go left," "Stop," "Give." He will be in full control. And He will bless you "real good" as a result!

He will say, "I can trust that one. He is going to support the things I want him to support. And I want him to have plenty. I want him to be able to fly wherever he wants, because if I lead him to a certain place, he will follow. He will go, and when the need is presented and I give the word, he will give."

Every morning, we need to wake up and say, "Good morning, Father. Good morning, Jesus. Good morning, Holy Ghost. What are my orders today?"

Do that every day of your life. Then if you get "fuzzy" or puzzled during the day, stop and talk to the Lord again. Ask Him to show you what to do. He will show you every time.

The Bible says in Philippians 2:9-10, **Wherefore God also hath highly exalted him [Jesus], and given him a name which is above every name: That at the name of Jesus every knee should bow, of things in heaven, and things in earth, and things under the earth.**

Jesus is the Name above every name, and He is the Lord. I remember in my own life when I moved spiritually from having Jesus as just my Savior to having Him as my Lord. I read these scriptures in Philippians and began to recognize that I couldn't run my life anymore—I had a new Master, and He was a *good* Master!

I realized that if I yielded my life to Him, He would raise me up in this life and then take me into the world to come. That's why I can boldly and frankly declare that I am who I am and where I am in life today because Jesus is the Lord of my life. I've turned my life over to Him. I've turned my ministry over to Him.

Without the Lord, I am nothing. I don't even know how to "come in out of the rain" without Him! But I've turned everything over to the Lord, and He just keeps blessing me. In spite of what others may say or do, Jesus is my Lord, and He just keeps on blessing me and my ministry.

Even if I try to move out from under "the spout where the blessing comes out," that spout follows me! I can't get away from it! I don't *want* to! And these things are so in my life because I follow God's laws of prosperity and always keep God first.

The Lord told me to teach these principles to others. He wants people to put Him first, to make Him the Lord of their lives, to understand the laws of prosperity and what He did for us and what He wants us to have.

God wants you to understand that Jesus became poor—He became poverty and a curse—because He wanted you to be rich, blessed and free.

Declare this out loud and mean it from your heart: "Jesus, You are my Lord and my Master. I yield everything I have to You—my home, my cars, my bank accounts, my talents, my family—*everything I have.* The world will not use what I have, Lord, because I yield it all to You."

When you consecrate yourself to God, He'll visit you. The visitation of His glory upon you will be evident. He is a wonderful, good Master. He will take care of His own. He will never let you be broke, "torn up" and ashamed. It is a *privilege* for you to let Him be the Lord of your life.

I preached this message once, and the Spirit of the Lord said to the people, "Stand still; the battle is not yours. The financial battle you're dealing with is not yours; it's Mine. Give it all to Me. I will 'fight' you out of your debts. Release everything to Me and stand fast in your consecration, and I will bring you out. And from this day forward, no weapon that is formed against you shall prosper, but I will see to it that *you* prosper."

In this chapter, we've been talking about some principles that a person must follow to make sure money is coming to him and that he is not going after money. Some people will have to make some adjustments and begin putting God first in their lives.

Others will have to get rid of their idols of money—always thinking about how they're going to get money no matter what the cost and then hoarding it for themselves, forgetting about God and His work.

Don't Let Money Become Your God

Anything you hoard and keep that the Lord has told you to give has become your god. I tell you, every person who is not tithing really loves money more than he loves God.

That's just the simple truth. I'm not saying that to condemn anyone. I'm saying that to *convince* and to convict and to help anyone who is not doing right. I want to help them get from the wrong side to the right side!

Thou shalt have no other gods before me.

Exodus 20:3

One of the reasons many in the Body of Christ have suffered and have not entered into godly prosperity is that, unknowingly, they have let money become their god, to a degree.

God is not going to give you other gods to put before Him. Therefore, He has had to cut off the prosperity of many. The more some people get, the more gods they will have before Him. Every new dollar becomes another god.

But the Lord reaches His long arm of grace to His children, even when they stray further and further from Him. He tries to get their attention. He says to them, in effect, "You don't have to go that way; come on back to Me, and I'll settle everything for you and put you in a sure place."

This is the God you want to follow! So make Jesus the Lord of your life today. Get all those other gods out of your life.

You know, one of the biggest hindrances to people's walking as they should with God is money. They always get upset about money.

But loose that money and let it go! Loose that dime off that dollar and let go of it. Stop letting that dime be a burden on you.

Too many are just looking for scriptures that say the tithe is not for today. They don't want to turn loose of that dime! But all they have to do is read Hebrews, chapter 7.

I tell you, instead of looking all over the world for ways not to tithe and not to be blessed by God in life, you ought to be looking for a way to give to God and be a blessing and be blessed yourself!

That's what is happening in my life, and that can happen in your life, if it isn't happening already. As long as you seek the Lord and always keep Him first, He will cause you to prosper.

Christian, you can't go after and seek money in life. You have to go after God, and when you seek Him and find Him, the money will be there! The money will be there waiting for you!

Seek God Through His Word

How do you seek God and go after Him? **If ye abide in me, and my words abide in you, ye shall ask what ye will, and it shall be done unto you** (John 15:7).

You seek God through His Word.

Let the word of Christ dwell in you richly in all wisdom; teaching and admonishing one another in psalms and hymns and spiritual songs, singing with grace in your hearts to the Lord.

Colossians 3:16

That's how you go after God—through His Word. And when you go after God, He will come after you. Now, He doesn't find people coming after Him every day, so when the Lord sees a man or woman turn his or her face from the world and toward Him, He is delighted. Whatever it is they're asking for, the Lord says, "Let them have it. They'll be blessed coming in and blessed going out. They'll be blessed in the city and blessed in the field" (Deuteronomy 28:3,6).

People in faith circles are always talking about believing something, then naming it and claiming it. That's true, but they have to line it up correctly. In other words, you can "name it and claim it" all you want, but if you aren't seeking the Lord properly—if you aren't obeying what He told you to do in the Word—you won't receive.

That's what many people have been doing to a large degree. Sometimes I wonder if the charismatic movement is not the "crazy-matic" movement! I mean, it's crazy just to confess a bunch of things without having any corresponding actions or obedience to God's Word.

For example, you could ask the Lord to help you financially. But if you can't turn loose of the dime off the dollar and give your tithe to the Lord and the local church, then your actions aren't lining up with the Word.

Actually, I don't know how some people have the nerve to say, "God, help me pay my bills" when they won't do what the prophets and preachers have been telling them to do to get in line with God's laws of prosperity.

Some people have the audacity to say things like, "I love You, Lord. You know I'd do anything for You. You're the Blessed Savior, holy be Your Name. I'd die for You, Jesus." But they're lying if they say they'd die for the Lord, because they're not tithing and giving and obeying God's Word in their finances! There's a long distance between "dying" and "diming"! And if they're not "diming," they're not doing God's Word. They don't love God if they don't love His Word.

What does the Old Testament say about the benefits, or results, of seeking the Lord?

> **And he [King Uzziah] sought God in the days of Zechariah, who had understanding in the visions of God: and as long as he sought the Lord, God made him to prosper.**
>
> **2 Chronicles 26:5**

As long as King Uzziah sought the Lord, God caused him to prosper. Why did God make him prosper? Because King Uzziah was putting God first in everything! In order to seek the Lord properly, you have to put Him first in everything.

> **The young lions do lack, and suffer hunger: but they that seek the Lord shall not want any good thing.**
>
> **Psalm 34:10**

Notice the word "seek" again. The Lord said that those who seek Him shall not want *any good thing.*

That goes right along with, **Seek ye first the kingdom of God, and his righteousness; and all these things shall be added unto you** (Matthew 6:33). Always keep God first, and all "these things" shall be added unto you. Always keep God first, and you shall not want for any good thing.

Well, what does "you will not want for any good thing" mean? Is it a *good thing* to have all your bills paid? Is it a *good thing* to eat the kind of steak or food you like? Then, you shall not want or lack for those things if you are seeking Him and putting Him first!

Some people think it's a sin to talk about some of the nice things of life in church. They will get "churchy" on you when you start talking about porterhouses or filet mignons. But who do you think God made the porterhouse and the filet mignon for? He made them for you and me to enjoy!

If having good things in life sounds a bit strange to you, just start seeking the Lord, and it won't sound strange after awhile! Those who seek the Lord shall not want for any good thing!

What Would *You* Call a Good Thing?

Could you call the house you want a good thing? Could you call the kind of car you want to drive a good thing?

You see, we who love God are seeking first the Kingdom of God. We're always keeping God first, so we have prosperity in the right perspective. We're not going after the car—we're going after *God!* Then, when we are seeking God, He'll say, "You can have the car!"

Listen, what I'm telling you is *B-i-b-l-e.* Let's read Psalm 34:10 again in its context.

> **O fear the Lord, ye his saints: for there is no want to them that fear him. The young lions do lack, and suffer hunger: but they that seek the Lord shall not want any good thing.**
>
> **Psalm 34:9,10**

In other words, God is saying to you who seek Him, "If you do what I tell you to do, I'm not going to let this world hold anything back from you, because you'll be stepping high, walking over this world's system."

You see, the world doesn't understand how the Christian who walks in prosperity is making it in life. People in the world are always worried about trying to climb the ladder of success. But you're on another ladder; you're on top of this world's system! The world doesn't understand that. But we serve the God of prosperity!

You need to recognize how big your God is and how much your God wants you to have prosperity. Your God's got it for you, and He will let you have it as soon as you begin to follow His laws and to walk consistently in His ways. When you do that, your "hustling-and-bustling-and-struggling-for-money days" will be over.

I dare you to seek God first and put Him first in everything in your life. I dare you to give everything you have to Him! The Lord said if we'll seek Him, we won't be wanting for any good thing!

Is Psalm 34:10 for everybody? Yes, it is if you've been born of God's Spirit, washed in Jesus' blood. When you get in His will, He'll pour down blessings upon you because He wants the world to know

He takes care of His own. It's not God who is holding things back from you. It's the devil who's keeping blessings from you. So separate yourself from the devil and his will and get in the Father's will so the Lord can pour blessings out on you!

God Is Faithful—If He Said It, He'll Do It!

God said in His Word, "I am not a man that I should lie; if I said it, I'll make it good" (Numbers 23:19). If you can find the promise in the Book, God will do it. He'll make it good. He said, **So shall my word be that goeth forth out of my mouth: it shall not return unto me void, but it shall accomplish that which I please, and it shall prosper in the thing whereto I sent it** (Isaiah 55:11).

The blessings of God are for you. All God is saying in these verses is that the blessings of God cometh; the goodness of God cometh! God just wants you in the position where you're not going after money the world's way, but you're seeking Him and putting Him first. Then "Money cometh" will be yours!

That is the truth, and truth that is known and acted upon will set you free. You see, it's not just knowing the truth; it's believing and acting upon the truth that bring results.

You really don't know the truth until you act upon it. Jesus said you shall know the truth, and the truth shall make you free (John 8:32)! You don't know something until you've proven it. It won't come to pass until you act upon it. But when you act upon it, it will come to pass, and then you'll be free. You won't be free by just memorizing truth, but if you'll become a *doer* of the truth, that truth will bring to pass in your life what it said it would.

You see, scriptures are not fulfilled in your life just because you know them or you've repeated them ninety-nine times. Scriptures are fulfilled in your life when you've acted upon them and they have produced exactly what they said they would produce in your life.

A lot of people have read John 8:32, **Ye shall know the truth, and the truth shall make you free,** many times, but they're not free. They've read other verses, and they're still not free. But if they will seek the Lord, He will not withhold any good thing from them. That is the truth, and when you act on the truth, the truth shall make you free!

If you will seek the Lord, He will not withhold any good thing from you. What are some more good things that you can think of that He will not withhold from you?

Well, is air conditioning a good thing? I tell you, I've been in my house when the air conditioner has been broken. I wanted to go to a hotel for the night until that thing was fixed! It gets hot in south Louisiana where I live.

Now a person who has never been introduced to air conditioning can tolerate the heat a lot better. But after he's been introduced to air conditioning, it's hard to live without it!

When we were kids, my two brothers and I used to sleep with the windows open to keep cool. We weren't able to buy screens, so when those windows were open, the bugs, the birds and anything else could come in those windows! We had what you'd call "automatic" air. You'd open the doors and windows and automatically have air!

So to me, air conditioning is a good thing!

Is it a good thing to have a nice car to go where you want to go with your family and get back safely?

I'm asking these questions because I just want to know if you know the difference between good and bad things. If you think these things are bad things, I'll pray for you not to have them! But you know they aren't bad things.

Is having a nice, new outfit a good thing?

And if you want your whole family of thirty-five people to come over for Thanksgiving, is having several turkeys and lots of good food to serve a good thing? If you have a house full of people over and you're able to set five or six turkeys before them to eat, that sounds like a good thing to me! If I walked into a house and saw five turkeys on the table with their legs stuck up in the air, I'd say, "The Lord is in this house. This is a blessed house!"

You see, all those things are good things. But the world and the devil have been eating those turkeys and enjoying all those good things. They tell us, "Yes, y'all are the Lord's people; we respect you."

Then they get in their fancy cars and laugh all the way home. They're laughing at us because they've got our stuff!

Let's look at some more benefits of seeking the Lord:

> I love them that love me; and those that seek me early shall find me. Riches and honour are with me; yea, durable riches and righteousness.
>
> Proverbs 8:17,18

Look at that word "durable." Do you know what that means? That means that the riches God gives you will last when everything else is gone. When the economic system of this world breaks down, God's Word, His riches and His financial plan of prosperity will remain strong, steadfast and durable.

When the stock market is crashing, major chemical companies are going under, banks are failing and family dynasties are coming to ruin, God's people will still have money in their pockets because God said His riches are durable. They are everlasting!

Even if Wall Street closed down, we're on God's system, and no matter what goes down or under or fails or falls, God's riches are durable. That means that God's riches can pass any test that comes against us!

How does this happen? Let's look at these scriptures again:

> Receive my instruction, and not silver; and knowledge rather than choice gold. For wisdom is better than rubies; and all the things that may be desired are not to be compared to it. I wisdom dwell with prudence, and find out knowledge of witty inventions. The fear of the Lord is to hate evil: pride, and arrogancy, and the evil way, and the froward mouth, do I hate. Counsel is mine, and sound wisdom: I am understanding; I have strength. By me kings reign, and princes decree justice. By me princes rule, and nobles, even all the judges of the earth. I love them that love me; and those that seek me early shall find me. Riches and honour are with me; yea, durable riches and righteousness.
>
> Proverbs 8:10-18

This passage is talking about the wisdom of God. What a treasure you have if you have the wisdom and favor of God!

We can see an example of this in the Old Testament in the life of a boy named Joseph. There was a famine in the land of Israel. Joseph, who had been in prison in Egypt, interpreted a man's dream by the wisdom and Spirit of God. And the wisdom of God eventually brought that boy from the pit, to the prison, to the palace as a top man in Egypt. (See Genesis 39-41.)

Joseph had the wisdom of God. He had something inside of him that was durable. And we, as Christians, have the same thing. The Lord Jesus Christ is inside of us by the Spirit of God, the Greater One. And **Greater is he that is in you, than he that is in the world** (1 John 4:4).

You Can Walk in the Wisdom and Favor of God

I can preach this because I'm living it. I'm not preaching another man's experience. I was preaching Christ and giving Him the glory, and God said, "Hey! You please Me. Come up higher." The world's system tried to block me, but God broke down the barrier!

I had some people come against me when I tried to build my house. I went to four or five banks and got turned down for financing. I had plenty of money, but the banks said the house I wanted to build was too big for the area of town in which I wanted to build.

Then one day I was coming back home on a plane from a meeting I preached, and I got to thinking about it. My wife was asleep next to me, and I just began to think, *Well, maybe I'll go to a smaller blueprint. These people have been giving me too much trouble.*

Then the Lord said to me, "Don't settle for less...." I wanted to ask Him, "Lord, what are You saying?" but He wouldn't let me finish. He said, "...for I have provided for you to have the best!"

I said, "Fine, Lord. Somebody is going to give us this money. Somebody is going to have to turn these papers loose." And, sure enough, somebody did! God caused all that mess to break up, and He came through for me.

You see, you can't quit when the first door shuts in your face. When God tells you He's going to do something for you, He's going to do it! But He's going to do it His way according to His Word, not according to the world's way.

I live in a very nice house—a very prosperous-looking home. Someone once said to me, "Your house would cost over a million dollars where I'm from!" Well, he was from Memphis, Tennessee, and I didn't pay that much for the house, thank God. But it is a very nice house.

Now you "lose" some people if you're a preacher and you tell them about how the Lord is blessing you, because they are "preacher-holders." They don't want the preachers to have things that are that nice.

I remember back before I built my house, I was in the home of one of my church members who was a doctor. He'd bought his house new, and he had a swimming pool. He once said something to me that will never leave me. We were walking around his swimming pool, and I saw a look of discontentment on his face. I said, "What is it, Doc?" He said, "I just won't be satisfied until you build *your* house."

He appreciated his new house, but he wasn't completely satisfied because I hadn't built mine yet! My goodness, that's "love gone to seed"!

Many people don't have that attitude. They don't want the preacher to have anything, and they've crippled themselves financially because they've tried to hold ministers back.

But that is foolish thinking; it's not God's wisdom. When you don't want ministers to go forward, you are really holding yourself back. God is not going to promote you if you don't bless your pastor. Do you remember what God said to His servant Abraham? He said He would bless those who blessed Abraham (Genesis 12:3).

If you are putting God first and seeking Him, God will see to it that you are blessed. So I encourage you to seek God and go after Him instead of going after money. Put His Word and His principles to work in your life by faith and let money come to *you!*

Part 2

I n the last chapter, we talked about two guidelines that will ensure that money will always be coming after us and that we will never be going after money. *First,* we must always keep God first. *Second,* we must remember that God owns everything; we own nothing. The things we have in life are things that God lets us use. We recognize that those things are temporal.

Keeping Divine Priorities Straight

Third, we must organize our priorities as follows: "God *first,* others *second* and me *last.*" Following that guideline will keep you humble and concerned for other people. Then when you get blessed, you'll know how to bless others.

Fourth, we must remember that *God* is our Source. Other people are not our source; and *we* are not our own source. We are to look to God and not to man for our financial prosperity. Remembering this will also help us keep our priorities straight in life.

These four guidelines will help you line up with God's laws of prosperity and get you away from the love of money and from always scheming to try to get money.

Reprogram Yourself
on God's Financial System

If you'll let Him, God can get you in His system of prosperity—in His "computer" of prosperity—so that your heart is programmed with the wisdom of God for your finances. Then, no matter which way the economic system turns in this world, you'll never have to worry about it.

God will tell His children what is coming on the earth and how to adjust themselves so they'll go through it as if nothing happened. God told Joseph to store up grain during the seven years of plenty to prepare for the seven years of famine (Genesis 41:36). He had Joseph stacking up the goods, and the people were able to have food as a result!

Remember this if you don't remember anything else: There are no shortages with God. God has plenty—a *full* supply! And He is our Source!

God Is a God of "Extras"!

You know, the Lord doesn't want us to barely get by. And when He blesses us because we take Him at His Word that He'll meet our needs, He doesn't just *barely* meet our needs. The Lord always gives a little extra. (That's why I had "extras"—amenities and upgrades—put in my car. The Lord deals in "extras"!)

God wants us to have the extras in life. I'm going to preach on this earth and get a lot of people saved and a lot of people turned on to the Word of God. But I am going to enjoy myself, too, with some of God's extras that He gives me.

I am enjoying my Lord. I love to preach. I love my job. I love to see that twinkle in people's eyes and the joy on their faces when the Word hits their hearts and becomes real to them. It's worth a million dollars to see somebody's life light up by the Word of God.

"Money cometh" is two English words. But the Lord has put them together by His Spirit and has endorsed them to cause those words to come to pass in your life when you continually speak them out in faith.

But in much the same way that the Lord has released the words "Money cometh," the *devil* has released the words "Money *goeth.*" And many people believe that and speak it out.

It's easy to say the negative thing sometimes. We've been programmed to say negative things, because this world's system is a negative system. To say something positive, such as "Money cometh," might cause people to think you're worldly and that you're just seeking after things.

There is nothing wrong with having good things if you love God. That's why the Lord built my house—to encourage the Body of Christ that the Lord wants us to have good things.

I invited one of my sons in the faith to my house once. He sat down and acted just as calm as can be. All of a sudden, he asked me, "Can I just be myself?"

I said, "Yes, sure. Go ahead." When I said, "Sure. Go ahead," that boy screamed to the top of his voice: "A preacher in a house like this? Hallelujah! Thank You! Glory to God!"

You see, all you have to do is love the Lord with all your heart, all your mind, all your soul and all your might. Then He knows He can trust you. When He can trust you, He can really bless you. He can give you some extras in life to enjoy.

The Lord Will Fill Your Treasures!

Look at Proverbs 8:21: **That I may cause those that love me to inherit substance; and I will fill their treasures.**

I like the Lord because He doesn't play around, saying, "I will *half-*fill their treasures." No, He will *fill* their treasures! Whose treasures? The treasures of those who love Him!

Can you stand for God to fill your treasures? Certainly, you can. We *all* could stand for our treasures to be filled up a little bit more. And we're on our way! Money cometh!

I've been studying prosperity over the years, and my wife and I have put it into action, word by word, line by line. We have stepped out to obey God and His Word concerning prosperity and to set in motion His laws of prosperity in our lives.

You see, you have to be consistent with the Word of God and stick with it. You can't be hit-and-miss with the things of God. My wife and

I stayed with what we learned about godly prosperity, and now the blessings are overtaking us and running us down! Our treasures are being filled!

One time a man practically ran me down to bless me. I mean, he was running and breathing hard. He was running toward my car at the shopping mall. When I saw him, I rolled down the window. He said, "The Lord told me to tell you to go into any store you want and get what you want." Then the man said, "I'm paying for it."

I told the man I didn't want anything, but the man persisted, so I went into the store I intended to go to anyway, and I picked out a sports shirt. (Some people are greedy. They would go to every store they could find if that happened to them.)

My two sons were with me. Actually, I wasn't shopping for myself, but I was glad that man ran me down to bless me in front of them. I've always told them, "Sons, if you live for God, His blessings will run you down." So it was good for them to see that man "running me down" to bless me.

When you understand how God's laws of prosperity work, those laws will start falling in place for you. So remember to always keep God first and think, *God owns everything; I own nothing. The things I have, God is letting me use.*

Then, you need to think, *God* first; *others* second; *and myself* last.

Also, you need to have the understanding that *God*, not man, is your Source.

When these attitudes are developed in your spirit, just watch what will happen in your life. I'm talking to you from a biblical perspective because God's Word cannot lie. But I'm also talking from experience.

The "Proof of the Pudding"

You can teach others better when you have experienced for yourself what you're teaching. I remember one older preacher said you need not preach something unless you have proven it in your own life. One of my favorite sayings is, "The proof of the pudding is in the eating."

I'm teaching these things from biblical revelation and personal experience. My wife and I have experienced these things in our lives again and again. So I have more than one motivation for teaching this message to you: one is the impartation of the revelation from my heart to your heart; the other is the fact that I'm actually walking in what I'm teaching.

Some people say, "You shouldn't talk like that as a minister. People are not going to give to you if they think you are already prosperous." But I always say, "Yes, they will; if God tells them to, they will."

I am on God's system of prosperity, in a divine hookup with God! God is my Father and my Provider. I don't have to whine and tell people I'm broke and barely making it just to get an offering.

Is God Your Father?

Whose child are you? If you are God's child, then your Daddy is saying to you, **Behold, the heaven and the heaven of heavens is the Lord thy God's, the earth also, with all that therein is** (Deuteronomy 10:14). He is saying, "I own everything. Farther than your eye can see and further than you can think or dream is Mine."

In effect, God is saying to His children, "I want you to have plenty of toys for Christmas, My child. Every day is Christmas with Me. I want you to be blessed and have all the toys you want. Just put Me first."

My youngest son can go shopping for toys at the drop of a hat! He doesn't have to wait for Christmas or for a special occasion. He's not thinking about any Santa Claus, either. That boy knows that *I'm* "Santa Claus"! There is no "Santa" coming down my chimney! If anybody comes down that chimney, it's going to be me!

If my son wants a new bicycle and new toys, for example, he needs to do what I tell him to do and love me, and I will bless him abundantly. If he doesn't, "Santa Claus" might not show up!

Similarly, when God's laws of prosperity are operating in your life, the prosperity of God begins to fall into place in your life. You will experience "life more abundantly" (John 10:10). You will experience the "gold and the glory"!

According to the word that I covenanted with you when ye came out of Egypt, so my spirit remaineth among you: fear ye not. For thus saith the Lord of hosts; Yet once, it is a little while, and I will shake the heavens, and the earth, and the sea, and the dry land; And I will shake all nations, and the desire of all nations shall come: and I will fill this house with GLORY, saith the Lord of hosts.

Haggai 2:5-7

I want you to feast your eyes on these scriptures so you can get that devil who made you broke out of your house! Verse 7 says God **will fill this house with glory.** God's glory is God's presence. So when God said He would fill the house with His glory, He was saying He was going to fill it with His presence.

Well, you know that where a king is present, his gold is. This passage is talking about the glory of God, but look at verse 8:

The silver is mine, and the GOLD is mine, saith the Lord of hosts.

Haggai 2:8

Then look at verse 9:

The GLORY of this latter house shall be greater than of the former, saith the Lord of hosts: and in this place will I give peace, saith the Lord of hosts.

Haggai 2:9

Notice, between two verses that talk about God's glory (vv. 7,9), a little verse that talks about the gold is sandwiched in (v. 8). Between two "glories," He's got gold!

Sometimes in meetings today, the shekinah presence of God will come rolling in like a cloud. The Bible talks about the presence of God, or the glory cloud, in Second Chronicles 5. Sometimes in my meetings, I see the glory cloud hover over certain people present in the service.

Sometimes, just before the Spirit will "break out" and manifest Himself in people's dancing and running in the Spirit, I will sense the glory cloud roll into the building. Sometimes I try to get away from the cloud because if it comes over me, I can't stand up at times. I have to hold on to a chair so I can stand up. People will see me rocking on the platform in church, but, really, any minute I'm about to fall or break out dancing or running in the Spirit. (You can hardly stand in His presence and do anything when that glory cloud comes in.)

So, in Haggai 2:8, God says, "The silver is Mine." You might say, "Oh, good, Daddy. You've got all the silver." But, then, God says, "Wait a minute, son. The gold is Mine too."

All the silver and all the gold are the Lord's. And we are His! The silver and gold belong to us because we are *in* Him!

God Wants "the Gold and the Glory" To Be in Your House!

A poverty spirit has tried to keep people broke and far away from God's gold and His glory. Those people are still in Egypt, so to speak—in bondage to debt and poverty—when they should come on over into the promised land. They need to forget the things they learned from religion and tradition that weren't true or in line with the Word. The teaching that people should be broke, poor and in lack is just something men thought up. It wasn't God.

Haggai 2:9 says, **The glory of this latter house shall be greater than of the former, saith the Lord of hosts: and in this place will I give peace, saith the Lord of hosts.** You see, the gold is only temporary, but you have to have some gold. The gold and the glory go together.

Some people shout in church because of the glory, but then they go home and "hell" is waiting for them, because they don't have any gold; they're broke.

I'm trying to teach you how to take the glory home with you— how to prosper God's way so that you have the glory *and* the gold. God wants you to go home from church and have glory and gold— glory and prosperity—at your house. He wants you to go home and witness the goodness of God in your life!

But there's not much glory in going home to a distressed and discontented husband or wife and hearing a bunch of nagging because you're always broke.

There's not much glory if you're broke, your spouse is broke and everything at your house is broke! Even the mouse in your house is broke! That rat doesn't have any cheese to eat because you can't buy him any; you're broke. That rat finally says, "Man, I'm moving uptown!" Then the roaches say, "We're leaving too! There are never any crumbs left at this 'broke' house!"

Roaches have better sense than some of us! They don't want to live in poverty! They know how to prosper and move out of "broke" places!

You know, some people will hear the truth about prosperity and how God wants them to live, and they'll just say, "Well, that was a nice message." Then they'll go right back into living in poverty.

But they need to come out of living in poverty, lack and bondage, and come into the glory and prosperity of God!

The Word of God Says, "Come up Higher!"

When I give you scripture after scripture about how the Father wants you to live, I'm not putting anybody down. I am telling people about the good things the Lord has blessed me with to help them, not to put them down. I am telling them how to come up in life.

You see, you have to be able to distinguish between down and up and know which way is up, so you'll know how to *go* up! So I just preach the Word of God to people, and they rise up from where they are to where they want to be in Christ.

Some people say that our church is just a "big-time" church and that you have to have money to attend. But it's the devil who tells people that so they won't come and get the Word and be fed spiritually.

A person doesn't have to have money to come to our church. He can come without a dime, but if he does, sooner or later, the truth will begin to rise up inside of him, and he will say, "Bless God: He wants me to prosper! I'm not where I'm supposed to be. God wants me to come up higher!"

Divine prosperity will not come overnight. Very rarely will God bring someone out of debt overnight. He will bring you out gradually as you stick with His Word.

And take heed how you hear. In other words, don't let anybody stuff doubt, unbelief and tradition down your ears while you're believing God and expecting a change in your circumstances. If you do that, you'll waver.

But don't waver! Continue to step on up into God's system of prosperity and blessing. I tell you, if you do, life will never be the same for you!

Why the World's Prosperity Can't Satisfy

We're talking about God's will concerning financial prosperity, and we're talking about the difference between your going after money and money coming after you!

Some Christians chase money. They go after money and prosperity instead of going after the *God* of prosperity!

You know, the world's system of prosperity cannot satisfy. But there is a satisfaction that goes along with godly prosperity. God wants you to have things, but there's a satisfaction with having those things *because you obeyed Him.*

The world's system of prosperity is empty. Most of the people who are wealthy the world's way are sad. Notice Ecclesiastes 5:10: **He that loveth silver shall not be satisfied with silver; nor he that loveth abundance with increase: this is also vanity.**

As I said before, there are movie stars and other celebrities who have so much money that they have to hide in seclusion in their palaces and can't even go out in public to get ice cream.

But when you release what you have to God, you don't have to worry about having policemen or soldiers around your house watching over you because you're rich. No, you who love the Lord and have received prosperity *His* way have those nine-feet, six-inch-tall boys watching you! You don't have to worry like the world does—you have *angels* watching over you!

Worldly Prosperity Will Become a Curse

God is the God of abundance, but the world's abundance is received by going after prosperity by methods other than God's methods. That's the kind of prosperity Ecclesiastes 5:10 is talking about: **He that loveth silver shall not be satisfied with silver; nor he that loveth abundance with increase: this is also vanity.**

Sooner or later, the world's kind of prosperity will become a curse. People who prosper that way are running around with God's tithes in their pockets! They may not all be millionaires, but they might have two cars and a nice house. When they hear preaching on tithing, they say, "Well, the reverend is not preaching to me; I'm doing just as well as he or anybody else is doing, and I'm going to handle my money the way I want to handle it."

But listen to me carefully. *Everyone* who prospers by methods other than God's laws of prosperity will find out sooner or later that his prosperity has become a curse.

Those who get their so-called prosperity by other methods than God's laws of prosperity may be laughing and "swinging free" as they're "out and about" riding around in those fancy cars. But the Bible tells you not to worry about the wicked. It says that they will soon be cut off.

> **Fret not thyself because of evildoers, neither be thou envious against the workers of iniquity. For they shall soon be cut down like the grass, and wither as the green herb.**
>
> **Psalm 37:1,2**

Have you ever seen some of those people, riding around in their luxury cars, all dressed up, wearing big gold chains around their necks, just living the high life? Some people wonder, *Those people are children of the devil. How do they live so well?* But the Lord is saying in this passage, "Just watch them. They'll be here today and gone tomorrow."

I've seen that happen. I've seen the wicked grow and thrive like a big bay tree, arrogant, talking their "talk," leaning back in their fancy cars, acting like they're superior. But I've also seen those same people lose everything they have.

But when the righteous go God's way, they're still here, standing strong tomorrow, the next day, the next week, the next month, the next year and so on! They will be here until Jesus says, "You servant of the Most High God, come up even higher now!"

You see, prosperity in God is a sure thing. But prosperity in the world is uncertain.

For the turning away of the simple shall slay them, and the prosperity of fools shall destroy them.

Proverbs 1:32

So, you see, a fool or an ungodly or worldly person can prosper, but it is a destructive prosperity. I see "fools" prospering every day, but those people are not going to last long. We'll still be here standing strong when those people are gone.

Listen, Brother and Sister, take hold of the revelation of prosperity and keep it in its proper perspective. Your Father does not mind your rising up in life. As a matter of fact, He *wants* that for you. (Remember how He bragged on righteous Job and told about all that Job possessed?)

Knowing these things will set you free from the things that have been holding you in bondage. This knowledge will get you out into the fresh, clean air of His prosperity, where He wants you to be!

If you haven't seen yet that God wants you to be prosperous, you're either stupid, hopelessly ignorant or you have somebody with a gun telling you, "You don't see it"!

Your Father doesn't mind your being blessed. As a matter of fact, you please Him more by being blessed than by sitting around like the rest!

Hang in There—Payday Cometh!

As I said, you won't rise up overnight to the level where God wants you. But if you'll stick with God and His Word, you will rise up. You won't have to go after money. Money will come after you!

For example, let me tell you a little story about an older minister who gradually rose up in the things of God.

Years ago, when this minister and his wife were just starting out, they went to a convention and were staying at another couple's house. The minister's wife had borrowed clothes to go to that meeting. She only had one good dress of her own that she could wear in public.

While they were visiting that couple, the woman of the house showed this minister's wife all her new clothes and her new coat with a fur collar.

The minister's wife became discouraged. (You know your flesh can really bother you in certain circumstances.) She went back to their room, and her husband noticed she was feeling down. He sat on the bed beside her and prophesied some things to her. He told her that God was going to bring them out and that they were going to prosper as they lived for Him and obeyed Him. And God did. That day came!

You can't serve God without prospering. That's not just true for ministers; that's true for everyone. That's why I'm telling you how to do it. You have to get ahold of the principles of God and keep God first. You have to stick with the Word of God and not think that you are unholy if you are prospering. The devil will try to accuse you, saying, "Why do you have that outfit on? You're just trying to show off."

But have you ever seen wild lilies growing in a valley or a peacock when he spreads out his tail feathers in a beautiful fan? Everybody stops to behold those colors that blend together more beautifully than any artist's hand can paint.

Well, God made the beautiful things that we see today. One reason He did it was to show us the way He thinks. By looking at those things, we can know that He wants to do good and beautiful things in our lives too.

Well, do you believe God thinks more of a peacock than He thinks of you? Of course, He doesn't. He wants you to have the best! And as you seek Him and put Him first and practice the principles of God's Word, I believe with all my heart that you will have it!

Your Prosperity Is Paid For!

We know by now that prosperity belongs to the Body of Christ! The Lord Jesus Christ paid for our prosperity that we might be prosperous. He died and rose again so that the Church could be prosperous in every way.

Jesus, the Classic Son of God, Our Living Example

We saw that Jesus became poor when He died on the cross. He stripped Himself, not only of His mighty power and glory, but of His ability to maneuver on the earth in the realm of the Spirit as the classic Son of God. When He rose from the dead, He became the first-born of many brethren. That "many brethren" is us!

In His earthly ministry, Jesus was setting a classic example of how a believer, a child of God, should live. He showed us what really belongs to us—prosperity spiritually, emotionally, mentally, physically and financially.

Jesus Christ is the classic Son of God. He's a living example to us, and we ought to follow His example as sons and daughters of God!

Prosperity is ours. Jesus paid for it, but if you're going to prosper personally, you're going to have to pay a price too. *First,* you're going to have to eradicate all the thoughts and ideas you've had of barely getting by, scraping the bottom of the barrel and being bound by those family ties that have been passed down to you—those family *lies* that told you you'll never make it and that you'll always be broke!

In some families, "brokeness" has been passed down from generation to generation. Their ancestors were broke. Their grandma and grandpa were broke, and *they're* broke. So all they talk about is being broke. Everybody in that family has a "broke" mentality. They have not read the Bible and found out what the Lord has said about it. They may even quote the scripture, **The Lord is my Shepherd; I shall** not want (Psalm 23:1). Yet they are full of want. They only think of that scripture as a "nice saying." They think, *Oh, isn't that nice?* It may be wonderfully said, but it's not being wonderfully *lived!*

Jesus paid a big price so we wouldn't have to live in poverty. Our divine prosperity has been paid for! But there is still a price we must pay.

The Example of Abraham

Abraham's name was "Abram" before God changed his name (Genesis 17:5). "Abraham" means *father of many nations.* But when God first changed his name, Abram and Sarah were childless! Abram wasn't the father of *one child,* much less of *many nations!*

Abraham had to walk out by faith the promise that God was going to give him a son. And Abraham did it. That's why God's blessing was upon him. And that same blessing can come upon us through faith because of what Jesus Christ did in redeeming us.

Some people just believe that Abraham lived a long time and had a child in his old age, and they call that the blessings of Abraham. That kind of thinking is a "sacred cow," or pet doctrine, that doesn't line up with the Word, because Abraham's blessing was more than just having a son in his old age.

So I'm going to kill that "cow" with some teaching from the Word! I'm going to show you an aspect of Abraham's life that will cause you never to doubt that a financial blessing was involved in the covenant God made with Abraham. Financial blessing was a part of the blessings of Abraham.

Our prosperity is paid for, but now watch this fellow Abraham and see some more of the price you're going to have to pay to walk in God's kind of prosperity.

Don't Let the Unbelief of Others Defeat You

The second price you're going to have to pay is to refuse to listen to the unbelief of others around you who will try to discourage you.

Even well-meaning friends and loved ones can discourage you and distract you from the Word with their unbelief.

The first words the Lord said to Abraham were, in effect, "Get out of that unbelieving company" (Genesis 12:1)! And in your own life, until you get on your feet financially, or while you're first putting the Word for finances to work in your life, stop inviting your unbelieving family members to your house who talk all that doubt and unbelief to you and drag you down!

When they're talking about how broke they are, you may say, "I don't want to talk about that," but they've already put that spirit of doubt and unbelief in your house. You may have to separate yourself from them for a while.

Now, that may not sound right, but the Lord told Abraham, **Get thee out of thy country, and from thy kindred, and from thy father's house, unto a land that I will shew thee** (Genesis 12:1).

You see, kinfolk can hold you down and hold you back if they're not flowing in the right vein. Now, you can thank God every day that they're coming into the knowledge of the truth, but until they do, you don't have to allow yourself to be influenced and affected by their unbelieving attitudes.

I thank God my entire family is coming in. And day by day, they *are* coming in. Some of them stood back for a while, but then the blessings on my life began to look so good to them that some of them went ahead and "dove in" with me. Now we're being blessed together!

There was a time when my sister-in-law was just satisfied in the denominational church she was in. But one day her sons joined our church. They went back home and told their mother, "We're members of Uncle Leroy's church now."

Those sons heard the truth and spiritually left their parents behind. But now all of them—my brother, his wife, their two sons and their grandbabies—have come in, and they attend my church!

God takes care of my family when I pray. Most of my family members call me first when something happens and they need God to do something for them. They have good sense enough to know who to call, not because *I'm* so great, but because I know a *great God!*

God will take care of His own. Now, you may want your kinfolks to come into the knowledge of the truth, but sometimes you have to leave them behind. They'll keep you in the dark if you don't. God told Abraham, **Get thee out of thy country, and from thy kindred, and from thy father's house, unto a land that I will shew thee.**

Now, that's what He's trying to do for us. He's trying to get us into a land of blessing, just as He did for Abraham. He is trying to get us into a new land. He's trying to improve our vision so we will no longer see Him as a barely-getting-along God, but as the God who's more than enough!

God was going to show Abraham a new land of prosperity, but He was saying, "The only way I can show it to you is if you come away from among your relatives here."

Then, verse 2 says, **I will make of thee a great nation, and I will bless thee, and make thy name great; and thou shalt be a blessing.**

Now look at verse 3:

> **And I will bless them that bless thee, and curse him that curseth thee: and in thee shall all families of the earth be blessed.**
>
> **Genesis 12:3**

Isn't that wonderful! Christ has redeemed us from the curse of the law so these blessings of Abraham might come upon the Gentiles through Jesus.

Abraham was very rich. The wealth God gave Abraham was part of his blessing that we have inherited in Christ.

Say the word "rich" out loud. Some people have a hard time saying that word. It's not a part of their regular vocabulary. Say it again: *"rich."* Doesn't that sound wonderful? I tell you, it makes those poverty demons just as mad as they can be!

Abraham's Blessing Belongs to Us!

Galatians said that the blessing of Abraham should come upon the Gentiles. Well, I don't just want Abe's healing. Thank God that I've got his healing, but I don't want to stop there. And I don't just want Abraham's lifestyle of faith. I've got faith, but you can have faith and still be broke and sick if you don't act on the faith you have. No, I want the healing, and I want the faith, but I want the money that goes along with Abraham's blessings too!

I need money to live in this life, and when the Bible talks about Abraham's being rich, it's not talking about his being physically rich. In other words, it didn't say God made Abraham to be very *healthy*. No, when you think of the word "rich," what is it that you think about? Do you think, *Well, Abraham never had to go to a doctor in his life because he was so healthy?*

No, when you refer to the word "rich," you think of *money*. So I argue that, undoubtedly, one aspect of Abraham's blessing was prosperity.

Then the Holy Ghost said that not only was Abraham rich, but he was *very* rich (Genesis 13:2).

Now the blessing of Abraham runs in our family—in the family of God! But, do you believe that the blessing of Abraham was intended for you? Are you working on fully receiving it by faith, or are you living below the covenant—below your rights and privileges as a believer?

When you start to think rich according to the Word and put into practice what you've learned about prosperity, things are going to start happening in your life. You are going to start prospering!

Now, persecution is going to come right behind it, as we've already discussed. But I always say, "That's all right with me; I want the blessings of God. I may not like the persecution, but I can stand it. I'd rather be persecuted than broke!"

Persecution comes with prosperity because when you begin tapping into the Word of God, your life becomes a mirror of the Word. And when others *aren't* tapping into the Word—when they don't have their hair combed right and they don't want to do anything about it and fix themselves up properly—they don't like looking into your mirror! In fact, they'd like to *break* your mirror!

A lot of people want to take financial prosperity out of the blessings that Abraham had. That's why the Lord told us that Abraham was very rich in cattle, silver and gold (Genesis 13:2). The Lord did that so we'd see what really belongs to us in Christ.

The Lord told us how He blessed Abraham in order to knock out of the boat, so to speak, every theologian who'd try to reason our financial blessing out of Galatians 3:13-14, which says Christ has redeemed us! That's why the Holy Ghost made sure the Scripture said that Abraham had silver and gold—so prosperity couldn't be argued out of this verse in Galatians!

Let's go a little higher in the Scriptures because the Holy Ghost explicitly tells how Abraham became rich.

> Now the Lord had said unto Abram, Get thee out of thy country, and from thy kindred, and from thy father's house, unto a land that I will shew thee: And I will make of thee a great nation, and I will bless thee, and make thy name great; and thou shalt be a blessing: And I will bless them that bless thee, and curse him that curseth thee: and in thee shall all families of the earth be blessed. So Abram departed, as the Lord had spoken unto him; and Lot went with him: and Abram was seventy and five years old when he departed out of Haran. And Abram took Sarai his wife, and Lot his brother's son, and all their substance that they had gathered, and the souls that they had gotten in Haran; and they went forth to go into the land of Canaan; and into the land of Canaan they came.
>
> And Abram passed through the land unto the place of Sichem, unto the plain of Moreh. And the Canaanite was then in the land. And the Lord appeared unto Abram, and said, Unto thy seed will I give this land: and there builded he an altar unto the Lord, who appeared unto him. And he removed from thence unto a mountain on the east of Bethel, and pitched his tent, having Bethel on the west, and Hai on the east: and there he builded an altar unto the Lord, and called upon the name of the Lord. And Abram journeyed, going on still toward the south.
>
> **Genesis 12:1-9**

Now after a while, the substance of Abraham and Lot was so great that the land was "not able to bear them" both. In other words, they had to go their separate ways.

And Lot also, which went with Abram, had flocks, and herds, and tents.

And the land was not able to bear them, that they might dwell together: for their substance was GREAT, SO that they could not dwell together.

Genesis 13:5,6

It says, **Their substance was great, so that they could not dwell together.** Now we know that the substance of Abraham and Lot was great, so that they were not able to dwell together. But it would not do harm to that verse to put the word "so" before the word "great" and come up with this statement: "Their substance was *so great* that they could not dwell together"!

Write that down on a piece of paper or in your Bible: *so great.* Just take the "so" and put it before the "great" for a little more impact.

"So great" is describing Abraham and Lot's substance! What was Abraham and Lot's substance? They had flocks, herds and tents. Somebody said, "Well, flocks, herds and tents aren't silver and gold." Yes, but those things were still revenue for Abraham and Lot. With those flocks, herds and tents, they got silver and gold (Genesis 13:2)!

Christ has redeemed us from the curse of the law that the blessings of Abraham may then come on the Gentiles, that we may receive the promise of the Spirit by faith! Now the just shall live by faith (Romans 1:17; Galatians 3:11; Hebrews 10:38; Habakkuk 2:4). And by faith, the blessings of Abraham are ours, including prosperity!

So we've established that Abraham was wealthy. In fact, the Bible says he was *very* rich. But, as I said, we need to know that Abraham had to do some things to cause these blessings to come to him. First, he believed God. Second, he separated himself from unbelief and would not allow himself to become discouraged or dissuaded, even by his own relatives.

Why the Blessing Came Upon Abraham

We already know that Abraham was consecrated to the Lord and to the things of God. When the Lord told Abraham to leave his kindred because He wanted Abraham to go somewhere else (Genesis 12:1), Abraham said, "All right, Lord." Then Abraham said to his relatives, "I'll see you later."

Abraham separated himself unto God. Abraham was obedient to the call of God, and the third reason God's blessing came upon him was that he was consecrated and devoted to fulfilling that call.

Abraham Paid God "Tithes of All"

A fourth thing Abraham did was to pay tithes, a tenth of all his increase, to God.

> And the king of Sodom went out to meet him after his return from the slaughter of Chedorlaomer, and of the kings that were with him, at the valley of Shaveh, which is the king's dale. And Melchizedek king of Salem brought forth bread and wine: and he was the priest of the most high God. And he blessed him, and said, Blessed be Abram of the most high God, possessor of heaven and earth: And blessed be the most high God, which hath delivered thine enemies into thy hand. And he gave him tithes of all.
>
> Genesis 14:17-20

Goodness! Look at verse 20! After Melchizedek blessed Abraham and said, **Blessed be Abram of the most high God...**, Abraham gave God **tithes of all.** In other words, of all Abe's increase, he gave God the tithe!

I see why Abraham was so rich—do you? Abraham was all tied up with God's laws of prosperity. Abraham was very rich, but when he met that priest, he gave him "tithes of all." That means Abraham gave him 10 percent of everything he had!

Concerning financial prosperity, you have to understand that, on God's system, you have to *release* it to *receive* it; you have to *give* it to *get* it. If you would just understand and act on God's laws of prosperity, you wouldn't have to live your whole life down here just barely getting by on the world's system.

Abraham Refused To Let Man Take Credit for His Blessing

A fifth thing Abraham did was to refuse to allow his prosperity to be contaminated.

> **And the king of Sodom said unto Abram, Give me the persons, and take the goods to thyself. And Abram said to the king of Sodom, I have lift up mine hand unto the Lord, the most high God, the possessor of heaven and earth, That I will not take from a thread even to a shoelatchet, and that I will not take any thing that is thine, lest thou shouldest say, I have made Abram rich.**
>
> **Genesis 14:21-23**

Abraham did not contaminate his wealth. In Genesis 14, it says that one time the king of Sodom tried to give Abraham all the goods and spoils of a battle. But Abraham said, **I will not take from a thread even to a shoelatchet, and that I will not take any thing that is thine, lest thou shouldest say, I have made Abram rich** (v. 23).

In other words, Abraham said, "I'm getting my riches from the Lord!"

We read in a previous chapter that **he that loveth silver shall not be satisfied with silver; nor he that loveth abundance with increase: this is also vanity** (Ecclesiastes 5:10).

That's covetousness, and that's the world's kind of prosperity. But we've got God's type of prosperity. And we're to receive our prosperity the same way Abraham did.

It's sad to say, but a majority of people won't ever walk fully in God's kind of prosperity. Why? Because it takes tenacity. It takes boldness. It takes separation. It takes self-control and singleness of purpose and mind. Abraham had all of these things working in his life.

So in your own life, you're going to have to go with what the Father has said in His Word to enter into the prosperity God wants for you.

In this world, people don't really like that. They want you to stay down on their level, where they're always complaining about how they'll never make it, and they're making excuses for why they won't.

It's sad to say, but unless you rise up and separate yourself from the unbelief of others and determine that you are going to let the truth of God's Word dominate your life, you'll never make it. Somewhere down the line, somebody is going to come along and try to preach it out of you.

Or somewhere down the line, you'll be tempted to fall back into the commonplace mode, where you're just satisfied with what little you have. You'll say, "Well, I'm not doing too badly." But you won't be doing too well either!

Are You Confessing "Money *Cometh*" or "Money *Goeth*"?

We've talked briefly about the faith of Abraham. But we really can't talk about faith without talking about confession.

We've heard so much confession about "Money goeth" and about money flying away. We've heard, "I don't have any money; I'm always broke. Maybe *one of these days* I'll have some money."

For example, some single women are just waiting for some rich "Romeo" to come so they can finally be prosperous. But if that "Romeo" doesn't have God's laws of prosperity working for him, he's not really going to have anything. Even if he has money, he won't be rich in his heart if he's not walking in line with the Word.

Or that "Romeo" may not have any money at all. He may just put on a front for that girl he's trying to impress. He'll take her out to nice restaurants, and he'll tip those waiters well!

But then, when they get married, he might say, "Honey, all I really have is $240 and $74,000 worth of debt"! (Now, my wife knew I was broke when she married me! She loved me anyway—she couldn't help herself! She said, "I'll take you, broke and all!")

We've heard people talking about money *going from them* or about money never coming to them and how they are barely getting along in life. But we haven't heard too many people talking about money constantly coming to them!

There's a joy in confessing "Money cometh," because when you're walking in God's will and you're keeping your confession about money straight, things will begin to change for the better in your life.

What I like about godly prosperity is that there's a joy with it. There's a peace with it. Those who walk in it are not God-robbers, so they have freedom and joy. The Bible says God has given us all things richly to enjoy, but worldly prosperity brings sorrow with it. Worldly prosperity brings sorrow because a person has to worry about how to get it, who's trying to take it from him and what the economical indicators are.

But when you are walking in God's ways, it doesn't make any difference what the economic indicators say. God is your Source!

The blessing of the Lord, it maketh rich, and he addeth no sorrow with it.

Proverbs 10:22

Since God's blessing "maketh rich," then the "rich" comes without the sorrow. Well, since the "rich" comes without the sorrow, there must be *joy* with the "rich"!

Some Christians are bringing sorrow upon themselves financially by getting caught up in gambling casinos, spinning those wheels and trying to get rich. But why are all those Christians in those places spinning those wheels when the Father has provided a sure thing for them?

Why do Christians go to those kinds of places? Because they want money. Some believers think, *Oh, I'll just go in there and buy a soft drink and say "hi" if I see anybody in there I know.*

But some of those same people are liable to put the Lord's tithe on that gambling table! Why? Because they want money, and they don't really believe what the Father has promised them concerning financial blessings.

The prince that wanteth understanding is also a great oppressor: but he that hateth covetousness shall prolong his days.

> He that hasteth to be rich hath an evil eye, and considereth not that poverty shall come upon him.
>
> Proverbs 28:16,22

My wife and I preached for a friend in Las Vegas once. The church put us up in a hotel where, instead of having enclosed elevators, they had glass elevators that ran up and down the side of the hotel lobby so you could look inside and see hundreds of slot machines. You could see people everywhere, pulling those levers.

But, you know, while I stayed in that hotel, I probably passed by hundreds, maybe thousands, of people gambling on those machines. Yet I never had a temptation to grab one single lever. Why? Because I wasn't broke. I could eat wherever I wanted to eat and buy the things I wanted to buy because the Lord had blessed me.

Now, if I were a broke preacher, I believe I might have been tempted to pull one of those levers! If I were a broke preacher who didn't know my rights in Christ, I might have pulled that lever, trying to make some quick money.

That's why a lot of Christians gamble; not necessarily because they are bad Christians, but because they're broke. They want to hit the jackpot and have some money.

But I've been talking about the "jackpot" throughout this book! I've been trying to tell you how to hit the jackpot with God and become prosperous. You hit the jackpot with God by obeying Him in your finances and by doing what His Word tells you to do. Prosperity is a sure thing with God when you're trusting and obeying Him. It's not a gamble.

Now, it might take you a little while; you can't make your order for prosperity at the speaker and then pick it up at the drive-up window! But if you "order" it and keep circling around that window, being faithful, it *will* come! Finally, the windows of heaven will open up and pour you out a blessing that you don't even have room to receive (Malachi 3:10)! Just order and keep circling the window, saying, "Money cometh!"

God wants us to prosper in life, legitimately and with joy, not with sorrow.

> **Thus saith the Lord, thy Redeemer, the Holy One of Israel; I am the Lord thy God which teacheth thee to profit, which leadeth thee by the way that thou shouldest go.**
>
> Isaiah 48:17

I'm telling you, the Lord put everything we need in the Bible! God wants to teach you to profit! He wants to teach you how to get prosperity, spiritually and financially.

My goodness! Look at that scripture again! He says, "I am the Lord, thy Redeemer, the Holy One of Israel." Make no mistake Who's talking to you! It's not John, Paul or any of the rest of the great men of the Bible. It's God, and He says, "I am the Lord which teaches thee to profit, which leadeth thee by the way that thou shouldest go!" And He *will* lead us in the way we should go!

What is the way that "thou shouldest go"? It's not to the casino. No, the *church* is where you ought to find your prosperity. You don't have to go looking for it anywhere else. The preacher at the church ought to teach you about the God of prosperity, Jehovah Jireh, the Lord our Provider!

The Lord is teaching us how to profit. That means He wants us to be financially blessed and prosperous. A god who wanted you poor certainly wouldn't teach you how to profit, would he?

Some people act as if that verse said, "The Lord who wants me to be poor teaches me how to be poor and how to just put up with it and be satisfied because I'm going to heaven one day." But, no! That verse says He is the Lord who teaches thee to profit!

If somebody says to you, "Where are you going?" you ought to tell him, "I'm on my way to church; I'm learning how to get prosperous. I'm going to the *prosperity* place!"

Your Prosperity Has Been Paid in Full!
What Are You Waiting For?

Remember, we read many scriptures that unmistakably prove God's will concerning your finances.

But thou shalt remember the Lord thy God: for it is he that giveth thee power to get wealth, that he may establish his covenant which he sware unto thy fathers, as it is this day.

Deuteronomy 8:18

Give, and it shall be given unto you; good measure, pressed down, and shaken together, and running over, shall men give into your bosom. For with the same measure that ye mete withal it shall be measured to you again.

Luke 6:38

Bring ye all the tithes into the storehouse, that there may be meat in mine house, and prove me now herewith, saith the Lord of hosts, if I will not open you the windows of heaven, and pour you out a blessing, that there shall not be room enough to receive it.

Malachi 3:10

But my God shall supply all your need according to his riches in glory by Christ Jesus.

Philippians 4:19

The Lord is my shepherd; I shall not want.

Thou preparest a table before me in the presence of mine enemies: thou anointest my head with oil; my cup runneth over.

Psalm 23:1,5

Now, make this confession: "The Lord is my Shepherd. He prepares a table before me in the presence of my enemies. He anoints my head with oil. My cup runneth over with blessings! Money cometh! God is opening the windows of heaven for me. He meets my every need according to His riches in glory by Christ Jesus. He is causing men to give unto me good measure, pressed down, shaken together and running over.

"God has given me the power to get wealth. I am redeemed by the blood of Jesus. I am redeemed from the curse of the law. I'm blessed going in and blessed going out. I'm blessed in the city and blessed in the field. I'm blessed with faithful Abraham. Money cometh to me!"

You may have the revelation of prosperity and of "Money cometh" burning in your spirit. You've conceived the revelation, and prosperity has come into your spirit.

Now, go ahead and act on it! By faith, shout your way out of debt and into financial prosperity. Give God praise and boldly confess, "My prosperity is paid for! Money cometh to *me!*"

For ye know the grace of our Lord Jesus Christ, that,
though he was rich, yet for your sakes he became poor,
that ye through his poverty might be rich.
—2 CORINTHIANS 8:9

We know the grace of our Lord Jesus Christ! Although He was rich, for our sakes He became poor, that we through His poverty might be rich!

Note that "Jesus" means *Savior,* and "Christ" means *anointed.* Some writers turn it around and, instead of saying Jesus Christ, they say Christ Jesus, which means *anointed Lord.* So we could say that Christ Jesus is the anointed Lord *over* poverty and the anointed Lord *of* prosperity! Let's look at our text again: **For ye know the grace of our Lord Jesus Christ....**

Jesus the Savior, who is also Lord, empowers you over poverty. And as the Christ, He is the anointing you need to overcome *any* situation, including any financial test or trial.

**For ye know the grace of our Lord Jesus Christ, that,
though he was rich, yet for your sakes he became poor, that
ye through his poverty might be rich.**

Jesus went to the cross as our substitute. We were supposed to be on the cross but, thank God, the Lord Jesus Christ took our place. He took our place in sickness, poverty and spiritual death so we could be free from those things.

Over a period of years in my Christian walk, I had been bothering the Lord, talking to Him repeatedly about prosperity. He corrected me because some of my thoughts and speech were not conducive to entering into the land of prosperity. So in order to get me to enter in, He had to rebuke me and correct my speech, or my confession. For example, when the man in that grocery store said, "Money really goeth, doesn't it?" I cheered him on, and it did not please the Lord. God said to me, "You cannot get prosperity talking poverty."

You cannot get prosperity with a bumper sticker on your car that says, "Too Poor To Pay Attention," or "Retired But Broke"!

Your prosperity is the Father's desire! It is His pleasure. The opposite of pleasure is *dis*pleasure. But God is not displeased with our prosperity. He is *pleased* with the prosperity of His servants (Psalm 35:27)!

Prosper in Life and Fulfill the Desire of the Father

Now, I believe that confessing this is the way God charges up and fine tunes our spirits. And I believe there's something about saying over and over again: "Money cometh! Money cometh! Money cometh!" It causes a heavenly blow to your financial situation and does something good in your spirit as well as in your circumstances.

One word from God can change your life forever! God wants His children blessed—not just a small group here and there, but *all* of His children! Jesus Christ is Lord *over* poverty and Lord of prosperity, and money cometh to the Body of Christ!

God wants His children blessed, but we have a part to play.

All of our needs should be met. We actually shouldn't have to preach to the Church about prosperity. We shouldn't have to preach about healing and long life. *That should be built into us!* Redemption is a package deal. We should be spending our time getting the lost saved, walking and living in the blessings of God provided for us through our redemption! But so many in the Body of Christ have been crippled by traditions and religious error.

But now we're coming back to the Word of God. We're going back to the book of Acts, the acts of the Holy Ghost. We're coming back up; now we will be able to do more for the Master. Jesus said, **Verily, verily, I say unto you, He that believeth on me, the works that I do shall he do also; and greater works than these shall he do; because I go unto my Father** (John 14:12).

Well, we're not going to be able to do those greater works like God wants us to if we're broke. But we are getting to the place where we are learning to walk in our full inheritance. I believe this is the generation that will do it.

Christ Jesus is the Lord over poverty and the Lord of prosperity! He became poor that through His poverty, we might become rich! Scripture says, **Christ hath redeemed us from the curse of the law, being made a curse for us: for it is written, Cursed is every one that hangeth on a tree** (Galatians 3:13). Now look at Galatians 3:29:

> **And if ye be Christ's, then are ye Abraham's seed, and heirs according to the promise.**
>
> **Galatians 3:29**

Notice again what the blessings of Abraham included:

> **Now the Lord had said unto Abram, Get thee out of thy country, and from thy kindred, and from thy father's house, unto a land that I will shew thee: And I will make of thee a great nation, and I will bless thee, and make thy name great; and thou shalt be a blessing: And I will bless them that bless thee, and curse him that curseth thee: and in thee shall all families of the earth be blessed.**
>
> **And the Lord appeared unto Abram, and said, Unto thy seed will I give this land: and there builded he an altar unto the Lord, who appeared unto him.**
>
> **Genesis 12:1-3,7**

> **And Abram was very rich in cattle, in silver, and in gold.**
>
> **Genesis 13:2**

Abraham was rich, and it was God who blessed him and made him prosperous. God is the God of prosperity! Jesus is the Lord *over* poverty, and He is the Lord *of* prosperity!

We have the blessing of Abraham because Christ has redeemed us from the curse of the law. We talked about reasons Abraham received his blessings, one of which was his *obedience to God.* When God chose Abraham and called him and told him to move, Abraham did it. He obeyed the Lord.

The Rewards of Obedience

Jesus Christ is the Lord *over* poverty and Lord *of* prosperity, but, as I said, we have a part to play in receiving the blessings of God. For example, we have to obey the Lord and His Word concerning finances if we want divine prosperity to come into our lives. Over the years, I have experienced many rewards for obeying the Lord. For instance, under the direction of the Spirit of God, I changed the name of the church I now pastor.

Years ago, Mount Zion Baptist Church in Darrow, Louisiana, was a historical hundred-year-old church. The Lord began dealing with me, as the pastor of that church, about changing its name, so I did it. I didn't have a meeting with anybody. I just changed it. The Lord gave me the new name: "Word of Life Christian Center."

When I announced the change, my secretary didn't say anything at first, but I saw her sad countenance and sensed the sadness of several others on my staff. But I knew the change was from the Lord, and I knew the Lord would do great things as a result of our obedience.

You see, no matter what the name, getting people delivered and blessed is what it all amounts to. I knew that the new name would take the brand, or label, off the church, which would, in effect, cause men and women of all different races, cultures and denominations to attend.

One day, after I changed the name of the church, my secretary came into my office, literally crying. She said, "But pastor, 'Mount Zion' is in the Bible." I told her, "Yes, but the Lord said, 'Word of Life Christian Center.'" I found out later that "word of life" was in the Bible too: **Holding forth the WORD OF LIFE; that I may rejoice in the day of Christ, that I have not run in vain, neither laboured in vain** (Philippians 2:16)!

I explained to my secretary, "When the Lord wants to do a new work, He changes names. That's why He changed our church's name." I cried with her and told her just to hang in there and see how things turned out.

Well, the "proof of the pudding *is* in the eating," because we really began to grow and prosper. My secretary finally came to me and said, "Pastor, I see what you were talking about."

You see, my people stuck with me. They didn't leave me. They didn't understand everything at the time, but they stuck with me.

Sometimes you don't understand everything, but if you obey the Lord and stick with what you know the Lord is doing, you'll get the blessing.

We know God changed Abram's name to "Abraham," which means the *father of many nations.* But before God changed Abram's name, He said to him, **Get thee out of thy country, and from thy kindred, and from thy father's house, unto a land that I will shew thee** (Genesis 12:1).

In other words, God made a promise to Abraham, but Abraham had to do something to get the full blessings. Abraham had to obey God.

Then, what did God further promise would be the result of Abram's obedience?

Genesis 12:2-3 says, **And I will make of thee a great nation, and I will BLESS thee, and make thy name great; and thou shalt be a BLESSING: And I will BLESS them that BLESS thee, and curse him that curseth thee: and in thee shall all families of the earth be BLESSED.**

Empowered To Prosper!

We saw the definition of "blessed"—*empowered to prosper.* We see it in the life of Abraham.

Say this: "I am blessed because I'm in Christ. And because I'm in Christ and I'm blessed, I am *empowered to prosper.*"

> **And I will bless them that bless thee, and curse him that curseth thee: and in thee shall all families of the earth be blessed.**
>
> **Genesis 12:3**

God told Abram, "I will make thee a great nation, and I will *empower thee to prosper.* I will make thy name great and thou shalt be *empowered to prosper:* And I will *empower to prosper* those who bless thee."

Do you know what God is saying to us today? He is saying, "Plant your seeds in good ground, and it will cause your crop to come up faster. You are empowered to prosper!"

When the devil starts talking to you, telling you you're not going to make it, say to him, "Look, Mr. Devil. I'm empowered to prosper. Christ has redeemed me from the curse of the law, so prosperity comes along with Christ's power. I'm empowered to prosper, because Christ Jesus is the Lord *over* poverty and the Lord *of* prosperity!"

> **But my God shall supply all your need according to his riches in glory BY CHRIST JESUS.**
>
> Philippians 4:19

Now I want you to look at the part of that verse that says, **By Christ Jesus.** As I said, "Christ" means *anointed* or the *Anointed One;* "Jesus" means *Savior and Lord.* Christ Jesus, the Anointed Lord *over* poverty and the Anointed Lord *of* prosperity, makes it possible for God to supply all of our needs!

Set Your Mind To Prosper

Christ Jesus is Lord of all. He is the Lord *over* poverty and the Lord *of* prosperity. But you have to set your mind to prosper.

> **And be not conformed to this world: but be ye transformed by the renewing of your mind, that ye may prove what is that good, and acceptable, and perfect, will of God.**
>
> Romans 12:2

Your mind has to be renewed toward prosperity before you can experience it. The first part of Romans 12:2 says, **And be not conformed to this world....** You see, you also have to understand that there is a difference between God's laws of prosperity and the world's system of prosperity. A lot of Christians don't have their minds renewed properly, and they want to take the world's system of prosperity and apply it to God's system of prosperity.

Then, there are some Christians who don't have their minds renewed who think they are doing something that's wrong if they prosper! They don't understand God's laws of prosperity. They don't understand the Father's will to prosper them. But remember, I said we are *empowered to prosper!*

When they see other believers prospering, they judge them by the world's system and automatically think those believers are being worldly. They'll say, for example, "Look at what she has on. That dress is too nice. Something must not be right." But I tell you, if anybody ought to be dressing nice, it ought to be a woman of God. It ought be an "Esther," not a "Jezebel"!

Heathen women should not be dressing nice while our women, the women of God, are dressing like vagabonds. Our Father owns all the cattle on a thousand hills! He owns all the silver and gold!

When some Christians begin living in line with godly principles and begin prospering, other good Christians who just don't know any better will start saying, "What in the world are they doing prospering like that?"

But those Christians who are living in line with God's principles are doing what the whole Body of Christ *should* be doing! They're preaching and they're prospering!

Don't let anybody rob you of your inheritance of prosperity. Your mind may have to change for you to enter in to what the Father has provided. If that is the case, then get your mind renewed! Get it in your mind that prosperity belongs to you and then be transformed by that truth. Don't be conformed to, or take the form or shape of, this world's beliefs and ways.

In essence, the Bible is telling us in Romans 12:2 not to be conformed to this world but to be conformed, instead, to the *world of the Spirit* so that what God has provided can take place in our lives.

You have to renew your mind because your soul—your mind, will and emotions—is not saved. James said, **Wherefore lay apart all filthiness and superfluity of naughtiness, and receive with meekness the engrafted word, which is able TO SAVE YOUR SOULS** (James 1:21). You have to renew your mind to get your soul into the realm of understanding prosperity. Your soul and your senses will gather against your spirit. The soul and the senses—the physical man—can gather against your spirit if your mind is not renewed. But the way to bring the soul and body under subjection to the spirit is through the renewing of the mind.

> But I keep under my body, and bring it into subjection: lest that by any means, when I have preached to others, I myself should be a castaway.
>
> 1 Corinthians 9:27

You see, your body doesn't know any better than to go the way of the flesh. Your body is lost and ignorant and will go its own way unless you "slap" it into shape and make it get in line with the Word and your spirit like it's supposed to. You have to make your body and soul get where they're supposed to be in the plan of God—in godly prosperity. Your body and soul just won't go in that direction by themselves.

Your body will either be dominated by your spirit or by the flesh, the senses and your unrenewed mind. If you let your body have its way, it will lie down with somebody else's wife or husband. The body is just as ignorant as it can be. It is selfish and wants to be indulged. That's why you have to keep it under control.

You know, your tongue would curse like a sailor, so to speak, and say every vulgar word it could if you didn't keep it under control. The Bible says that no man can tame the tongue (James 3:8). You need the Holy Ghost inside of you, taming your tongue. You have to get your tongue to the point at which it doesn't speak words of poverty. You have to get your mind to the point at which it doesn't think poverty and lack.

One writer once vividly explained that the word "transformed" means the same thing as the word "transfigured" in Matthew 17:2 and Mark 9:2 where it talks about Jesus' transfiguration.

> And after six days Jesus taketh Peter, James, and John his brother, and bringeth them up into an high mountain apart, And was TRANSFIGURED before them: and his face did shine as the sun, and his raiment was white as the light.
>
> Matthew 17:1,2

So when you get your mind renewed, your life is transformed or transfigured "from earth to glory"! In other words, you start living like God lives. Paul said in Romans 12:2 not to be conformed to this world but to be transformed or transfigured from a worldly lifestyle to a godly lifestyle! But it all starts with getting your mind renewed. That's the first thing you have to do—get your mind set on the Word of God.

Jesus was on the mountain they called the Mount of Transfiguration. The glory came down and rested upon Him, and the Bible says Jesus' face shone as the sun. I tell you, if you speak prosperity from the Word of God, the glory of God will shine upon you too!

Money cometh to the Body of Christ! And God has empowered each one of us to prosper because Christ Jesus is Lord *over* poverty and Lord *of* prosperity!

I'm preaching this message to you from three platforms—Bible *information*, personal *revelation* and *experience*. I have walked through what I'm teaching others. My mind got set on the Word of God and on the prosperity of God, and I ran away from the denomination I was in that didn't believe God wanted His children to prosper.

Actually, they gave me the left foot of fellowship as I was running away! Then I got out of all the ministers' clubs and cliques because a lot of those cliques were unbelieving too. They would meet seemingly just to talk about all of their problems, so I wouldn't go to any of those meetings.

Renew Your Mind and Fellowship
With Those of Like Faith

But "no man is an island unto himself." You can't make it by yourself, because we are interdependent. So I had to find some new company to fellowship with. I found it first in another state. I went to a man's church that had thousands of members, and I got some good fellowship with this minister and his group.

I also found at that church that there really wasn't any such thing as a "black church" or a "white church." I found black, white, Japanese,

Spanish and many other cultures and races there. And everybody praised the Lord together. It looked like the *Lord's* Church to me! It was another world to me—to someone who'd come from a place where there was still a lot of tradition.

Well, I started renewing my mind. I got my hands on another older minister's books, and I couldn't go to sleep at night—sometimes I'd read those books and meditate all night about what I'd read! I learned about being redeemed from sickness and poverty and about the authority of the believer and how to be led by the Spirit of God. It was raining spiritually, and I needed to get under God's rain of blessings, but I didn't even know it was raining blessings until then even though I had been teaching for ten years.

Through renewing your mind, your life can be transfigured from the world of debts and bills and financial troubles to the world of the will of God, where it says, **Beloved, I wish above all things that thou mayest prosper and be in health, even as thy soul prospereth** (3 John 2).

Jesus is the Lord *over* poverty and the Lord *of* prosperity! The Judge has already slapped the gavel on the rostrum. I've argued the case with you, so to speak, and I've won! It's as though the Judge said, "You've presented My Word, and you've won your case. You've won your case whether they believe you and go on with you toward prosperity or not."

You see, whether people accept what I'm saying or not, I'm going to keep on declaring the truth that Jesus is the Lord over poverty and Lord of prosperity.

"Let This Mind Be in You..."

Jesus Christ is the Lord *over* poverty and the Lord *of* prosperity. And He taught us on the "before-side" of the cross how we should live on the "after-side" of the cross.

> LET THIS MIND BE IN YOU, which was also in Christ Jesus: Who, being in the form of God, thought it not robbery to be equal with God:

> But made himself of no reputation, and took upon him the form of a servant, and was made in the likeness of men: And being found in fashion as a man, he humbled himself, and became obedient unto death, even the death of the cross. Wherefore God also hath highly exalted him, and given him a name which is above every name: That at the name of Jesus every knee should bow, of things in heaven, and things in earth, and things under the earth.
>
> Philippians 2:5-10

Verse 5 says, **Let this mind be in you, which was also in Christ Jesus.** Well, what kind of mind did He have? For one, He had such a mind that when 5,000 people needed something to eat, He fed them with one little boy's lunch! Then He sent twelve baskets full of leftovers home to that boy's mama!

Jesus was giving us an example. He lived on the *front* side of the cross—before He died for you and me—a lifestyle that we should live after He went to the *other* side of the cross.

Jesus could have gone directly to the cross without ministering to people for those three years. But He stayed on earth three years to set the example of how He wanted us to live—a life in full cooperation with the Father!

That's why Paul said, "Let's have the mind of Christ." Christ's mindset was, *I'm serving the Father. Whatever I need, My Father has it, and He's willing to give it to Me.* Jesus proved that in His earthly ministry.

Well, the Lord wants our mindsets to be like that. He wouldn't tell us to renew our minds, to learn to think like He thinks, if He didn't mean to bless us by it. The Lord is not a crook, and He doesn't talk loosely. He wouldn't tell us to "let this mind be in you" if it couldn't be in us!

Let's look again at the mind, or attitude, of Christ.

> Let this mind be in you, which was also in Christ Jesus: Who, being in the form of God, thought it not robbery to be equal with God.
>
> Philippians 2:5,6

Look at verse 6: **Who, being in the form of God, thought it not robbery to be equal with God.** You see, the Lord wants you to be just like Him in your thinking. Your religious mind will give you trouble with that. The Lord wants you to be just like Jesus. No, we are not the Savior. And we are not God. But all that God has is available to us. He wants us to have it!

You see, when you come to the knowledge of your rights in Christ as a joint-heir with Him, you become master of your circumstances.

No, we are not equal to God in the sense that we can get on His throne with Him. But He wants us to walk in equal ability to that which the Lord Jesus walked in when He was on the earth. Christ Jesus paid for us to have that ability. That's why He gave us His Name. He is *Christ;* we are the *Body of Christ.* Jesus is *the* Son of God; we are *sons and daughters* of God. We have equal rights with Christ because Christ *gave* us equal rights with Him. We are not the King of kings and Lord of lords. Only Jesus can fill that position. But we are heirs of God and joint-heirs with Christ.

No, I never said we are the Savior, but we are saved! And we are to boldly live a full, abundant life in the Savior and be on display for the Body of Christ and the world, living in holiness and sanctification and walking in the blessings He has provided for us.

We Are Rulers Over Circumstances!

We know from reading the Bible what kind of mind Jesus had. Jesus was ruler over circumstances too. He didn't pay any attention to "newscasts" that said a storm was going to wipe Him out. Jesus would just stop the storm!

And the water didn't bother Jesus. When He had somewhere to go, He just walked on it (Mark 6:48,49)!

The lack of food didn't stop Jesus. We read that when He had more than 5,000 to feed, He just took a loaf of bread and two fishes and fed them!

Jesus didn't let tax deadlines bother Him. When it was time to pay taxes, He just told Peter to go get a certain fish in a certain sea and get the tax money out of the fish's mouth (Matthew 17:27)!

Jesus didn't let any circumstances bother Him. Peter told Jesus, "What do You mean by telling us to let down our nets? We've fished all night and have caught nothing." Jesus answered Peter, "Yes, but you're not a fisherman like Me! Let Me renew your mind. You've been on the wrong side of the ship. Cast your net on the other side." I'm paraphrasing that, but when those boys did what Jesus told them to do, the ship almost sank—they had so many fish! (See Luke 5:1-7.)

I tell you, when you're a partner with Jesus, your "ship" will get full of blessings too!

That's the kind of mind you need to have! You need to "buck" against the devil and the world's system. You need to buck against those bills that you want paid. You have to resist what society might be telling you—that you won't make it and that you'll never be able to enjoy the good life.

You have to buck against this world's system and boldly say, "No! You're not going to rule me and have the final say in my life." It doesn't matter if you're making minimum wage at your job; just stand up and take your ground by faith. Declare that you are prosperous. It's up to God to do the rest. And He will do it!

It's not in the power of your own might or strength. You don't have to *make* "Money cometh" come to pass in your life. You only have the power to believe it, speak it and seek the Lord. It's up to Him to cause it to come to pass. You don't need to be concerned with where you're working or how much you're making. Just get the revelation. Renew your mind and speak the Word.

Speak the Word and Seek the Lord

It doesn't make any difference where you're from, what side of the tracks you were born on or what your background is. It doesn't make any difference what kind of job you have or even if you don't have a job at all! If you're seeking the Lord and speaking His Word in faith, then money cometh to you! (If you don't have a job, go out and look for one and keep speaking the Word and seeking the Lord.)

Somebody said, "Yes, but I'm just a janitor." Good! You will show God all the more strong in your life! The man down the street from you will say, "Even that janitor is prosperous and blessed abundantly because He is a child of the Lord. I've never seen a janitor so blessed!"

The Lord will raise the janitor up who believes and trusts Him, because "Money cometh!" It's not who you are, anyway, even if you have a good-paying job. It's not how much you know, how educated you are, what color you are or what inheritance you received from your family.

The only thing that counts is that you get the revelation of God's Word in your spirit and on your tongue—and that you're speaking that revelation constantly. Speak it and seek Him! Speak the Word and seek the Lord! It's not *where* you are now; it's not *who* you are; it's *whose* you are in Christ! If you've been born again, washed in the blood of Jesus, you belong to God. And you've got the sword of the Spirit, which is the Word of God, to "cut" your way to prosperity! You can cut that poverty down and rise up to where your Father wants you to be.

God has given us His life and nature. It is not wrong for us to have the things He intends for us to have. Jesus is our Elder Brother, and He stripped Himself of all His mighty power and glory and came to earth, not to minister as God, but as a man empowered by the Holy Spirit with *lordship.*

Jesus died and rose again, victorious over death, hell and the grave! Now you and I have been empowered with lordship; we are masters over circumstances.

If you are not living as master of your circumstances, you are living below your means.

You are to be master over situations and circumstances because the Lord lives on the inside of you to empower you. One of the Holy Spirit's names is "Helper." With the help of the Holy Spirit, you are victorious—more than a conqueror through Christ who loves you (Romans 8:37).

Smith Wigglesworth was a great example of someone who lived boldly as more than a conqueror. Wigglesworth used to get up and dance before the Lord, first thing every morning. I once read that about Wigglesworth and said to myself, *Smith danced; I'm going to dance right now!*

We are heirs of God and joint-heirs with Christ Jesus! We have every reason to be glad. Jesus Christ is the Lord over poverty and Lord of prosperity!

Don't Allow Yourself To Be Robbed

We read Galatians 4:1, which says, **Now I say, That the heir, as long as he is a child, differeth nothing from a servant, though he be lord of all.** We could read this verse like this: "Now I say that the heir, as long as he is a child, is uninformed and ignorant in certain things because he hasn't grown to maturity."

We could apply that to a Christian's growing up in knowledge and receiving his inheritance that belongs to him in Christ. Many are "old enough" to receive it; they're not that child Galatians 4:1 talks about.

They're old enough, but they've been robbed through ignorance of what was rightly theirs.

One way they've been robbed is through men. Paul talked about that in the book of Colossians.

> **Beware lest any man spoil you through philosophy and vain deceit, after the tradition of men, after the rudiments of the world, and not after Christ.**
>
> **Colossians 2:8**

Philosophy and vain deceit "after men's traditions" have robbed people of taking their rightful place in Christ. But the Word of God and *this* word from God, "Money cometh," are full of power to prosper you! Those words will propel you, like a jet, out of poverty and into prosperity!

There is a certain place you "hit," or arrive at, in pursuing Christ, seeking the things of God and speaking the Word. There is a certain place you reach where you're actually over in that realm of prosperity, but you're so busy seeking the Lord, you don't realize you're there.

In my own life, when I first got hold of the fact that it was God's will to prosper me, I got so busy seeking Him and speaking the Word and telling the same truth to others that there was a season in which I began looking back over the months, and I suddenly realized I was living "Money cometh." My circumstances had changed and were changing every day, for the better. I was in that flow of prosperity!

Somebody said, "Well, Preacher, you've got to watch that pride, talking the way you're talking." But how could I have pride, knowing it was all the Lord's doing? It wasn't my own ability. It's not pride if you have the attitude that you don't own anything, and God owns everything.

Christ Jesus is the Lord *over* poverty and the Lord *of* prosperity, and He'll let you become lord over poverty in your own life. Actually, if you *don't* take authority in your own life in the area of finances, He is held back from working on your behalf.

God is able to do exceeding abundantly above all that we ask or think (Ephesians 3:20)! The only reason a person doesn't have "exceeding abundantly above" is that he's holding the Lord back.

Don't Hold God Back From Working in Your Life

If you're not prospering, the only reason is that you are holding prosperity back! You are holding the Lord of prosperity back from being able to make you lord and ruler over your finances.

Somebody said, "What do you mean by that, Preacher?"

I mean, according to Ephesians 3:20, God is ready to prosper you exceeding abundantly above all that you can ask or imagine, according to the power that works in you. If you give His power place in your life by living according to the Word in your finances, the Lord of prosperity will come in, and, in time, He will flood you with His goodness and blessings! But you have to obey and trust Him, and part of doing that is having the mind of Christ and totally renewing your mind to the fact that God wants to bless you.

Again, let's look at the mind of Christ. Christ never had the thought that His Father didn't have whatever He needed. And He never thought that God wouldn't get it to Him. No, in every situation, Jesus declared, in effect, "I and My Father are One. Where I stay, He stays. We are One."

I wonder what kind of suit God would wear if He were here physically? I wonder if He would have a seersucker suit on—something that wrinkles up every time you sit down? Or I wonder if He would have on a nice, wool, pinstriped suit!

You might say, "Brother Thompson, that's sacreligious." No, that's good sense. I *know* what kind of suit God would have on—a *good* one—because I know what kind of house He has. He told us, **In my Father's house are many MANSIONS...** (John 14:2)!

You know God has nice things, because when you read about heaven in the Bible, you read about pearly gates and streets of gold! When you show up at those pearly gates, you'll be face to face with those big pearls. Then, after the gates open and you get inside, you'll look down and see gold here, gold there—gold *everywhere!*

Someone who paves His driveway with gold has no problems wearing a good suit! But many people have been serving the wrong god—the "barely-get-along" god. But our God is a God of prosperity! And, as long as you keep Him first, He doesn't mind your being prosperous too. It doesn't matter to Him what you have that's good; He *wants* you to have it. He just wants you to preach the Gospel and remember that that's the main reason we are here.

If you will do those things, He will say to you, "Go ahead and enjoy yourself while you are doing My will."

God Is the Sum Total of Everything You Need!

Once when I was praying in other tongues I heard these words from the Spirit of God: "I am the sum of the whole matter." I looked up that word "sum" and started thinking about it. The word "sum" means *the total amount*. The Lord said, "When you get through adding up all your bills, I am the sum of the whole matter, and My sum is prosperity."

The Lord is your prosperity! When the devil gets through talking to you, your bills get through talking to you and unbelieving people around you get through talking to you, God is the sum—the total amount—of everything you need!

I looked up another word, "summary," in connection with what the Lord showed me, and I found that that word means *a short restatement of the main points*. You see, when you get through adding up all your bills and adding up the unbelief that tries to come to make you doubt God's Word, God never changes! He will continue to restate His main point that He is Lord over poverty and the Lord of prosperity!

Why haven't Christians experienced more of this prosperity then? It all boils down to the fact that we've been robbed. We've been lied to, and we haven't been ministered to in our spirits concerning the truth.

But as we learn the truth, we can rise up and take our rightful place in Christ and boldly declare that "Money cometh! I'll never be broke another day in my life. I am a child of God. My Father is the God of prosperity. If I seek Him first and keep Him first, acknowledging that He owns everything, I can have the prosperity He has given me. God's kind of prosperity is mine now."

As I said in the very beginning of this book, you have to "talk up" if you want the blessing. The blessings of God don't just fall on us. We have to receive them by faith.

The Bible says, **Now FAITH is the substance of things HOPED for, the evidence of things not seen** (Hebrews 11:1). Faith is the substance of things hoped for. You have to build your hope so you can add your faith to it. Then the substance of your hope will come running after you!

Get Your Hopes Up—God Will Not Fail You!

When you hear the truth of God's Word, you get your hopes up. When the Word gets in you, a ray of light comes in. You begin to think, *Hey, it's really possible for me to rise up and not just stay down here where I am.*

Have you ever heard the story of the eagle that was raised as a chicken? I'm going to tell the story a little differently than you may have heard it so I can help you better understand some things I've been talking about.

This eagle was caught as a little eaglet and put in a yard with chickens. He grew up with chickens. He thought he was a chicken. He'd walk around that yard, picking up what he could find on the ground to eat. He'd look up from time to time and see birds flying overhead.

But then one day, this "chicken-eagle" saw another eagle flying in the sky above him. That eagle he saw flew like a master!

That little eagle kept pecking away at the ground, but he began noticing those eagles flying above him day by day. Pretty soon, he began flapping his wings, one at a time, and he saw that his wings were stronger than the wings of those chickens hanging around him in that chicken yard. That's because that eagle's wings were not made for the *ground*; they were made for the *air!*

One day, this eagle got to flapping his wings again, and he decided he was going to give flying a try. He flapped both wings at the same time and came off the ground. He looked down at the chickens and said, "I'll never see you again. Good-bye, chickens! You had me fooled for a long time, but I'm not fooled anymore. I'm an *eagle!*"

Much like this eagle flew away from those chickens, if you don't like the neighborhood you live in, you should change neighborhoods! When you get ahold of this prosperity message in your spirit, you are going to "flap your wings" and say, "Good-bye, chicken yard. I'm flying away. I've been in the chicken yard too long. Good-bye, poverty. I'm an eagle! I am a prosperous child of the Most High!"

We're flying away with the eagles! Too many of you have been in the chicken coop too long, pecking around on the ground for worms and bugs, and you haven't even tried your wings! If you'd try your wings, you'd know that with God's Word, you can fly out of that situation you're in.

God has given you wings of the Holy Ghost, revelation knowledge and the blood and the Name of the Lord Jesus Christ. If you'll start mounting up with those wings like an eagle (Isaiah 40:31), you will come out of the chicken yard. You will fly out of the coop into the sweet atmosphere of His blessings where He wants you to be.

So don't be a chicken, pecking around and scraping to get by the best you can. Flap those wings and get on out of that chicken yard. Get up high where God wants you to be and live in prosperity so you can bless others and be a supporter of the Gospel.

I like that eagle story! I found out a few things about eagles. They have more sense than some human beings. When they get old, they go into hiding and beat off their old beaks and grow new ones. And I have heard that they regrow their feathers and won't set out after molting until a certain oil is secreted onto their wings. The oil comes out onto the eagle's wings, and he says, "I'm ready to fly again."

I liken that to the Holy Ghost "oil," or anointing, that we need before we set out to doing anything for God!

I believe that in the Body of Christ, we need to beat off some of our old "beaks and feathers"—that old poverty mentality that has robbed us and weighed us down. We need to go ahead and get some new feathers, new wings, and let the oil of the Holy Ghost anoint us to come on up to prosperity!

Body of Christ, we've been in the chicken yard too long! Let's come on out and fly away with the Father! This world's system will fry you like a chicken if you let it! But the Father has given you wings of faith, love, joy, understanding and wisdom that you might fly above the world's system.

Come on out from the limits the world has placed on you! You've been in that old chicken yard long enough, fenced in and held captive, eating those old bugs and worms. You haven't been able to go where you've wanted to go. You've been broke and fenced in. But now you see the eagle gliding through the air—he's free!

That's us, Christians! We're free! We can mount up on wings of eagles because we can rise above this world's system. So tell that chicken yard good-bye!

You know, when a storm or hurricane comes, the eagle doesn't worry about it. He has a special "mechanism" in his wings; he sort of locks those wings in place, gets in the eye of the storm and just rides the current.

So when things get rough in your life, and the storms of life rise up, lock your wings in place! Be bold and say, "I will never go back to that chicken yard!"

But don't try to make it in your own strength. Just ride the wind of grace and mercy and glide on the goodness of God!

> To whom then will ye liken me, or shall I be equal? saith the Holy One. Lift up your eyes on high, and behold who hath created these things, that bringeth out their host by number: he calleth them all by names by the greatness of his might, for that he is strong in power; not one faileth. Why sayest thou, O Jacob, and speakest, O Israel, My way is hid from the Lord, and my judgment is passed over from my God?
>
> Hast thou not known? hast thou not heard, that the everlasting God, the Lord, the Creator of the ends of the earth, fainteth not, neither is weary? there is no searching of his understanding. He giveth power to the faint; and to them that have no might he increaseth strength. Even the youths shall faint and be weary, and the young men shall utterly fall: But they that wait upon the Lord shall renew their strength; they shall mount up with wings as eagles; they shall run, and not be weary; and they shall walk, and not faint.
>
> **Isaiah 40:25-31**

It is God who gives power to the faint. He gives power to the "broke"; and to them who have no might, He increases strength! He increases our strength so we can fly on to prosperity and the blessings God has provided for us in Christ Jesus—the Lord *over* poverty and the Lord *of* prosperity!

We talked previously about the balance of this prosperity message and said that God has provided for His children to have the very best in life but that it wasn't wise to try to live above one's faith and one's means.

In this chapter, I'm going to cover some things that will help you not to be "flaky"—for example, following some uninspired dream that flounders, leaving your faith shipwrecked. You don't want that to happen, and neither do I, so I'm going to "tie up" some loose ends to make sure you fully understand what the Spirit of God is trying to tell you through this book.

A person has to be established in the laws of prosperity before he can prosper properly. And what I'm going to share in this chapter will help you to keep yourself in balance in God's divine system of prosperity. God wants to bless you, but He wants you to keep His Word and to put Him first always.

> **For the Lord thy God bringeth thee into a good land, a land of brooks of water, of fountains and depths that spring out of valleys and hills. A land of wheat, and barley, and vines, and fig trees, and pomegranates; a land of oil olive, and honey.**
>
> **Deuteronomy 8:7,8**

Now notice in particular verse 9:

> **A land wherein thou shalt eat bread without scarceness, thou shalt not lack any thing in it; a land whose stones are iron, and out of whose hills thou mayest dig brass.**

I like that part: **A land wherein thou shalt eat bread without scarceness, thou shalt not lack any thing in it....** Goodness!

Then look at verse 10: **When thou hast eaten and art full, then thou shalt bless the Lord thy God for the good land which he hath given thee.**

Now the Lord has provided a good land for us! When we follow His laws and commands—His Word—there's a good land of prosperity for each of us!

But we have to know how to put first things first to have God's kind of prosperity. And I'll tell you from firsthand experience, when you support the Gospel first, and you do it consistently, you'll soon have plenty, plenty, plenty! You'll have plenty left over for you and your family.

So let's look at what the Lord has to say about putting Him first and keeping balanced in this message of prosperity:

> **When thou hast eaten and art full, then thou shalt bless the Lord thy God for the good land which he hath given thee. BEWARE THAT THOU FORGET NOT THE LORD THY GOD, in not keeping his commandments, and his judgments, and his statutes, which I command thee this day. Lest when thou hast eaten and art full, and hast built goodly houses, and dwelt therein. And when thy herds and thy flocks multiply, and thy silver and thy gold is multiplied, and all that thou hast is multiplied; Then thine heart be lifted up, and thou forget the Lord thy God, which brought thee forth out of the land of Egypt, from the house of bondage.**
>
> **Deuteronomy 8:10-14**

The reason God is warning us about keeping His commandments is that most people forget God when they come up financially a little bit. So you have to keep God's Word; you can't let money ruin you and cause you not to live right.

In essence, God said in verses 11 through 14, "Beware that you don't forget the Lord, lest when you have eaten and are full and have built houses and have prospered, your heart be lifted up and you forget the Lord."

You see, the only reason some people serve God is that they need something. Then when they receive what they need, they slack off in their Christian walks or forget God altogether. They haven't grown to the point that they'd serve Him no matter what.

I'm not saying that to condemn anyone or make anyone feel badly. I just want you to look carefully into what I'm saying to make sure that attitude will not get hold of you.

We are to love God for who He is, not for what we can get from Him.

You know, in the natural, I can "smell," or sense, when a person is hanging around someone else just to get something from him. People like that are not really interested in you; they only "like" you because of what you have, and they're just hanging around, thinking you might drop a little something for them.

You know, some people stick to their wealthy relatives just because they have a little something. And many times, those relatives treat them any kind of harsh way they want to. But a person who just tries to hang around wealthy people, looking for a handout, needs to learn to make *God* his source.

I didn't want any handouts—I wanted to get into the hand of God for myself! I wanted to learn how to receive from the main hand—the hand of God. And the way you do that is by getting in His will.

God gave us guidelines in His Word for dealing with godly prosperity because if you don't know how to deal with it, it will become more of a curse than a blessing.

Divine Prosperity Is by Degrees

We've been taught about prosperity, but often there's not enough balance in the message, and some people have moved too quickly after they've heard the message of prosperity. But there are levels to prosperity. Most people prosper in levels.

First of all, a person has to get the foundation of his faith built properly so that, no matter how high he builds—no matter how many floors he goes up—he knows he's got a firm foundation, and his prosperity won't crumble.

We already talked about always keeping God first. Keeping the Lord first is your foundation.

That's why we need to get the foundation straight and solid. Too many people are trying to build skyscrapers without a proper foundation.

Don't Neglect Your Foundation

The Holy Spirit gave me this message "Money cometh," but He wants to turn the prosperity message inside out, so to speak, so it will be taught properly and people will stay balanced.

As I said, many try to go too quickly with this message. They don't realize that *true prosperity is prospering on the level where you are.* In other words, one dollar extra on the other end of debt is prosperity! It's surplus. You don't owe that dollar to anybody; all your bills are paid and you have money left over. You have just hit the realm of prosperity!

People always look at the corporate executives, doctors, lawyers, widely known ministers, certain politicians and some others in the business world as truly prosperous. They tend to look up to those people as if they were the ones who had the greatest advantage in life.

But God doesn't want you to get your eyes on those people. If you are a janitor or custodian making minimum wage, just take off and begin prospering right where you are! Begin honoring God and His Word with your giving. If you keep doing what God wants you to do and continue to trust Him, you may pass up some of those people in their corporate positions as though they were standing still!

Some people think, *Well, I have to have this or that type of job to really prosper.* But, no. You just have to love God and keep Him and His Word first. Then that Word will elevate you like a skyscraper!

Whatever you have now, just turn it over to God and be happy. You don't have to have a brick or stone mansion; just turn whatever you have over to God. Just keep up the house you live in like it is a mansion. Plant flowers, paint the house and keep it looking good. Be happy and thank God for it. Give it back to Him and watch what He will do for you.

We need to be thankful for what we do have and take care of the things God has given us.

Now, as you're building your foundation for prosperity, you have to make sure you are rooted and grounded in faith.

Have you ever lived financially from payday to payday? Have you ever been in a "bill-wrestling match"? Those bills tug one way, and you tug the other way, struggling to pay them. It's hard to stay solidly rooted in prosperity when your circumstances are saying *poverty*. But you can do it through faith!

I know all about walking by faith in the midst of terrible circumstances. There was a time my wife and I lived from paycheck to paycheck, but we broke out of that by faith, glory to God.

We didn't do it overnight. My own family and others in my church watched us work the Word over a period of time. They remember a time when we didn't have anything. But we were faithful to work the Word and do God's work day in and day out, week after week, month after month and year after year.

It Pays To Be Faithful

Faithfulness pays off! You may start out like one of those men who was in distress, in debt and discontented who gathered themselves around David. But if you stay faithful, you will be promoted; you'll come out of debt, distress and discontentment. Further down the line, those men under David's care turned out to be captains of David's armies. They got out of debt. They got out of distress. They got out of discontentment!

As I said, "in debt, in distress and discontented" describes the Body of Christ at large, but that shouldn't be so. Churches shouldn't have to borrow money to build buildings. There is enough money coming into the homes of the Body of Christ to pay tithes so that churches would never have to go to banks. The Lord wants banks to come to *us!*

According to the Old Testament, God's people were supposed to be the lenders and not the borrowers. But Christians have not been taught properly. Many of them have not honored God in their giving. And many have let credit cards become "demons" in their lives.

As I said before, it's not wrong to use credit cards, but it's wrong for credit cards to use you. It's wrong to spend more than you can repay so that you sink deeper and deeper into debt. It's called the credit-card syndrome. For example, if a person who's in the credit-card syndrome has a credit card with an $800 credit limit, he uses the card up to the limit. Then, when he gets his balance down to about $400, he runs his account back up to $800. But God has a better way for you!

Some people are looking for a "get-rich-quick" plan with God. In other words, they will tithe for a while to see if God will open those windows quickly. Then, when things don't happen quickly, they forget about tithing.

You have to take prosperity step by step and develop your faith. If you read one book or go to one prosperity revival and decide, "Yes, I want what so-and-so has," you can't just expect to "arrive" overnight at the place you want to be. Your faith may not be developed as much as the other man's. But if you'll take it step by step, you'll get there.

You see, there is a price to pay to walk fully in the Word of God. You have to be hungry for the Word. When I first got the revelation of the faith message and the power of God's Word, I read the Bible so much, I think some people thought I was crazy. But I was hungry for the Word of God.

Make God's Word Your First Priority

I remember something I read about Smith Wigglesworth concerning the Word. When he was alive, he wouldn't go more than thirty minutes without reading the Bible. He was known to have said things while traveling, such as, "Let's talk to God now. Stop this car. Pull over and stop all this unbelief and get out your Bibles!"

I may be paraphrasing what Wigglesworth said, but I think you understand how important it was to him to keep God and His Word first in his life. And you need to do the same in your life. God wants you to have the best in life, and the way to become a possessor of prosperity is through His Word.

God doesn't want you to settle for less than His perfect will in your finances, because He has provided for you to have the very best! He doesn't want you to settle for less in any area of life. Young person, don't settle for drugs when God has provided for you to be free! Don't settle for selling drugs to try to get to the top financially. God has provided for you to rise to the top in *His* program.

You don't need the world's program; all you need to do is get in God's will and stay there. Abide in Him and His Word (John 15:7). Love Him and walk with Him, and you will rise to the top. The drug dealers will wonder what in the world you're doing to be so prosperous, but you will have a "clean bill of sale"! You won't have to duck and hide and be ashamed because of your lifestyle. You will have gotten your prosperity God's way—decently and in order.

God wants you to have the very best in life, and He's made a way for you to have it. God wants His ministers to have the best too. That's why I said that it's wrong to want to hold the preacher back when it comes to God's program of prosperity.

God gave me the revelation that He wanted His children to have the very best in life. As I said before, when I was getting ready to build my house, I had some problems because the banks didn't want me to build such a big home in the area I wanted to build in. I was about to begin looking at some blueprints for a smaller house when the Lord said to me, "Don't settle for less, for I have provided for you to have the best!"

God as my witness, had I not built the house that I have now, I would have been out of the will of God! That's hard for people to understand, but it's true. The Lord told me to build that house. As a matter of fact, He "manifested" that house in New Orleans, led me to it and said, "There it is; there's the house. Build yours like this one." When my wife and I first walked in that house, we both said, "This is the house!"

God had somebody build that house in New Orleans, and then He showed it to me! My wife and I went to look at the house in New Orleans, believing God and turning our faces toward Him for His perfect timing. He said, "Now's the time." Then He gave me a scripture from Proverbs to back it up.

I had been reading a chapter from Proverbs, the book of wisdom, every day for a few years. I'd read Proverbs through and through. But He took me to this particular verse, and it just blew me away—it almost blew me out of my car!

The Lord gave me Proverbs 24:27: PREPARE THY WORK **without, and make it fit for thyself IN THE FIELD; and afterwards build thine house.**

Our ministry didn't build our house. I don't have a parsonage. I built my house myself. It's my family's home that God has provided for us.

In *The Amplified Bible,* Proverbs 24:27 reads, **[Put first things first]....** Then it says, **Prepare your work outside and get it ready for yourself in the field; and afterward build your house and establish a home.**

Our church has been out of debt, owing no man anything, since 1987. The church has plenty of money in the bank earning interest. We own all of our land, many acres. Well, I believe that all the Lord has accomplished in this ministry is a field prepared!

Since 1987, the only bills the church has had to pay have been utility bills. The church accounts have just been drawing interest. Our major problem has been finding enough banks to split up our accounts so there would be enough insurance to cover them! That's a good problem to have—if you'd even call that a problem!

Somebody asked, "Brother Thompson, do you have as much money yourself as the church has?" No, but I do have a full supply.

Remember, I said that "rich" means not being in debt and having a full supply. "Rich" is being able to shout without sorrow!

I don't apologize for what the Lord has done for me. God wouldn't have been able to bring me to the place in ministry where I am today if I preached about a god who won't do anything for His people. He wouldn't have been able to do what He wanted to do if I lived in a shack, had busted britches and wore a necktie that was fourteen shades different than the color of my suit! People wouldn't come and listen to me preach!

Don't Be Afraid To Brag on the Lord

God is my Source, and I want to brag on Him. He takes care of His children well! Sometimes I weep while I'm telling it—God has blessed me so much. I'm blessed from head to toe, inside and out. I'm blessed because I got hold of God twenty years ago, and I haven't turned Him loose yet!

I teach the way I do because I'm here to help people. I'm for them; I'm not against them. And I'm teaching about "Money cometh" because if I don't, I'll be in disobedience to God and will stop the blessings from flowing in my life.

God has blessed me so I can share with the Body of Christ without being arrogant. I don't want to be arrogant. I don't want to hurt anybody; I just want people to be blessed.

I maintain a humble attitude before the Lord. I have money, but money doesn't have me! I got ahold of the revelation of "Money cometh," and I'm not being arrogant when I say that I'll never be broke another day in my life. I'm rich!

You need to say that word, "rich," out loud, often. I have people do that in my meetings when I teach on this subject. The Body of Christ has been in poverty so long that we need to change our mindsets about money. We need to get used to saying "rich"and hearing "rich."

We will not rise any higher in life than our confession. Our lives are run by our confessions, but in the past we have said things such as "Money flies away" or "Money really goeth" or "I'm always broke."

You'll Become What You Confess

And then, some person who was totally ignorant of the Bible made a bumper sticker that said, "I'm too broke to pay attention." And some people actually put those bumper stickers on their cars, and everywhere they go in those cars, they confess that they are broke. Well, you know the devil is going to tap into that confession!

Then, there are people who work until they're sixty-five and receive a pat on the back and a watch, which breaks not long after they leave the company they worked at for so many years. Many companies don't want to pay retirement benefits like they should to retirees who practically gave their lives for the companies. So what do those retirees do? They'll put bumper stickers on their cars that says "Retired But Broke."

But, we read in the Scripture that if you are a Christian, you are Christ's, and all things are yours. You don't have to settle for less when God has provided for you to have the very best!

Don't misunderstand me. There has to be balance in this message. You have to stay on your level until you're ready to go on to the next level. Make sure you don't jump or act on another person's experience, or level. That's where the enemy can defeat you.

Make sure you don't buy a house or car just because you see somebody else with a new house or car. If you do, you're going to jam your faith, so to speak. In other words, your finances will become a struggle.

Faith is never a struggle. Yet some people will do foolish things beyond their levels of faith and then say, "Well, the devil's fighting me."

But the devil's not fighting them. They've made a mistake. They've messed around and punched the wrong floor on that elevator. They got off the elevator on the wrong floor and it's too high for them. They did it in the flesh and now they're struggling. They need to go down to the floor they're supposed to be on until they develop their faith a little bit more.

Avoid That "False Prosperity" Monster!

False prosperity is a monster. People have been trapped in that syndrome of buying cars they can't put gas in, houses they can't furnish or entertain guests in. Why? Because they're really broke. They can hardly pay their utility bills. They can't run their air conditioners like they need to, because they have to cut back.

It's hot down here in the South. I've been to people's houses, and I've just come out of those houses sweating because it was so hot! (I hurry up and finish those visits!) They say they're economizing (and I certainly believe in economizing), but many of them are broke. They can't afford the houses they're living in.

Now, my oldest sister is an example of how Christians ought to live concerning this prosperity message. She doesn't have any mansion, but she lives like a queen in the house she has! She can eat what she wants to eat, and she turns her air conditioner on as low as she wants. She doesn't drive a luxury car, but she has a nice car. And she keeps it looking good and running well.

I know there are people who have big money, but they don't know what money is for. They're tightfisted, and they'll keep their air conditioners turned way up, not because they're *broke,* but because they're *tight.*

But when a person buys a house and can't even afford to heat or cool it, that's not prosperity. That's *false* prosperity.

Many people have shipwrecked their faith by trying to go too quickly with this prosperity message. They might listen to people on TV and send them all their money, thinking they're going to get rich overnight.

Most people don't get rich overnight. Most people have to work their faith and develop it and come up through the ranks, so to speak.

Besides developing your faith, you have to fulfill the will of God before "money cometh" to you. So it's by developing your faith and fulfilling the will of God that money cometh.

"Money cometh" is not complicated. It's very simple. Some people are always wanting some new revelation, but they've never done anything with the revelation they have!

God told me once during a ministers' conference that I needed to preach the same messages over and over again, not just once or twice. One older minister told me, "You haven't really preached a message until you've preached it fifty times!"

So we don't need to be as concerned with new revelation as we need to be concerned about doing something with the revelation we have and getting it to work and produce something in our lives.

Money cometh to the Body of Christ! The *balance* to this message is walking prosperity out, step by step, according to the Word. When everything is done decently and in order, you have balance and you won't stray into error, just going after money to consume it on your own lusts (James 4:3).

But we who love God and His Word are not going after money; money is coming after us, good measure, pressed down, shaken together, running over and exceeding abundantly above all that we ask or think according to the power that worketh in us (Luke 6:38; Ephesians 3:20)!

The Lord Is Our Shepherd

God is establishing His covenant in the earth realm through those who will trust Him and take Him at His Word. If you do what God says to do, God will take care of you. Psalm 23:1 says, **The Lord is my shepherd; I shall not want.** Some people are quoting that verse, but by the way they act, they should be saying, "The Lord is my shepherd, and I'm *full* of want"!

Psalm 23:5 says, **Thou preparest a table before me in the presence of mine enemies: thou anointest my head with oil; my cup runneth over.**

Then look at Psalm 23:3: **He restoreth my soul....** You see, your soul needs to be restored and your mind renewed so you can get your thinking straight about biblical prosperity. Then you will begin to think in agreement with God's Word. You will begin to say, "I claim what God says is mine. I'm not moved by what I feel or see. I'm only moved by what I believe. And I know that if I keep believing, the Word will change what I feel and see!"

There's more to "Money cometh" than just instantly becoming rich. Certainly, you can become rich, because that's what God wants for you. But I have to teach all sides of the subject so people will be balanced.

Learn the Secret of Being Contented

So don't get in too big a hurry. Don't go build that house that you've been wanting too soon. I once told someone, "You don't need your dream house now; you need a starter home first. Get your family in a starter house and dress it up really nicely. Then be happy with that starter. Shout and jump for joy in that house."

You know, before I built the house I'm living in now, I was happy with the house I had.

Some people want to go too far too quickly. They want a luxury car, but maybe they just need to get one that *looks* like a luxury model until they can get the car they really want.

Don't put yourself under stress and strain to buy a car you can't afford—that is, a car you can't afford to make repairs on or put gas in or pay the insurance premium for.

I'm talking about balance. Having a luxury car doesn't make you wealthy. In fact, having a luxury car before you're ready for one will make you *broke!* You have to have enough money to support your buying a luxury car. If buying a luxury car puts you in the "hole," you're going to have to get in debt further with those credit cards just to get by.

If I could get people to see what I'm talking about, and if the Body of Christ would rise up like a giant in this earth and take their rightful place as sons and daughters of God, they would come out of debt, distress, discontentment and financial bondage.

The Lord Will Increase You More and More!

If you're in debt, God not only wants you out of debt, He wants you *way* out of debt! He doesn't want you broke. He wants you to have a rich, full life, and He wants you to leave something for your children to enjoy too.

I sometimes think about the inheritance I'm leaving for my children if Jesus tarries His coming. All my children have to do is stay in line with God's Word and follow Him, and I know they will come right along the same prosperity line I have come.

The Bible says, **A good man leaveth an inheritance to his children's children: and the wealth of the sinner is laid up for the just** (Proverbs 13:22).

Some children fight over the fifty dollars their parents left them when they died. Then the children have to pay to bury their parents!

You need this prosperity message so you can leave your children something. That's why I recommend writing a will to keep the courts from getting all your stuff when you die.

I tell my church congregation, "All of you need to take care of your family and write a will."

Somebody argued, "I'm not going to write a will," as if writing a will showed a lack of faith! I said, "Everybody alive today is going to die sooner or later if Jesus tarries His coming. The *will* is not going to kill you!"

> **Ye that fear the Lord, trust in the Lord: he is their help and their shield. The Lord hath been mindful of us: he will bless us; he will bless the house of Israel; he will bless the house of Aaron. He will bless them that fear the Lord, both small and great. The Lord shall increase you more and more, you and your children.**
>
> **Psalm 115:11-14**

Verse 12 says, **The Lord hath been mindful of us: he will bless us....** Remember I said the word "bless" actually means *empower to prosper.* In other words, we could read this verse like this: "He will empower us to prosper." Verse 13 says, "He will *empower* to *prosper* them who fear the Lord, both small and great!"

You see, if you fear the Lord—if you revere the Lord and keep His Word as holy—He will empower you to prosper. If you practice these principles I've shared, God will cause you to prosper.

God's Word is more real than the word of a banker. God's Word is more real than any situation or circumstance you may face.

Now look at verse 14 again: **The Lord shall increase you more and more, you and your children.** That is what the Lord wants for you. He wants you to increase so you can work on His covenant. God's major concern is not that we know about the gifts of the Spirit. It's not that we know about talking in tongues or building big houses. God is most concerned about evangelizing the world, and when He finds a vessel, or reservoir, who will work for Him in that matter, He will bless him.

Remember, all the silver and gold belong to God. The cattle on a thousand hills belong to Him. The earth is the Lord's and the fullness thereof!

I tell you, this world's system is out of whack. I personally don't believe women should *have* to work to keep a household going financially. I know a lot of people don't like to hear that.

I'm not saying a woman who has a job or a career should just quit her job. The bottom would fall out if some wives stopped working, because the family has already bought too much on credit. They have to pay for it. But I don't believe it was God's original intent that women should have to work.

God's Reward for Faithfulness: A Real Life Example

Years ago there was a woman in my congregation who had been faithful in the church for years. One day, I was riding in a car with a pastor friend from another state, and this young woman's name just came up in my spirit. This pastor was a single man, and I knew God was talking to me and that I had to get the two of them in each other's presence.

I arranged a meeting and flew the woman to the state where this pastor lived. Well, in just a short time, they were in love. I said to the pastor, "Now this woman has a little boy; she's been married before." He said, "I'll take him and give him my name."

Then the woman told the man about some bills she had, and he said, "I'm going to take care of that, too, and wipe those bills out!" This woman seemingly moved from poverty to prosperity overnight. But, you see, she had been working the Word for a long time and had been faithful in our church for years.

Some of this woman's friends from where she'd worked thought she was crazy when she first met this pastor and fell in love. But the Lord did the work, and "the proof of the pudding is in the eating." We tell her testimony all over the United States. The two of them serve God in the ministry today. The ministry is so big, you have to ride around in a golf cart to get from one building to the next. They just bought a big, new house, and she rides around in a luxury automobile. And they support our ministry. They are constantly sending money to our church to spread the Gospel.

You see, there is a blessing for being obedient to the Lord and His Word. If that woman in my congregation had not been faithful and submitted and teachable, her name would have never come up in my spirit so I could introduce her to my friend.

This woman trusted us, too, and believed in our ministry. She had respect for the things of God, and she took time off from work to go meet that pastor just because I told her to go.

Another girl came up to me after all this happened and said, "Pastor, whenever the Lord speaks to you about me, go ahead and speak that out. Just feel free!" Actually, several young ladies have said similar things.

I'm just trying to show you that God wants the best for you in life, and He has provided for you to *have* His best. I believe you will begin to put into practice the principles of God's Word that I've outlined in this book because you believe that prosperity belongs to each one of us. Money cometh to the whole Body of Christ! That means money cometh to you!

About the Author

Dr. Leroy Thompson, Sr. is the pastor and founder of Word of Life Christian Center in Darrow, Louisiana, a growing and thriving body of believers from various walks of life. He has been in the ministry for twenty-two years, serving for twenty years as a pastor. Even though he completed his undergraduate degree and theology doctorate and was an instructor for several years at a Christian Bible college in Louisiana, it wasn't until 1983, when he received the baptism in the Holy Spirit, that the revelation knowledge of God's Word changed his life; and it continues to increase his ministry. Dr. Thompson attributes the success of his life and ministry to his reliance on the Word of God, being filled with the Holy Spirit and being led by the Spirit of God. Today Dr. Thompson travels across the United States taking the message of ministerial excellence, dedication and discipline to the Body of Christ.

To contact Dr. Leroy Thompson, Sr.,
write:

Dr. Leroy Thompson, Sr.
Ever Increasing Word Ministries
P.O. Box 7
Darrow, Louisiana 70725

*Please include your prayer requests
and comments when you write.*

Other Books by Dr. Leroy Thompson, Sr.

What To Do When Your Faith Is Challenged
The Voice of Jesus—Speaking God's Word With Authority

Available from your local bookstore.

HARRISON HOUSE
Tulsa, Oklahoma 74153

The Harrison House Vision

Proclaiming the truth and the power
Of the Gospel of Jesus Christ
With excellence;
Challenging Christians to
Live victoriously,
Grow spiritually,
Know God intimately.

Divine Prosperity & Health Academy Ministry